Byng's Tours

The Journals of the Hon. John Byng 1781–1792

Edited by DAVID SOUDEN

Every summer for over twelve years at the end of the eighteenth century, the Hon. John Byng set out on a two- to three-month tour in England or Wales. With a few friends, or riding on his own, he sampled the landscape and historic delights of the countryside, visited country houses and sketched ancient ruins, staying in inns that were by turns comfortable and seedy. He was often outspoken, sometimes funny, sometimes biting in his descriptions of what he saw, confiding his thoughts to his journal. Byng's accounts of his travels record a Georgian world that was on the point of vanishing.

These journals came to light in the 1920s and were published in four volumes soon afterwards. They have been unavailable for many years. Now David Souden has produced a new single volume, highlighting three of the tours, for a modern reading audience.

Byng's Tours

Byng's Tours

The Journals of the Hon. John Byng 1781–1792

edited by David Souden

CENTURY

LONDON   SYDNEY   AUCKLAND   JOHANNESBURG
in association with The National Trust

First published in 1991 by Century
Random Century Ltd
20 Vauxhall Bridge Road, London SW1V 2SA

Random Century Australia (Pty) Ltd
20 Alfred Street, Milsons Point, Sydney, NSW 2061, Australia

Random Century New Zealand Ltd
18 Poland Road, Glenfield, Auckland 10, New Zealand

Random Century South Africa (Pty) Ltd
PO Box 337, Bergvlei 2012, South Africa

Printed and bound in Great Britain by
The Guernsey Press Ltd, Guernsey, The Channel Islands

A catalogue record for this book is available
from the British Library.

ISBN 0-7126-3765-6

—

Acknowledgments

I am grateful to Margaret Willes, Publisher for the National Trust, and Random Century Ltd, for the invitation to produce this edition. The texts have been reproduced with the kind permission of the Keeper of Western Manuscripts in the Bodleian Library, Oxford and Brighton Public Library.

—

Contents

Introduction

Sometimes it seems that in the later years of the eighteenth century, the roads of England and Wales were thronged with well-to-do travellers. Hundreds of 'itinerant view takers' were doing their tours of natural scenery, taking notes and drawing pleasing aspects, or paying their compliments at country houses and being shown round by some ancient family retainer. The vogue for landscape and the search for antiquities brought out the visitors. Some of them, like William Gilpin, set out on their travels with an eye to publication and to educate others in the proper taste. Some were professional artists, like Hieronymus Grimm, commissioned to record views and antiquities. Others, like William Wilberforce, were young men finding out more about their country, in the same way as others of their age and class were imbibing continental culture on the Grand Tour. There were also those men – and very occasionally women – in the prime of life who were satisfying their curiosity and perhaps learning lessons for the future.[1]

The Honourable John Byng was one of the latter. Every summer for at least twelve years he set off on horseback for a period of weeks, and sometimes months, on a tour of a different part of England or Wales. He might stay close to home, venturing into Sussex or his family's county of Bedfordshire, or he might travel for hundreds of miles into northern England or furthest Wales. Sometimes he had a companion, sometimes he travelled alone (except for a servant). His travel journals are a day-by-day account of his sightseeing and his feelings, written up from notes made at the time, which he intended for his family and for others who cared to read his opinions.

Occasionally, one suspects that he hoped posterity would heed his views.

Everywhere Byng went, he would seek out antiquities: an old church, a country house, a ruined castle. He relished rustic epitaphs in country churchyards. He swore at innkeepers who ran a poor establishment or provided bad food or damp beds – and he found many of those. Occasionally, very occasionally, he had praise for someone who kept a good, clean establishment. He lamented novel fashions in interior decoration or landscape gardening; he was intrigued by modern manufacturing industry as England was set on the road to industrialization, yet he feared for the consequences. He was opinionated. He was arrogant. He was often funny – and often vexed. Everywhere he went he kept a chatty, lengthy journal, writing up his notes at the end of a day by the rushlight in the bedroom of some inn which he was damning as he wrote. Occasionally he painted or sketched, sometimes he was moved to compose verse. He was not particularly accomplished in either of these arts, but they give his travel journals an extra freshness.

Why should we read Byng today? Although most tourists of his day – and they used the term readily – were moved by natural scenery, which they imbued with wildness and grandeur, John Byng was much more interested in buildings and man-made places. Often he wished for some book to point him in the right directions; the word 'guide-book' had yet to be coined. He speaks to a modern generation of country-house visitors and church-crawlers. His tastes were certainly not those of most people today, for he abhorred almost every style since the mid-seventeenth century, and reserved the term Adamatic for those modish structures he hated most. Sometimes he seemed alone in his appreciation of older houses. On his tour of Derbyshire in 1789, he found the then-neglected Haddon Hall 'aweful and melancholy' and Hardwick Hall 'the foremost old manor I ever saw', verdicts which few other tourists of the time seemed to endorse. Yet the interest of visitors like Byng kept some of the older country houses intact to provide an inheritance we still enjoy.

Byng was by no means averse to country scenery either, and he provided thumbnail sketches of people he came across or curious incidents that make his characters come alive to us. The slatternly alehouse keeper who cooked an evil-tasting mutton chop, or the tall, handsome farmer who guided Byng and his companion to some out-of-the-way natural wonder, have as much place in the journals as a petrifying well, a sweeping landscaped park or any of the other curiosities of the Georgian touring age.

The Honourable John Byng was born in 1743. For a brief fortnight at the very end of his life he was the 5th Viscount Torrington, in succession to his brother George (from whom he had been distant for most of his adult life), and he died on 1 January 1813. In between there is curiously little to relate; he provided his own biography in the poem he included in his Sussex tour (see pp. 61–64 below).[2] After an unhappy time at Westminster and being George II's page, he entered the Army at the age of seventeen and pursued that career for twenty years – first in the Royal Horse Guards and then in the 1st Foot Guards. He left in 1780 with the rank of Lieutenant-Colonel – at which time seems to have come the rift with his elder brother. It seems likely that fear of arrest for debt forced him to flee to the continent in 1777, probably as a result of many cases being brought against his profligate brother. After a short spell in Lord North's government, he became a civil servant, working in the Inland Revenue Office at Somerset House as a commissioner of the Stamp Tax. Byng himself put his career more briefly even than that:

> His early days were spent in camps,
> His latter days were passed at stamps.

He was still passing at stamps in 1794 when his touring days seem to have ended. He retired in 1799.

Although he was evidently interested in sightseeing during his years in the Army, the free time of civilian life gave him the opportunity to go off each summer for perhaps six weeks at a time in pursuit of different parts of England. The extant journals of his tours cover the years 1781, just after he left the armed forces, until 1793 when he was perhaps becoming too old and crusty to indulge in such rigours. With the exception of the West Country[3], few areas of England or Wales escaped his critical gaze during this period. His own drawings, engraved views he collected and the bills he paid at inns were all pasted into the pages of the finished manuscript journals and annotated to enhance the narrative. In one instance – in his 1789 Midland tour – there are still grasses and flowers pressed between the pages which were picked on the way.[4]

Were it not for these journals, Byng would be remembered today for being the husband of Bridget, one of the women loved by William Windham II, the politician and owner of Felbrigg Hall in Norfolk whose letters and papers provide such a rich view of the *beau monde* of the middle years of George III's reign.[5] Bridget Byng, often racked with pain, makes occasional appearances in her husband's journals, and Windham accompanied Byng on a number of expeditions including early ones for which there are no manuscript accounts. On the Tour of Sussex, Windham and Mrs Byng turn up together, to John Byng's surprise. Or perhaps affected surprise, since he assuredly knew of his wife's place in Windham's affections – a place made easier to access by Windham being married to Bridget's sister Cecilia.

John Byng's manuscripts entered the public domain in the early years of this century, following their sale and dispersal in the 1920s. Through spirited and ingenious enquiry, they were all tracked down by C. Bruyn Andrews, who published transcriptions of them in four volumes between 1934 and 1938.[6] Writers and historians have been grateful to Andrews ever since. With the exception of a one-volume edition which appeared soon after his death, no subsequent version has been published. In providing a new edition, I have been governed by a number of considerations. Since the 1930s, Byng has been used as a quarry by writers searching for an apposite (and often critical) quotation. It seemed appropriate to render certain tours more or less in full, so as to give the flavour of his opinions and writings. I have chosen three tours, which cover the range of his travelling – his first and one of his last; a short tour and a long tour; one to the south-east, one to the west and one to the north. The manuscripts for them were conveniently accessible in the Bodleian Library, Oxford and in Brighton Public Library and I am grateful to the staffs of both libraries for the assistance they have given me on my visits.[7]

Since this edition appears as part of a National Trust series, the fact that many properties and tracts of countryside which Byng visited are now in the Trust's care enhances its interest. Visitors and guide-book writers may not always agree with Byng's judgments today, but the fact that he went, appreciated what he saw and tried to persuade others to save the remains from the past, has in itself helped to preserve them for us and for the future.

NOTES

1 There is now a considerable literature on Georgian travelling. The most recent are Ian Ousby, *The Englishman's England. Taste, travel and the rise of tourism* (Cambridge, 1990), and Adrian Tinniswood's *A history of country house visiting* (London, 1990), although this covers a wider period. One of the important older studies of the phenomenon is Esther Moir, *The discovery of Britain: the English tourists 1540 to 1840* (London, 1964). Ann Paine, *Views of the past* (London, 1987) is an illustrated brief guide to the wealth of mainly eighteenth-century topographical views among the manuscripts of the British Library, including the drawings of Grimm. William Gilpin's *Observations* on various picturesque beauties, first published between 1782 and 1798, are available in a number of modern editions. William Wilberforce's *Journey to the Lake District from Cambridge, 1779*, was edited by C. E. Wrangham (Stocksfield, 1983).
2 Dr Joanna Innes has produced a new biographical notice of Byng for the revised *Dictionary of National Biography*, for which she has unearthed a number of fresh facts about his life. I am very grateful to her for permitting me to see the article in advance of publication.
3 Although Byng had clearly toured in Devon in 1780; see p. 18, below.
4 Bodleian Library, MS Eng.misc.d.517, fos 184v–185r.

5 R. W. Ketton Cremer (ed.), *The early life and diaries of William Wyndham*, (London, 1930); Mrs Henry Baring (ed.) *The diary of the Rt. Hon. William Wyndham 1784–1810* (1866); R. W. Ketton Cremer, *Felbrigg. The story of a house* (London, 1962 edition).

6 C. Bruyn Andrews (ed.), *The Torrington diaries, containing the tours through England and Wales of the Hon. John Byng (later 5th Viscount Torrington) between the years 1781 and 1794*, 4 vols (London, 1934–8).

7 Bodleian Library, MSS Eng.misc.d.237 (1781 tour), Eng.misc.d.215–217 (1792 tour); Brighton Public Library, MS S9/T63 (1788 tour).

Editing Policy

In producing the text, I have attempted to provide modern spellings, punctuation and equivalents for what Byng wrote, without altering too much the rhythm and the sense of his prose. The original form is now as much a barrier as an aid to understanding, for he used dashes, commas, semi-colons, colons and full stops almost indiscriminately. The punctuation has been silently amended to fit modern conventions, as has spelling except where an archaic form seemed appropriate. (Byng was liberal with the use of exclamation marks; these I retain for their effect.) Often he abbreviated the names of people and places; when those are identifiable, they have been expanded to their full form. A short list of *dramatis personae* is included in this introduction.

In his edition, C. B. Andrews incorporated the annotations to hotel bills and printed views into the running text, and sometimes re-ordered passages to include them. I have excluded the commentary on accounts, and have followed the text of comments on pictures wherever possible, so occasionally a comment such as 'these pictures' will not obviously relate to an illustration, which is however preserved in the original. Various words or passages which needed elucidation or translation from the Latin, have been marked and a footnote added. Byng's own footnotes are marked by an asterisk.

Various portions of the original text have been carefully removed from the manuscripts themselves at an earlier date: a sentence here, a paragraph there, occasional pages. Perhaps these relate to Mrs Byng or to John's elder brother the 4th Viscount Torrington, and were excised for reasons of family embarrassment (certainly, they seem not to interrupt the main flow of the text). Only occasional, tantalizing, words can be discerned. I have only noted those excisions when a word or two are still visible.

Some longer passages of Byng's poetry have been excluded, although I feel I have left sufficient to provide a full impression of its quality and metre. Occasionally he included lengthy quotations from other authors, which have also been excised.

The intention throughout has been to provide a reading text which is true to John Byng yet accessible to a present-day audience.

The Characters

Honourable John Byng, later 5th Viscount Torrington (1742–1813).

Mrs Bridget Byng, *née* Forrest (d.1823).

'Frek', George Frederick Byng, their beloved younger son (1784–1831).

I.D., Byng's unidentified travelling companion in 1788.

Albemarle Peregrine Bertie, of Wooburn, Bucks, afterwards 9th Earl of Lindsey, Byng's friend and frequent companion.

Tom Bush, Byng's breezy servant who accompanied him on many journeys.

Garwood, Byng's more efficient servant who accompanied him on the later tours.

Poney, Byng's beloved horse on most of his earlier tours.

Bumper, the horse that carried him around the north in 1792.

Ranger, Byng's dog which also travelled with him in 1792.

I

An Excursion Taken
in the Year 1781

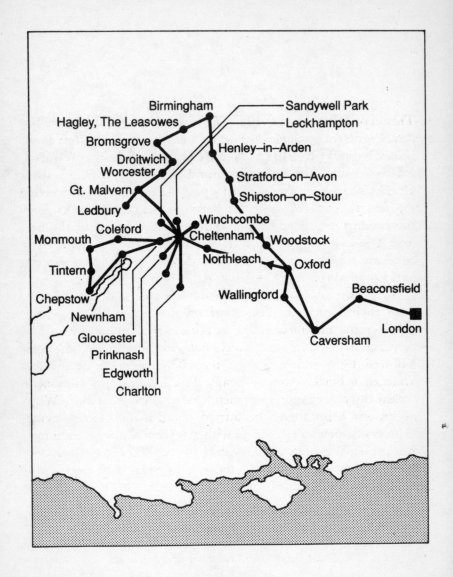

Birmingham
Hagley, The Leasowes
Bromsgrove
Droitwich
Worcester
Gt. Malvern
Ledbury
Coleford
Monmouth
Tintern
Chepstow
Newnham
Gloucester
Prinknash
Edgworth
Charlton

Sandywell Park
Leckhampton
Henley–in–Arden
Stratford–on–Avon
Shipston–on–Stour
Winchcombe
Cheltenham
Northleach
Woodstock
Oxford
Wallingford
Beaconsfield
London
Caversham

This expedition was began on *Thursday, May 31st*, on a very hot day. I rode gently to Hounslow, on a newly-purchased bay horse (most happily named by Mrs Byng, for his agility, Vestris), where I found Mr P. and Edmund, Mrs Byng and her sister Harriet soon after arriving in a post-chaise. We all proceeded together to Salt Hill; there Mr Bertie joined us, and we enjoyed the comfort of a good dinner at the Windmill (one of the best inns I know) and at six o'clock parted company, Mrs Byng continuing her journey into Oxfordshire, Mr P. with Harriet and Edmund returning to London.

No people can be better known than Mr and Mrs March, from their having so long kept an inn upon this road; her ugliness and notableness are as notorious as his cringings and cunning. Mr March, who always hobbles forth to the equipages, followed by a waiter with a tea board of cakes etc., lately accosted a black coach company with his usual salutation of, 'What do you choose, gem'men; biscuits, cakes, jellys?' When no answer being made, he turned round to the waiter saying, 'The gentlemen so oppressed with grief don't choose anything.' But presently a post-horse, putting his head into the coach, tore out the bowels of one of these gentlemen who were only mourning cloaks stuffed with straw.

> Most happy I, after my ride,
> With wife and Edmund by my side,
> So lively and so arch;
> Who freed from London's nervous noise,
> Can taste the country's tranquil joys,
> Welcomed by Mrs March.

3

So very good, so very slim,
So very stiff, so very prim,
With ancient visage starch;
Lovers must certainly endure
A radical and lasting cure,
From sight of Mrs March.

The wine of all sorts being brewed,
Instead of doing any good,
My tongue and bowels parch;
No stomach they can e'er befit;
I wish you would your vintner quit,
My worthy Mrs March.

Her feeble spouse to gout a prey,
Almost worn out, now was grey,
And peevish, tedious, harsh
Of negus[1] takes a plenteous fill,
Unable now to make a bill;
All's left to Mrs March.

I jogging on with Mr Bertie to his house at Wooburn, near Beaconsfield, which is a pleasantly situated house in a valley watered by a trout stream, and surrounded by well-wooded hills. It was built within these 25 years on the site of the old mansion formerly belonging to the Wharton family.

2 *June*   I left Wooburn on the Saturday following, and crossing the Thames at Cookham Ferry, and again at Sonning Bridge, arrived at Mr Loveday's house at Caversham on the banks of the river, which commands a charming view over the town of Reading.

This house, confined within walls, yet retains its ancient form, and contains an old gallery wherein are some good copies of old portraits.

[1] Hot, sweetened wine and water.

3 June   We passed the Sunday here, and on Monday after dinner pursued our way. The turnpike road from Reading to Oxford, that Mrs Byng went, is particularly charming, lying on the banks of the Thames and by several pleasant villages. Having travelled this way often, I preferred going the old road, which leads through delightful shady lanes and a country thick of woods; and by Lady Hardy's at Woodcote, a spot commanding rich and extensive views. Descending thence into the champaign[1] country, four miles brought me to Wallingford.

I was struck with the view from the bridge, up and down the river, with Benson Church to the north filling up the scene. The repassing the River Thames again at Shillingford Bridge is very picturesque. During our short stay at Wallingford a set of morris dancers pranced away in the street; these, with other old rural sports, I feared had been lost. We made Newnham House in our way, where the charming grounds and excellent house must delight every eye; though I wish for a library and could spare some of the gilding and French taste.

Mrs Byng was much pleased with Oxford, and saw its particular beauties to great advantage by the assistance of my old acquaintance, Mr Reynolds. Everyone must wish that the new bridge had been wider; and I think that the gateways of the town, which added dignity to the entrance and bespoke it to have been a place of arms and antiquity, might have been preserved.

Amidst the general demolition, which the hurry of modern taste occasioned, fell Friar Bacon's study. There is a tradition that a study of Friar Bacon built on an arch over the bridge will fall when a man greater than Bacon shall pass under it.

Oxford has been lately much improved in its inns (which were so justly complained of), and the new stables at the Angel are excellent. Mrs Byng in the evening had the satisfaction of hearing Miss Reynolds play upon the harpsichord, whose taste and judgment are generally admired.

[1] Good fertile, open countryside.

5 June   On Tuesday morning, after our walk through many colleges, I rode to see the poor remains of Godstow Nunnery whose owner has suffered the road and causeway to be repaired with its dilapidations. This is a common lounge[1], either by land or water, of the Oxonians though there remains but little worthy of observation; and nothing but the memory of fair Rosamund could inspire curiosity. At four o'clock in the evening I left Oxford. On the hill above Eynsham are the marks of castellated ground; this is called the Beacon Hill, but no beacon has been remembered. Whenever I enquire about ruins I always get the same answer, that it was some popish place and destroyed by Oliver Cromwell, to whose share is laid even much more devastation than he really committed. I wish with all my heart that half the turnpike roads of the kingdom were ploughed up, which have imported London manners and depopulated the country. I meet milkmaids on the road with the dress and looks of Strand misses; and must think that every line of Goldsmith's *Deserted Village* contains melancholy truths.

However I had my fill of bad roads in crossing from Eynsham to Stanton Harcourt to see the old seat of the Harcourt family, of which nothing curious remains but the old kitchen (resembling the Abbots' at Glastonbury, the smoke in like manner passing up the walls and issuing out under the roof), and the old lodge, where Pope wrote part of his *Iliad*; and near which the two lovers were struck dead by lightning. To the top of this building (which seems only fitted for a place of confinement) a winding staircase leads, affording a tolerable view of the country. In the church are several good monuments, which have been lately most unskilfully beautified and daubed with colours by some housepainter. The farmer who attended me was a very civil man and, what is yet more extraordinary for a farmer, well contented with the dispensations of Providence.

In three miles from this place I joined the high road at Witney, a long ill-built town, and arrived at eight o'clock at

[1] Place to be visited.

Burford. The neighbourhood of this town, formerly so noted for hunting, is now spoilt by enclosures; and both the hunters and the poor are driven into other countries. As a sportsman I hate enclosures, and as a citizen I look on them as the greedy tyrannies of the wealthy few to oppress the indigent many, and an iniquitous purchase of invaluable rights. Burford is a poor declining place, having lost the clothing trade and almost the saddle business, once so famous that when King William passed through the town on a progress, he was presented by the Corporation with two hunting saddles.

The church is large, and contains some old monuments of a bishop and the Sylvester family (now tanners), but, laying low, is half overflowed in winter. Near the High Street is the family seat of the Lenthalls; it is in very bad plight, but possesses several excellent portraits of the last century, particularly three of Charles I, one of Henry Prince of Wales, of the Duke of Buckingham, and three of the Speaker Lenthall (of whom Clarendon says, writing of the Parliament of 1654, that as Speaker Cromwell having designed him, for luck's sake and being well acquainted with his temper, concluded that he would be made a property in this, as well as he had been in the Long Parliament, when he always complied with that party that was most powerful).

Two large pictures of Sir Thomas More's and the Speaker's families I apprehend to be copies. The present owner may have employed to repair his pictures the same person that painted the Harcourt monuments, for they are sadly spoiled by varnish and retouching; and I should fancy that Dr Smollett satirized this gentleman in *Peregrine Pickle* as putting large wigs on the heads of the van Dyck portraits. I had some thoughts of going out of the road here to see a house that is to be let, but was advised against it, as the road would be bad and my time probably thrown away.

We are tolerably well accompanied with touring, road books, maps etc., and I am also stocked with James's Powder; so should a fever overtake me, I will hope that by taking some of his doses and being well wrapped up in blankets I shall chase away sickness, without consulting the medical country blockheads who kill or cure by chance. (The many maps I shall have with me are very ancient, and before the baneful luxury of turnpikes was very public, when the horseman travelled in quiet and cheapness in countries filled with game and timber, and where he met with civility, honesty and good cheer.)

Our tour of last summer into the west was made agreeable by the company of a friend whose according, quiet, never-fretful manners made bad inns appear good and stony roads feel easy. Besides, we had our dummy whist every evening; and I now begin to feel that no day can pass well without it, and every day of summer or winter afford some uncomfortable weather, when this game comes well into season. Perhaps at Cheltenham I may pick up a party of my way of thinking in this article, which will then figure away in this book.

The road from Burford leads through a bleak country, part of the Cotswold Hills, and affords some good views.

> Or to thy Downs
> Fair Cotswold, where the well-breathed Beagle climbs
> With matchless speed, thy green aspiring brow,
> And leaves the lagging multitude behind.
> *Somerville's Chase*

On our right we saw Barrington Park, the seat of Lady Talbot, which (either from bad report or want of curiosity) we did not visit; to our loss, if it resembles this print. We also passed near Mr Dutton's at Sherborne and Lord Chedworth's at Stowell. When within four miles of Cheltenham, there opens a most glorious view of a well-fertilized vale through which the Severn rolls, and with a prospect of the Malverns and the more distant Welsh hills. In our way is Northleach, a small market town with a well-built church.

After the descent from the hill country, the soil changes to sand, and by a shady road we soon arrived at the Swan Inn at Cheltenham, where we stopped to dine and make enquiries. In an hour's time I was lucky enough to fix at the Grove House, Mrs Field's, the best lodgings in the place and nearest the well. This was absolutely necessary for Mrs Byng, who could not walk far without pain. I left my horse at the Swan Inn and took possession of my new lodgings that evening, which are comfortable, neat and spacious, detached from the town and overlooking lovely meadows. These and all sorts of provision seem to be dear; even salmon is 7 or 8 pence the pound, owing to London's powerful indraught.[1]

There being no boarding, we had trouble enough in buying necessaries, the family servants being to market and cook for us. The walks both public and private are shady and pleasant; opposite to the pump is a new long room where the papers are taken in, as also sometimes fortunate young gentlemen. On the other side is a band of fiddles, to assist with their music the operation of the waters. Sorry I am to own that such music is to me as delightful as the opera band or Bach's concertos, for I think no music is pleasant but when you can choose your distance, or time of attention, otherwise I suffer worse than a young fiddler's elbow.

Much company is here and more is expected, as the waters are in high vogue and the last season the best ever known (the opinion being that the sea coasts are dangerous in war-time); but, in general, our company are a scurvy set.

I intend, on every day that the weather is tolerable, to skirr[2] the country round, and hope to find sandy and gravelly roads, the only ones proper for castle building; for many have I had overthrown by my horse's blundering on a stone. After a long continuance of dry weather, a change to wet prevents my stirring out, which I doubly wish for both to see the country and to ride off the heat which the waters give me. I already begin to dislike Cheltenham and principally for the dearness of every article which is equal to the most polished places of public entertain-

[1] Demand.
[2] Ramble over.

ment, where for money every pleasure and luxury may be procured; whereas I hoped by being debarred of these, cheapness and quiet had here dwelt together. This place, like all others, is divided into two factions: the greater and most powerful party (who are Republicans), headed by Mr Miller's who has built the new rooms and by Mrs Field (who keeps the Grove Boarding House, where we have the honour of lodging), are averse from a master of the ceremonies in the person of Mr Moreau, supported by Mrs Jones of the town rooms and the generality of the company. I have heard both parties, and neither liking the character or manners of my hostess, am inclined to yield subjection to Mr Moreau, who to be sure is only self-elected and never was properly crowned here; at Bath, indeed, he has the honour to be *arbiter elegantiarum*[1] to the Corporation. If Mr Moreau continues to behave with decency, I hope he may preside as such a character seems necessary at a public place; and his opponents seem to be guided by ill humour and self interest.

There are no manufactories or trade at Cheltenham, and the market is not much used. Cheltenham waters were first discovered by a grandmother of the present owner, Mr Skellingcoat, who, observing the pigeons in great numbers frequenting the spring, tasted the waters and finding them mineral drank of them herself, as well as several others, with great success; and then their merits were soon noised abroad.

My first ride was to see the ruins of Sudeley Castle; but I found the road so deep and stony as to sicken me of riding again that way. I passed through Prestbury, a village a half mile distant, and then by Southam, an old seat of the De la Beres, which with the family continues in the same state as described in Sir Richard[2] Atkyns' *Gloucestershire*; thence mounting the hills, and soon descending from them by the worst of roads, I came to Winchcombe, a mean dirty market town, from which Sudeley is

[1] Master of etiquette.
[2] Sir Robert.

one mile distant. The ruins are truly magnificent and prove it to
have been a very noble place.

SUDELEY CASTLE. June 1781.
Here on deserted and sequestered ground,
Whilome of chivalry, the vaulted hall,
On each remaining arch, and mould'ring wall,
The ivy and the bramble creep around;

Bethink me of the knight returning home
From sadly desolate Judea's land,
Who views with transport Albion's whitened strand,
Then hastes him to his native lofty dome:

But first before the cross devoutly bowed,
Offering to saints within their blessed shrine
The armour of a haughty Saracen;
Tender indulgence holy church allowed.

Before this porch his villeins met their Lord,
Whilst bards and minstrelsy did hither hie;
His trusty helm he forthwith did lay by,
And for the lute exchanged his glittering sword.

What sad reverse! there's now the sound of mirth,
That once was heard with pleasure and good will?
All, all is fled; e'en echo's self is still,
And vile ill-favoured weeds bestrew the earth.

If time such waste and havoc can effect,
That castles, with their warders, must decay;
Warning let's take, repent us whilst we may,
Nor wilfully the present hour neglect.

It seems to have been built at three different periods; first the
old castle towards the north, then the dwelling house round a
very large quadrangle, and thirdly the chapel which appears to
be of later date. The southern gateway makes the residence of
the farmer, Mr Lucas, who holds it of Lord Rivers. It formerly

belonged to the Chandos family of whom several lie buried (as also Queen Catherine Parr) under an aisle of the old chapel, in which divine service is sometimes performed. The chapel has only lost its roof and windows and disfigured by being in the farmer's garden; many old statues and monumental pieces are dug up around it. On one side of the quadrangle are the remains of an old galley, still roofed in and so planked that I could walk to the further end and admire a chimneypiece (yet reparable) on which is written in ancient characters '*Maintien Le Droit*'. The only old piece of furniture that was lately left in the place was a bedstead which the Duke of Chandos, by permission of Lord Rivers, has taken away. At the end of this galley are the ruins of a magnificent chamber called the dining room. At some distance from the house are the great barns. Adjoining this noble pile were two parks – one called the home park, now totally destroyed and all the fine timber cut down; and, I believe, within the memory of man. I returned home in a violent storm through large pasture grounds; and by a great old mansion called Postlip, belonging to Lord Coventry and surrounded by a rabbit warren.

Hitherto there have been no public meetings at the rooms, as the weather has continued bad and people choose to make their parties at home or at the inns. On *Sunday June 10th*, I attended divine service; as irreligiously performed here as at most other places. The inhabitants are of different sects, which is owing to the want of discipline in the Church of England; for thither would the people flock were pluralities in general abolished and more spiritual comfort to be had; which not being the case, the religious fly into other persuasions. The vicar of this place must be a Welshman from Jesus College, Oxon, and his stipend is £40 per annum, which is considerably augmented to the present incumbent by subscriptions and his skill at whist. The best house in Cheltenham is Mr De la Bare's, a relation of the owner of Southam.

In the evening I rode out and was soon driven back by the rain, but not before I had gone through some pleasant lanes and crossed several pastoral streams in the village of Charlton, a mile distant; near which is a neat house, belonging to Mr Prin, with a small deer park, and in a dry clean soil, which is a rarity about Cheltenham. At my return I found Mrs Byng at tea with some ladies of our house; and joining them, passed a dull hour in the much no-discourse of a tea table. The old lady (Mrs Parish) who presided complained that there were too many '*Pre*(sub!)scriptions' here; she is accompanied by a daughter of 30 years of age, and of weight 15 stone, who is a spoiled pet and is by her mother eternally called dear.

My next ride was on the London road and round Leckhampton Hill (the only tolerable way I have yet found), whence is a wonderful prospect of Tewkesbury and Malvern Hills to the right, Gloucester (seven miles distant) in front, and to left the wide and saltwater part of the Severn, backed by the woody hills of the Forest of Dean. This is a truly fine prospect; yet prospects please me but for an instant, for they fatigue my eyes and flurry my nerves, and I always wish to find myself in the tranquil vale beneath.

From this view I descended by the Gloucester Road down Cricklade Hill, which is steep and stony; at the bottom Witcombe Woods form a fine amphitheatre. Here unluckily I turned to the right, and through a labyrinth of dirty lanes found with difficulty my way back to Great Shurdington and Leckhampton. At the former place I passed by a well-looking seat of Mr Lawrence's with a good summer prospect and a view of Chosenhill church, situated on a pleasant hill starting out of the vale. (This church was built in the bottom, but some saint in the night-time removed it to the top of the hill.) Mr Lawrence keeps a post-chaise, but to what purpose I know not unless to visit his neighbour Madame Chester, the roads being so very bad. I also passed by a third mansion, of Mr Andrew's, on which is written a Dutch inscription. As I think a tolerable dinner (even bread and cheese) with good wine, superior to a feast with bad wine, so I prefer an ordinary house in a dry situation to a palace in a deep, dirty soil. I am therefore displeased with the vicinity of

Cheltenham for the want of safe and smooth riding, so necessary for health and pleasure around a place of this sort. On the adjacent hills are vestiges of Roman camps; several of them unhurt by the plough.

The walks at the back of the town through the meadows and by the banks of the trout stream are very pleasant; and particularly now, being the hay season.

The weather continues so wet (*June 12th*) as almost to prevent the possibility of going out, though Mrs Byng in a chaise and I on horseback did set out for Gloucester, but the increasing rain drove us back before we had got three miles.

It should never rain at a public place, as it prevents intercourse and drives everyone to his own bad lodging to breed spleen and ennui. The first public meeting of this season was held last night at Mrs Jones's room, where was sufficient company to form six couples of dancers and one card table. As Mrs Byng was not well I stayed at home after my walk. Our way of life has been hitherto very dull, but then the weather has been bad; and at the early season of a public place, the world does not associate comfortably together, and we meaning a retired life are the last to embark in noise and diversions. We have risen early, commonly by seven o'clock; at eight have crossed the meadows to the pump room, there passed an hour in walking and taking two glasses of water (which heating me, I shall leave off), at nine we breakfast, and from that time till dinner at three o'clock I am seeking out new rides; we pass another hour in the evening at the wells, and to bed early after our strawberries or some slight repast. This has been the outline of our life. But the balls are now begun, and the players from Tewkesbury open their theatre on Saturday next.

Today (*June 13th*) I took a ride on the Tewkesbury road; and in the evening had the company of a family of the place to tea, and for the first time played at whist.

14 June   We do not abound in beauty, or odd characters; and the war[1] and the camps have taken away all the young men. My next day's ride was in company of the Revd Mr Tracy through the village of Charlton and Dowdeswell, where the roads are as bad as the country is beautiful; from the parsonage of the last (lately built) is a delightful view. The minister guided us through fields to Sandywell Park; the seat of Mrs Tracy, aunt to Mr Tracy, which formerly belonged to the Hertford family, is in the hill country in a neat pleasing park. We stayed an hour with Mrs Tracy and then returned by Whittington over Northfield and down Radmore Hill. No one can pass Northfield in the summer without stopping to remark the glorious prospect, perhaps one of the most extensive in the kingdom, commanding a view of the River Severn and Gloucester city (broken by Robin Hood's and Chosen Hills in the valley), the Forest of Dean, the Black Mountains of Radnorshire, Stoke Lodge (Mr Foley's) in Herefordshire, Malvern Hills, Clee Hills, the town of Worcester and the Wrekin Hill in Shropshire, though sixty miles distant.

My eyes were soon fatigued with (even) these beauties; and I do not envy Mr Bagot the possession of his house on Radmore hillside; I should like to visit him for one day in the summer, and then leave him with more in view than others can boast. What must be the look or enjoyment of such a winter prospect I neither know, or wish to feel.

The players begin on Saturday with *The School for Scandal*, which I shall not see, as I propose setting out tomorrow on a long-intended Tour.

15 June   I have now begun my short Welsh tour, and I hope with good weather. I arrived here [in Monmouth] this evening, rather tired (owing more to weak nerves than to any other cause), and am now sitting in a mean room at this bad inn; which may be the best here. The stables are new and good,

[1] War of American Independence (1776–83).

that's a comfort; for if my horse does not fare and sleep well, why, there would be an end of my travel.

Resolved I was to set out, though it is very dull to be alone and to have no communication of what one sees and observes. Mrs Byng attended me in a post-chaise to Gloucester. The road from Cheltenham is very bad and rocky; though I came by the roundabout way of the London road, down Cricklade Hill and through the villages of Witcombe, Brockworth and Wooton. Mr Brereton has a large house near the turnpike by Gloucester; and behind it are almshouses and a chapel, called The Margaret and Magdalen Charities (from two maiden sisters) and well endowed for old men and women.

Gloucester Cathedral makes a fine appearance on every side. The town is entered by two old gateways, and looks clean and gay from the width and new pavement of the streets. The tower of the Cathedral is very handsome and very light; which is more than can be said of the pillars in the body of the church, which seem gouty and immoderately swelled. The choir is neat; and the great window over the altar, as also that of the chapel beyond it, are much to be admired. They boast of the fine voices of their choir. The annual meeting of the Three Choirs[1] will be held here in August next.

I walked quite round the town, saw the quay, etc. etc. At four o'clock I parted with Mrs Byng, as I had a long ride to take; everyone agreed in the distance, and that the road was intolerably bad, but nobody had travelled it or could give me information; the first person met in Piccadilly could tell me more of the country than I could learn in the Bell Inn, Gloucester. From Gloucester I crossed two branches of the River Severn, and the Isle of Alney; and soon passed by a house of Mr Gage's, who has a good prospect and a grove of old oaks before him. I was surprised to find that the road mended at every step, and before I had gone four miles became very good. The country about

[1] The Three Choirs Festival continues to be held in Gloucester, Hereford, and Worcester in rotation.

Gloucester is well-enclosed; and near Huntley (whose chapel stands pleasantly) begins to grow very woody. The road through Longhope, and all the way to Mitcheldean, is by most pleasant lanes (good riding) surrounded by orchards, hills of wood and several tall plantations of fir trees. The houses are white, strongly ribbed and seamed with oak timber; a proof how plentiful this country was of wood, and indeed still is, notwithstanding the frequency of the iron furnaces whose smoke, impregnating the air, felt to me very wholesome and agreeable. Mitcheldean, twelve miles from Gloucester, is a small market town (overlooked by Mr Colchester's house The Wilderness, situated as woodily as I could wish one to be), and here the Forest of Dean begins, which I was very anxious to see (as a place of fame) and was one principal object of my ride. It fully answered my hopes, being as enchanting as a profusion of noble trees, hawthorns, hollies on bold scenery can make it.

The woods are suffering, and have suffered much lately, from the axe, and can never recover, owing to the flocks of sheep which will prevent the growth of young timber. For seven miles from Mitcheldean, a very good road leads through this noble forest, and for the last mile particularly abounding with princely beeches. The irregularities of ground are charming; and the noble waving woods, hill above hill, aided by a gloomy, still evening made me feel all its awful grandeur. Some of these woods seem to be enclosed by stone walls, a defence, I hope, both from verderers and cattle. I quitted the forest a mile above the town of Coleford, which is of the same size and sort as Mitcheldean and equally surrounded by hanging woods. At the end of this place (seemingly the worse for wear) I stopped at a dairy to drink some warm milk (my common practice on the road); and there held discourse with the civil farmer, who fancied me a wool-dealer and questioned me much about its price.

The streams here run brown, from the neighbouring coal pits whence the happy inhabitants are supplied at one penny the bushel. The Forest of Dean is full of coal.

The people about this country are stout and tall, as I fancy all men are in warm rich soils and where fuel is plenty. Those men here who are not blacked by coals and furnaces are redded by the iron ore. Oxen are used in their ploughs. Some I also saw near Burford, and think it most surprising that this custom is not more generally adopted in preference to horses, who are only better for road or hasty work. The legislature should lay increasing taxes upon horses, to force farmers into common sense. At two miles from Coleford I passed by High Meadow, a seat of Lord Gage, which seems large and ill kept-up: the north front is to the road, but the south front not only commands a view of the church at Staunton, with beautiful turrets, but also of some thousand acres of woody hills in the forest, a prospect scarcely to be equalled in this island. Hence the road twines by a brawling stream, overhung by woods, to the village of Radworth; and in my way, passing by an iron furnace, I entered therein and was well received by the devils who can bear the infernal heat, which soon drove me forth. They showed me the iron melting and the immense bellows moved by water, eternally keeping alive the monstrous fire; for they work day and night, and make about 4 tons in the 24 hours.

> Yet from these flames
> No light, but rather darkness visible
> Served only to discover sights of woe.
> *Paradise Lost*

No sooner had I quitted the furnace than I found myself on the coal shore of the River Wye, where the road turns to the right and for two miles keeps close to the river's bank. I could now only go a foot's pace, that I might sufficiently admire the banks of this charming river, steep and wooded to their very summit, sometimes with white houses intermixed, and in the bottom a torrent of wide water; altogether infinitely surpassing all I had seen in Derbyshire, and rendering poor in my idea the Totnes River from Dartmouth which I went up last year.

Monmouth looks well from the descent of the hill, with a good bird's-eye prospect that makes it appear almost the size of Gloucester; the bridge view is very fine and of a very different scale of country from that seen from Wallingford Bridge. In short I determine (even with a headache) that the road from Gloucester to Monmouth is the most beautiful I ever took. Indeed I am mounted upon such a clever horse that if, at the end of forty miles, I do but shake my whip or close my legs, he instantly curvets from playfulness, disdaining to trip on any stone. There is a great deal of venison in the larder, which the waiter says comes from gentlemen's parks in the neighbourhood; but I rather guess that it belonged to King George III. I saw the parade of the Monmouthshire militia this evening, and a stout body of men they are, to make good my observation. The landlord (who seems tolerably intelligent) tells me, to my sorrow, that a boat to Chepstow will cost one guinea and a half, and that I had better ride, and save my money. Good counsel this, and I will embrace it for the sake of novelty.

16 June   I slept very ill last night. It is a plague to be in an inn with troops, for the officers employ and occupy the whole house; on this account the landlord oppresses the traveller and the officer, from remembrance, takes pleasure in eating up a landlord. Nothing strikes a man more dead than a good reckoning in a little room.

I rose this morning at seven o'clock, and it being market day I took a survey of the market which seemed to be well furnished; there were store of kids of six weeks old, at 5 shillings price, and of old goat at 2 pence per lb, with plenty of salmon. The landlord's son walked with me to their public gardens, which are across the River Monnow (for the town is surrounded by the Monnow and the Wye); here when the weather permits, the company of all the neighbourhood meet every Thursday, at five o'clock in the evening, and dance till nine o'clock upon two bowling greens from which the views are delightful. Surely this must be a famous place for cuckoos! The rent of houses and prices of provisions here are not so cheap as I expected to have found them; but the grand saving by quitting London is getting rid of its idle expenses. Sir C. B. has a house here, and his lady is now at home.

The body of the great church of Monmouth Caley, rebuilt, is very elegant, and the inside resembles St Stephen's Walbrook[1] or the New Church of Buckingham. Benefactions to the town are written up therein very conspicuously, especially those of Mr Jones, who has endowed almshouses and given other charities, both here and at Newland near this place. Jones fled from this town a poor ragged boy, and becoming at last a rich Turkey merchant returned in a shabby dress to this his native place; when, being disowned by his relations, he left all his money in charities.

But little remains of the old castle; part of it and an old arch have been lately pulled down by the owner, of happy taste! From its ruins have arisen a boarding school for young ladies. In this town, Welsh is as much understood and spoken as English.

Having now pretty well surveyed Monmouth, which is most cheerfully situated in a charming country and on every side surrounded by lofty well-wooded hills, I mounted my horse and proceeded to Troy House (1 mile distant), an old seat of the Duke of Beaufort's, placed low and in a very damp vale. The rooms are but barely furnished, and its antiquities are a sumptuous bed (called Henry V's) and two fine old wainscot chimney pieces; one of them in a servant's room below, is curiously carved. Rummaging old corners I found a suit of armour (John of Gaunt's very probably), and an old sumptuous velvet cradle reported to be of King Henry's: in this we will suppose he made his holiday appearance, and that this other – from which a print is engraved, and which was preserved in Monmouth Castle – was the common receptacle of young Harry's body.

Here every piece of antiquity will be dignified by his name. Deprive antiquity of its titles and it becomes like majesty deprived of its externals, a jest.

[1] Sir Christopher Wren's parish church in the City of London.

The armour has been magnificently gilt, and should either be repaired by His Grace of Beaufort or given to me.

A small white house (1 mile distant) belonging to an old military comrade of mine, I could not in friendship pass by; so I rode up to the door. The captain was at home but the servant said could not see me, being shut up; which he explained being still in bcd. At 10 o'clock I sent up my name, and entered the house, from which are delightful and extensive views of the town and bridge of Monmouth, the river, the house of Mr Milbourn on the opposite hill, the church in the bottom and the distant Sugar Loaf hill in Glamorganshire. The situation is so steep that should anyone slip out of the parlour window, he might roll to the next hedge. The parlour was (ill) furnished in the modern taste, with French chairs, festooned curtains and puffed bell ropes; this and his keeping in bed informed me that the gentleman was not master of his own house. At length (in a loose bed-gown) he appeared; then never gave me an invitation to stay, or could possibly ride a mile with me, for his wife being big with child he never stirred abroad.

Risum teneatis Amici![1] Observe that by riding this way, I made curosity subservient to economy!

In three miles I reached Trelleck, a small village, where a storm of rain drove me into a public house with whose landlord I conversed about goats and the Welsh language: he told me that many goats were kept in the neighbourhood; that in his village they spoke English, but at the distance of six miles understood it no more than my dog. To Trelleck Grange (a small village) is through an opener country, but on the left, brush woods, intermixed with rocks. From Grange I descended into immense woods, with a rippling stream on my right hand, heard but not seen; and, embowered with lofty wood, here and there a cottage appeared, with scarcely ground sufficient for their small garden and apple trees. To this succeeded the incessant thump of furnace hammers, which might appall (in

---

[1] Smile at that, friend.

the night) a stouter heart than Sancho's[1] by their 'dreadful note of preparation', and terrified poor Jock most exceedingly. Here I approached a noble foundry of cannon; and now, continuing by and often crossing this rapid stream, which turns a variety of mills, soon arrived at the village of Abbey Tintern on the banks of the River Wye. I alighted at the Beaufort Arms alehouse (the sign of all this country); and then finding I could hire a boat a no very dear rate, I sent my horses forward and desired a share of the salmon in the pot.[2]

Now for Tintern Abbey. All description must fall short of its awful grandeur, situate amongst woods on the banks of the River Wye, and in the highest preservation a ruin can be in. The Duke of Beaufort, its owner, often comes here, and has removed all filth from within and guarded it from without by doors and locks.

Over this stile and by this door I entered the abbey, accompanied by a boy who knew nothing and by a very old man who had forgotten everything; but I kept him with me, as his venerable grey beard and locks added dignity to my thoughts and I fancied him the hermit of the place. Most of the pillars, and stone work of the windows, are complete, and it is well overgrown by ivy and properly inhabited by choughs and daws; but I wish His Grace would adorn it (instead of the well-mowed floor) with evergreens, cypresses etc. And make the doors in Gothic character.

This rudely carved, mutilated figure of Strongbow still remains, and is of the same intention (though of inferior size) as that of Guy, Earl of Warwick, at Guy's Cliff. His remains were found (within this century) in the orchard, at the east end, where many stone coffins have been dug up. His bones were of prodigious size. At some trifling expense, the surrounding cottages and orchards might be removed, and then the abbey

[1] Don Quixote's companion.
[2] Byng's painting of this view is reproduced on the cover.

would stand nobly backed by woods and open to the water; at present it is shamefully blocked up.

The way to enjoy Tintern Abbey properly, and at leisure, is to bring wines, cold meat, with corn for the horses. (Bread, beer, cider, and commonly salmon, may be had at the Beaufort Arms.) Spread your table in the ruins; and possibly a Welsh harper may be procured from Chepstow. I next visited several of the iron works up the stream, and with wonder observed the gradations of the iron ore from the smallest wire to a large cannon. All the iron ore is brought from Lancashire; and the dross, already a crystal, is sent to the glass houses at Bristol. Much is employed in mending the roads, but I rode over them in fear. Mr Tanner, who lives here, farms all these and several neighbouring mills, and pays daily 1500 workmen, most of whom earn from 18 to 20 shillings per week.

At my return from these surveys I dined in the kitchen of the alehouse on salmon and tolerable ale.

> Come, our stomachs
> Will make what's homely savoury: weariness
> Can snore upon the flint, then restie sloth
> findes the downe pillow hard.'
>
> *Cymbeline* (1st ed.)

Opposite to me sat an impudent talkative fellow, who bragged of his angling salmon by scores and of his shooting deer by dozens. He well remembered my face, and that I lived at Shadwell; he invited himself into my boat to act as steersman (*comes jucundus in via, pro vehiculo est*)[1] and the tide now serving, we embarked for Chepstow at about 2 o'clock p.m. Wind S.S.W. blowing fresh.

The first object is the abbey, at which I gazed for some time with admiration and wonder. The river continues its course betwixt the most lofty hills, covered with wood from the water's edge to their summit; some deer are in these woods, but scarcely

---

[1] (A pleasant companion on the way, as a book is).

any game or singing birds as they abound with flights of hawks and kites. We often spoke to the salmon fishermen, who catch great numbers (some of 60 lbs weight) which are generally sold at 3 pence the pound.

On our right soon appeared Mr Morris's walks at Piercefield, with the seats and alcoves peeping from amongst the woods and cliffs. The boatmen and steersmen exerted themselves during our voyage in telling miraculous stories, and in hunting a duck for half an hour. We passed a small oddly-shaped rock, called St Peter's Thumb; and on our left (two miles from Chepstow) the white chapel of Lancaute and a gentleman's house on the hill, with some few warm enclosures about them. As an honest historian I should own that, by the wind meeting the tide, the water began to be too rough for me; but my company spoke lightly of it, after bragging of their skill in swimming.

Chepstow Castle now displayed itself most superbly, placed on the very edge of the rock which serves as a lower wall. The ruins seemed very magnificent. The bridge, lower down, is built very lightly of wood and covered only by planks, to yield to the strong tides which sometimes rise fifty feet. On the quay were immense piles of bark for exportation to Ireland; and incredible numbers of iron water pipes (like cannon), each nine feet long and weighing about eight hundredweight, which are going to France (by permission), but whether for the Paris aqueducts of the King's water works is not known. Near 21 miles of them are sent; judge the height and expense. Chepstow looks very neat from the water, as the houses are all whitened. It is distant two miles from the Severn and from Beachly Passage.

At every town I have passed it has been market day and [I] find this place crowded for their wool fair (which as being a dealer, you know, I must understand).

The women here are handsome, having fair skins, with very long eyes and noses; no face (in my opinion) can be handsome without long eyes and nose. A Frenchman may think otherwise, from being accustomed to their apple-faced, smirking beauties. At the inn door (the Three Cranes) was a bevy of Welsh squires intoxicating themselves; and round the market place plenty of puppet shows, balance masters, etc. etc., but the heat of the weather prevented my going in to see them.

After a complete shaving and dressing, and drinking two pint basins of tea, I walked through the town to a stone gazeabout[1], half a mile distant, whence is an immense view down the Severn to the sea, over the Bristol hills, and to the left to Thornbury, Berkeley Castle etc., etc.

I met two ladies at this seat, who were devouring with eager eyes a departing vessel which contained something very dear to them; so I hurried away (not to interrupt the luxury of their grief) and returned to the survey of Chepstow Castle.

The front is very perfect; the gates (the only ones of the kind I ever saw) are strongly cased with iron; and above them, an opening to pour down molten lead etc. on the assailants. Every part is not only overgrown with ivy but decked with valerian, foxglove and red and white ladytire, a most glittering flower. On the right, after entrance, are the remains of the old kitchen, and a good descent into the cellars, from which there is a fine view of the side rocks. From the kitchen, the old stairs lead (by the part, now a dwelling house) to the old hall. The chapel is very lofty. There are two courts beyond, sadly overgrown, as all the bottom is, with nettles and brambles; which being removed, one might easily walk around the ramparts, and an active man may climb the stone staircases of several towers. On many of the walls are the remains of stone chimneypieces. The gunpowder room is entire, and so is the place called the dungeon. The most perfect building is opposite to the dwelling house in the first court, one floor of which is planked and glazed, with stairs in good repair leading to the battlements, whence is an extensive view. This was the prison of Harry Marten, one of King Charles's judges, who was confined here till his death, at which time (I believe) there was a small barrack for soldiers.

[1] A view point.

Within the outer walls is an extent of five acres. Cannon balls are yet found in the rubbish. One day is not long enough for the proper survey of Tintern Abbey and of Chepstow Castle. I employed two hours here, and was happily startled in my reveries by the distant (puppet show) trumpet, which reminded me of ancient chivalry and made me expect the approach of an armed knight. (The Duke of Beaufort seemed to be a grand possessor of antiquities, as Tintern Abbey, Chepstow and Raglan Castles all belong to him; and it grieved me to leave the latter behind, unseen.)

I spent another hour in walking round the outside of the castle; and afterwards till dark in reading several ridiculous verses upon tombstones in the churchyard. Those upon Capt. John Leask are a happy mixture of religious and profane: about Neptune, and Admiral Christ.

In the churchyard I was offered by a ratcatcher a certain cunning receipt to kill rats or to cure horses of the staggers; which he would not communicate to the natives, but he said he saw that I was a foreigner and must be an outrider. This is the third character that has been allotted to me in this ride: viz. a wool-dealer, an inhabitant of Shadwell, and now an outrider.

I bought a Pontypool snuff box, a beautiful and dear ware and much to be admired. The Cranes Inn (where I stopped) and the Beaufort Arms Inn, being both hired by the same person, brings on a certain imposition from which the traveller cannot fly. The may-pole of this town, as of others I have passed through, is well hung round with garlands.

17 June   I rose very early that I might in the cool morning air walk to and round Piercefield Woods, and be able afterwards to return home in the evening; besides, the early morn is the best time for prospects and for long walks in very hot weather. Mr Morris's seat in Piercefield is two miles distant from Chepstow; the house stands in a park, now sub-divided and of considerable extent. It is let to Mr B. at forty pounds per annum, without either ground or garden. Having been long known to Mr B., I was fearful that his reception of me might be either similar to, or very different from, that of my Welsh friend (both equally embarrassing), so only asked for the gardener (to whom the gardens are leased) and with him took the circuit of the walks.

The view from the house, and a neighbouring seat, commands the bridge, castle and town of Chepstow, with a long extent of the River Severn; and the several prospects from the grotto, cave, battery etc. are singularly grand and romantic, affording every charm of rock, wood and water.

In these shades one might pass a happy day, and dine as I had before proposed in Tintern Abbey; for there is a well near the Elm Walk that would serve to cool wine in; the grotto or cave will protect from bad or sultry weather. The quiet situation of the former must inspire in youthful pairs every tender sensation; and being dry and pleasant (with that proper light described by Ovid) would form a delicious *speluncam Didonis*.[1]

The opposite rocks, with Lancaute house and chapel, highly enrich the delicious scenery. The Lovers' Leap is well railed, so that none but the very desponding would take it; I have never heard that it was attempted: the first leap would cure the most heart-felt pangs. The walks are ill kept, some of them are almost impassable, viz the zig-zag walk to the water and that to the cold bath. As horses would not spoil the walks, men and old women who cannot traverse them should be allowed to go in any carriage; and how highly would it repay the gardener to keep a garden chair with a small horse, as it is so profitably and agreeably practised at Mr Hamilton's at Painshill. At the end of the walks is a temple, where horses and carriages should be ordered to, to prevent the fatigue of the return of the company on foot. The view from this temple towards Wales is very full of objects, as the village of St Arvans, The Grange, Mr Carr's house, the village of Shire Newton and the River Severn with the ships in Kings Road. The return from this walk is by the Elm Avenue; the trees whereof, tall and beautiful, are now

[1] Dido's cave.

marked and numbered, so that I tremble for their approaching fate. The gardener sells the fruit of the garden and hot-house, which would add much to an entertainment in the woods. I returned to Chepstow by nine o'clock, to breakfast; and soon set forward to the bridge, where my horse awaited me.

The country from Chepstow is very green and enclosed, full of inhabitants. The prospects are rich with, to the right, an almost continued view of the Severn; the similarity of ground makes it much to resemble the road from Rochester to Dartford.

Tidenham church stands pleasantly. Strode parsonage seems very good. The rain drove me into a public house at Woolaston, where was an excellent promise, before the fire, of a good dinner. Though I stayed an hour at this place, it was with difficulty I could force a present upon the civil landlord for my lodging. A second shower confined me under the market house at Lydney, where, and at Alburton just passed, are the remains of two of the most magnificent old crosses I ever saw. At the end of Lydney stands a large house of Mr Oathurst's, called Lydney Park, and an iron forge, the water to which is brought from some distance through meadows on a pillared aqueduct. The village of Blakeney is pleasantly watered by a lively stream; and from the hill above the village the Forest of Dean presents itself to the left, and to the right a distant view of Gloucester and its Vale.

From every rise is Berkeley Castle, on the opposite land, to be seen; where also Hill House makes a grand appearance.

At Newnham, a small market town, the churchyard is much to be noticed for a noble view over the Severn etc. and also for the curious monument of Jenkyn Wyrrall and the gravestones of his wife and daughters.

I entered the Bear Inn at Newnham with a good appetite, and found a round of beef just taken from the pot, which I strove to devour, and likewise a gooseberry pie. It is always my rule to stop (if possible) about noon, at second-rate inns, and take the family fare; as one commonly dines much better in that way, and at half the expense of an ordered dinner.

Passing through Westbury and Gloucester without stopping (at which latter place the bells ringing merrily at a funeral, I enquired the reason and was told that it was usual at the interment of a ringer), I arrived by the nearer, and duller, road at Cheltenham at six o'clock.

18 June   I had every reason to be highly pleased with my expedition; had it been in company, it should have been extended; for alone one soon tires, and a single expense becomes very heavy.

I found Mrs Byng tolerably well, though she had been much fatigued with the rumble to Gloucester and had only gone abroad to the play which, she said, was decently performed. On Mondays there is always a public breakfasting, where is the only opportunity of seeing the company here and that of the neighbourhood; this morning were assembled about eighty people, but at the full of the season the number amounts to 200 or 300 people.

There is a gaiety in a public breakfast in a summer's morning, with music, that is to me very pleasing; everyone then looks fresh and happy; the women are more in their natural looks, not disfigured by over-dress and paint, and the men are civil and sober. Being rather jaded by my ride, and my horse wanting shoeing, we both kept holiday. In the evening I took my old walk by the stream in the meadows, and returned in time to see the first minuet (for this season) danced in the Pump Room. I played two rubbers of whist and won £2 12s. 6d. of the vicar, whose stipend is forty pounds per annum. Sedan chairs are to be had, but their fare is very exorbitant; and as the master of the ceremonies dares not, and the company care not, to make alterations, many such exactions and abuses continue here unrectified. A brick kiln is close to the walks burning bricks for the new house of Lord Fauconberg, who is expected at Mrs Field's tomorrow.

The actors here were tolerably good, with decent dresses and decorations, Mr and Mrs Fullam the best performers. The play was not ended till the late hour of eleven, when Mrs B. was so overcome by heat and fatigue that I think she will not undergo a second trial.

20 June   On Wednesday, the heat of the forenoon and the storminess of the evening prevented my riding the whole day. Mr Miller of the Long Room continued his impertinence and tyranny of Mr and Mrs Moreau by refusing them the waters (though Mrs C.'s mangy dog drank of it constantly) and by turning his subscription book out of the room. I hate oppression; and as this is particularly against the sense of the company, Moreau should be supported. After dinner, at the walks, this affair was canvassed and some gentlemen meeting in Mrs Field's room (from which they have absented on this account) determined not to subscribe to Mrs Field's room unless Mr Moreau's book was suffered to be there; especially as the lodgers of her house, if supporters of Moreau, were to be refused the water. We sent to Mr Miller, who returned this polite answer, 'That anyone who wanted him, might call on him.' Accordingly a deputation of four gentlemen waited upon the great man, who at first was very violent, refused to have connection with Moreau, etc., etc., but at last all was compromised, and by a shaking of hands a kind of peace was established; poor Moreau was in agonies of joy, and at his return home fell into hysteric fits. After this treaty was concluded, we played whist in Mrs Field's rooms.

21 June   I rode on Thursday (according to promise) to meet Mr Palmer, whose servants and baggage arrived yesterday; and on the road near Frogmill had a pleasant and cordial meeting. He has bought two new horses, one lame, one broken-winded, and both tumblers; so he intends sending them both instantly back to London. After a late dinner and showing him the lions, we went to a Cotillion Ball[1] at Mrs Jones's, which from want of

[1] A country dance.

skill ended in country dances. Our business was at the whist table, a station I am very fond of. Even that great leviathan of learning, Dr Johnson, regrets him of his ignorance of whist, etc: 'I am sorry I have not learnt to play at cards. It is very useful in life: it generates kindness and consolidates society . . .'

I have received a good seaman-like letter from my son, George, with an account of their late action off the Bay of St Iago. Lord, Lady Fauconberg and their daughter Lady Anne Belasys arrived today, which 'frights our house from its propriety'. An intercourse of civility subsists with our next room neighbours, the P.'s. The mother is an old talkative good-humoured fool, and the daughter (Pet) is commonly out of her mind; they are very civil and often send us such dishes from their table as they think we should like. Mr Moreau puffs for them and says that Miss has refused 33 offers (one for each year) and that she meets a new admirer in every town. My next excursion was to see a surprising large oak tree at Boddington, four miles distant.

> Whose boughs were mossed with age
> And high top bald with dry antiquiry.

It is shortened and hollowed by time, which has formed in it a grotto that would hold two men on horseback, and serves as a shelter for the cattle; several of whom we turned out. The circumference at bottom must be fifty feet. Near the tree has stood a large manor house, surrounded by moats, orchards etc.; most of it is now pulled down and what remains serves for a farmhouse, in the centre of which is a curious turreted chimney. In my way back I rode around the marsh near our town which is the Rotten Row of the place and has pleasing views of the hills.

In the evening we drank tea at the Miss Tracy's and were entertained there by a singing boy of sweet voice, accompanied by his master. Afterwards there were two card tables at Mrs Field's rooms.

The Revd Mr Tracy and his daughters left us the next

morning, much to our regret, he being a plausible man and they amiable, pleasing-looking girls. Wits speaking of him have said (in allusion to his height, 6 feet, 4 inches) that he was never meant for the church but for the steeple. After breakfast (*Sat. June 23*) I took an airing with Mr Palmer (Mrs Byng in a post-chaise) up Rodden Hill, to view the prospect from Northfield, and then kept the high ground to the Roman camp on Cleeve Hill, one side of which is defended by steep rocks, with perfect ramparts and ditches, having never been ploughed. What number of their troops two acres of ground were supposed to contain, I never heard, or how they were supplied with provisions and water, for descents into the vale must have been very dangerous.

We dined with my old schoolfellow and riding-house companion Lord Fauconberg. Much discourse about our former days and modern politics, with too much wine; and I went, rather heated, to the playhouse to *Love in a Village*. Sing-song performances are generally ill-performed, and always make me melancholy, as I feel for their want of abilities and pity their distress: what can become of a failing actor, or a failing running horse, being both unequal to the business of common employments? Harry, my stupid servant, announced his Lordship and daughter, Earl Fauconberg and Miss Fauconberg; and on my reprehension improved his cotterellship into General and young Lady Fauconberg.

Sunday June 24th was a day of the most distant visiting I made; for I rode with Mr Palmer to breakfast with an old German acquaintance, whom I met on the walks some days since and pressed me (beyond denial) to perform his civility as far as breakfasting. As for dinners they are affairs of form, distressing to all parties, and to be followed by a disagreeable ride home in the evening. It requires more resolution than I am master of to follow mine own intentions, and to live quietly and happily; in some respects I act pretty stoutly, but in general, like others I am hurried away against my consent and do not begin with boldly saying no. Of all words the most useful. On the road my friend's servant met us to show the way (whch was very intricate) from Birdlip through deep shady beech woods to the mansion, where the lady of the house, with a friend and her husband, were prepared to receive us; and after praising the prospect, etc., etc. we sat down to the tea table and a profusion of fine strawberries of the Surinam kind (a novelty to me). After breakfast and our promise to return to dinner (to escape sleeping there was a great point), we were escorted by our landlord to the village of Edgeworth, 6 miles distant, and were shown in the way a variety of views; those overlooking the clothing vale are very rich, the hill prospects I did not admire. Edgeworth House and another that we saw in our return (both advertised to be let) are too miserable for description. The roads are bad and stony, the hills steep, the country without beauty or shade, and spoilt for hunting by the new stone enclosures. We returned to dinner at 3 o'clock. Mr H.'s house was the seat of the Abbots of Gloucester, and commands a fine and extensive view over the Vale and town of Gloucester and to the Welsh mountains. The owner has a miserable little taste, ignorant of necessary improvements; for the roads are bad within ten yards of his door and he does not know it. There are some good trees about the house, but they are not taken into the grounds, as also a handsome long walk of sycamores. With difficulty we got away at 7 o'clock from civil form and Germanic remembrances, and came home with as much haste as the road would permit – ten miles in an hour and to open twenty gates, and to ride up and down stone stairs, is pretty good riding!

25 June On Monday I did not ride till twelve o'clock; the first part of my morning being passed at the public breakfast (which was not so full as the foregoing Monday), and afterwards in viewing with Lord Fauconberg the situation for his new house, where they have begun to dig the foundation. It will be pleasantly placed, two fields from the pump, and will command agreeable views; the water of the well, now sinking, has the taste

of the pump-water. I endeavoured to dissuade Lord Fauconberg from building his kitchen under the house, for which there can be no reason in the country. In the village of Swindon, to which I rode today, there are some genteel-looking houses, and the church is remarkable for a septagon tower whose sides are not equilateral; in the way is a wonderfully fine elm tree. In the evening, Lord and Lady Fauconberg, Lady Anne Belasys, Miss Tracy, Mr H., etc., etc. drank tea with us; and the singing boy and his master helped to while away the time, and to save me the trouble of conversation. After this gallantry I took a quiet walk till supper time. An attempt was made, in vain, to muster a dance at Mrs Jones's room.

After some stay at one of these places, there is nothing left to see, say or do; and that is the case at present with me, for my life passes in the dullest gloom. At one's own home there is always something to amuse; but in these places I soon lose my happiness, and retain only noise and unsettledness.

26 June   Tuesday I made my morning ride about the village of Charlton, where are neat cottages and shady lanes; and then to review the diggers at Lord Fauconberg's, which is a business of twice a day to me. Could I afford it I would be ever employed in some building, as a great and additional enjoyment. In the evening we went to the play, *The West Indian*, which was particularly well-adapted to the powers of the actors.

Wednesday, June 27th, the last day of our sojourn (I feel like a schoolboy near the holidays) afforded nothing particular; it consisted of a short morning ride, making parting visits, drinking tea at the Tracy's, and playing two rubbers of whist at Mrs Field's rooms.

Cheltenham, I quit thee with pleasure and hope never more to revisit thee! I believe I may aver, and be agreed with, that Cheltenham is the dullest of public places; the look of the place is sombre, the lodgings dear and pitiful, and no inns or stabling fit for the reception of gentlemen or their horses. Most of the company come from Bristol or its neighbourhood.

Without advantage to Mrs B.'s health and without comfort to myself have I been spending much money. The only thing that has answered my expectations was the Monmouthshire excursion.

28 June At the Talbot Inn, possibly in the same house that Tom Jones and his Sophia stopped at; I am as poor as he and Mrs Byng (no doubt) as fond as she was.

There were, at Mrs Field's last night, a commerce, and a whist table at which I was successful. We supped pleasantly with Lord Fauconberg. This morning after the pump, and being pumped out of my money by Mrs Field, etc., etc., we began our new voyage. Mr Palmer accompanied me on horseback, and Mrs Byng went with the baggage in a post-chaise. In our way we saw the Boddington oak, which Mr Palmer thought as large as the Green Dale oak; but then this is in much better state and would yet make a good park tree. At Tewkesbury we stopped to survey the great church which did belong to the abbey. The outside is august, but the inside is clumsy and disfigured by ill-built pews. The elegant monument of the Duke and Duchess of Clarence, and those of the Duke of Somerset and Lord O'Brien, killed at the Battle of Tewkesbury, are worth attention. A very large gravestone covers the remains of Prince Edward.

> How sweet a plant have you untimely cropt:
> You have no children, butchers, if you had
> The thought of them would have stirred up remorse;
> But if you ever chance to have a child,
> Look in his youth to have him so cut off.

Nothing of the abbey is left but two old gateways, one of which serves for a prison. The town is large, old and ill-paved. The bridge over the meadows and river is very extensive; above them are several neat houses.

The road from Tewkesbury is very pleasant, and the Malvern

Hills in approach very magnificent. The Severn and the bridge here make a good appearance; but the new church is an ugly clumsy building.

The road from Upton is very cheerful; we soon began to ascend the Malvern Hills, and passing by Little Malvern church in two miles reached Malvern Wells, whence is a most wonderful prospect to the left over Worcester to the Clent Hills; in front Upton, and at the distance Edge Hill; and to the right Gloucester and the Cotswolds. This house stands alone, has been built about forty years; but a long room etc. have been added to it within 16 years. It is now quite full, not being able to contain above 25 visitors, with their servants. The first entrée is rather embarrassing.

After tea we walked to the well; the water has no particular taste, it is reckoned a restorative and as a lotion good for weak or sore eyes. The living at The Wells is 14 shillings, and the Red Rooms from 5s. to 7s. 6d. per week; dinner is served at two, and supper at 9 o'clock. Our supper was a hot one; at ten o'clock we all rose from table.

29 June   The next morning I was early up to climb the hill, which rises steeply from the house, and to whose summit by winding paths is more than a mile, whence fourteen counties, and the Bristol Channel, are to be seen; the Worcester side is charming, but not comparable to the Herefordshire view which is a continuation of woods, pastures, orchards and houses thickly scattered, which with the backing of the Welsh hills gives the eye an ample gratification. After breakfast I rode by the hillside to Great Malvern, once famous for an abbey, of which nothing remains but one beautiful structure, which seems so compact and well allied in all its parts, strong in substance and rich in ornaments, I have since grieved that I did not explore every corner of it. It is now like other old grand and religious houses, abandoned of comfort and peace, and affording shelter only to a wretched family. The thought of what was, and what is, gave occasion to the following hasty verses.

View these sad remnants of monastic pride,
In which stern bigotry did long preside;
The distant corner of the cloistered hall
Serves for one cow a solitary stall,
And where the crozier reverently hung,
A pitchfork quivers in a bank of dung;
Each orchard felled and every fish pond dry,
That did their Lenten penance well supply.
Once the grave majesty of yew was seen,
In silent pomp of everlasting green,
Now only ragged briars in wildness run,
To lift some tattered linen to the sun;
Regardless of the ashes of the dead,
From abbots' coffins pigs are daily fed;
The dortor long left by the sleeping cowl,
Becomes a station for the watchful owl,
And where the prelate kept his robes of silk
Appear two scanty pans of wretched milk.
Perplexed by want, the shivering peasant lies
Praying for warmer hearths, and kinder skies,
Whilst round him throng a miserable brood,
With agues fainting, and the want of food,
A squalid race enervated by woe;
Not of that make which drew the English bow
At Creçy, or at Poitiers' famous field,
When France defeated saw her sovereign yield:
But why so altered at the present day,
Let overseers and new enclosures say!

A tyrant monarch with rapacious hand
Of greedy power, usurped the Church's land;
Rebellion followed next in spacious show
To give religion an o'erwhelming blow.
With fiery zeal a Puritanic flood
Deluged the state, and bathed the throne in blood.
By glare and pomps the vulgar are confined,
'Tis those that gratify the human mind;
'Tis holy robes that swell the prelate great,
And with his wig the judge would quit his state

For if the mystic veil be once withdrawn,
The reverence were lost for sacred lawn,
The law itself would quickly be o'erthrown,
And all its blunders, all its quibbles known.
'Twas awful mystery that linked the band
Of order, regulation, thro' the land;
That once dissolved, fair freedom went astray,
Lost and bewildered in the thorny way,
From prudery, an harlot she became,
Of frantic liberty she took the name;
And like this ruin, with destructive haste,
Must sink (too soon) a venerated waste.

(As for what I said in the verse about a cow, pig, milk, etc. that was all ideal, and the *licentia vatum* [soothsayers' license].)

The Great (Abbey) Church much resembles that of Tewkesbury, and is on the outside very beautiful; the inside is damp and dirty, and the pillars heavy, the windows abound with painted glass. The floor is covered with old mosaic pavement, which about the altar is in particularly good preservation, the back front whereof is cased with large glazed tiles, and upon them the arms of all the benefactors to the abbey. At the dissolution it was granted to a family of the Norbrooks, whose monument is very costly; at their feet is their daughter kneeling, with her hair finely carved *en tête de taureau*, and her hoop exactly of the modern make. Here is also a fine recumbent figure in stone of a Knight Templar. From the size of all old monumental figures, I doubt not but that the men of former ages were infinitely taller and stouter than the present race. Within the memory of man, the stalls have been removed to give way to paltry pews; they yet remain in one of the aisles and are curiously carved (the bottoms of the seats particularly); not only with scripture history but with most ridiculous and indelicate compositions. The churchyard is most indecently kept; even under the church walls are receptacles for ducks, hogs, etc. and a gallows for horse flesh; in it is a large new tombstone, saying that:

'Fatigued with swet and toil is gone to reap his hearvist.'

The old house adjoining was probably built from the ruins of the abbey. Worcester and the Clent Hills are seen to great advantage from this spot.

In the evening (after the public dinner tolerably well-served amidst a violent noise), I took a long walk under the hill, to the right, to Little Malvern. Here I must observe that by being placed under a prodigious east hill, the sun retires (and in fact to us sets) at half-past four o'clock; so that the walking at that hour is very pleasant. From Malvern by the Ledbury road, which twines through the hills very romantically, I was led to the opposite view under a Roman camp, one of the most perfect in the kingdom. I then attempted to return back over the hilltops, which at last I effected exceedingly fatigued, and my nerves much harassed, from being unused to such heights and declivities. This place could not be endured by those in sickness or pain, from the unavoidable continued uproar.

30 June   Next morning, crossing the hills and descending into Herefordshire, I arrived in 7 miles through a woody country, and by stony roads at Ledbury, a market town so hid by woods that even the spire (a very tall one) is scarcely discernible. The day was very warm, and my horse's back (sad to relate) galled by the breaking of the saddle tree. The streets of Ledbury are very slippery, being paved with a marble stone brought from a neighbouring quarry which furnishes chimneypieces etc. I passed, on entering the town, by some well-built houses and a small paddock of Mr Skipp's. On the window of the inn, where I put up my horse, are written the following lines:

> Yes, virgin window, I presume
> The first to scribble here;
> But with a wish to save thee from
> Each brother sonneteer.

Oh, never here may word obscene
Offend the virtuous eye;
Nor vicious passion crimson o'er
The blush of modesty.

Sure the abandoned wretch was born
Of Erebus and night,
Who writes but with design to shock
Those eyes that seek the light!

The church is strong and well-built, and detached from the steeple and spire. The churchyard is flanked on one side by a wet fosse[1] and on the others by well-built houses, which give it the look of a cathedral close. In the church are some old monuments, and several of a later date of the Skinner family, in most prodigious wigs; the inscription of Capt. Skinner says, that, 'Having served 40 years in the navy, he was not *proficient* in maratime knowledge'.

The chancel has had stalls and a beautiful screen, half of which is just taken down. I should fancy that the wood where Tom Jones is supposed to rescue Mrs Walters must be that above Malvern. The soreness of my horse's back prevented an evening ride, and my walk was only to the hill top.

This journal appears to me (as it must to any reader) one heap of egotism and tautology: I am bewildered in . . . I rode, I went, I . . .

1 July   Arrived here this morning at 8 o'clock; for dreading the heat I resolved to be early stirring, so left Malvern Wells at half-past six o'clock, and a very bad bed, and bedroom, and company that I am not likely to meet again. At Powick, a pretty village, are several smart houses; it appears to be the Clapham of Worcester.

The new bridge (now building here) will when finished be very ornamental, and a good approach to the town.

[1] Ditch.

The players, to our sorrow, are gone away. Our inn is large and showy, and the streets, in general, are well-built and newly paved. I attended morning service at the cathedral, which was very ill performed, with chanting, and began with the Litany. I examined the seats of the stalls, and found the carvings to be of the same nature as those of Malvern. Mrs B. and Mr P. arrived at one o'clock. At dinner we feasted on fresh-caught salmon and drank good perry. In the evening I went with Mr P. to evening prayers at the cathdral, where (I believe) he thought with me there was a great relaxation of church discipline; the psalms were slurred over most irreverently, and the organ is a hoarse unpleasant instrument; the cathedral is called the College.

2 *July*　　This morning (Monday) I walked early to see the building of the new bridge, and to make the circuit of the town; Mr K—t, whom I met in my way, returned with me and stayed with us till our departure.

At eleven o'clock we sallied out in a hired coach, and first to the cathedral, which is clean, newly paved and with fluted pillars, not like those I have lately seen. The tomb of Prince Arthur is in the most beautiful state of Gothic magnificence; that of King John reverend from age. The cloisters have been lately repaired and look better than at most other places. There is a total want of stained glass, so necessary for church grandeur to cast a dim religious light. Thence we went to the china manufactory, of which we took an accurate survey, from the first handling to the last removal from the furnace. The trade is now very flourishing, owing to the great demand from Holland; for the china is very clumsy and probably suits their taste. The races are held on a little meadow called Pitchcraft, which is the fashionable drive and ride; and opposite are bird gardens at Henwick Hill (a bread and butter manufactory) to which we crossed [by] a ferry; whence is the best view of the town and the adjacent country.

The Foregate Street is the ornament of Worcester, being of good length and width, and well built with genteel houses.

At five o'clock in the evening we left Worcester, and in seven miles came to Westwood, the old seat of the Packington family. The house is very ancient, with lofty turrets, placed in the midst of a wood in which great avenues are cut, and through one there is a view of the great pool of water, now much contracted from its former largeness; and the timber is also greatly diminished. Here is a striking appearance of wood and old grandeur; but the house is sadly improved by modern glazing, and the trees being at some distance afford no immediate shade. The approach to the house is bad and formal, not leading (as it ought to do) through the wood. It is surrounded by gardens and walls, in the old taste, but the inside retains nothing ancient except the hall, the staircase and one large room upstairs. The rest is fitted up in a style ill-corresponding with an old house; the chapel, particularly (which should appear grave) is decked out in the Adamatic fashion.

The servants were very civil (not often met with) and offered us all kinds of refreshments.

Droitwich (one mile distant) has a canal to the Severn, is a dirty, ill-built town, famous for its salt works which I was very sorry I had not time to see.

Bromsgrove (where we passed the night, after a shabby supper) is a large town with a manufacture of linen and cotton spinning; the spire of the church is very tall, and the churchyard, to which I ascended by sixty steps, commands an extensive view. There is a good ring of eight bells, which the clerk said were lately put up by *Cription*.[1]

In the church is an old monument of one of [the] Lytteltons and four large alabaster figures of the Talbot family; one of whom, whose head is supported by a helmet with a boar's snout, is supposed to have killed the boar that infested this grove, and hence should be name of Boars-, not Broms-grove.

3 July   The way from Bromsgrove to Hagley would be pleasant but from the badness of the road, which is sand mixed with

[1] Subscription.

large pebbles, and worse than most seashores; it passes through the villages of Catsell, Fairfield and Clent, where are the houses of Mr Blair and Mr Waldron.

I hope I shall not appear either peevish or self-opinioned to say I was disappointed with Hagley; which must, and should happen, when any place has been over-praised. Hagley is deficient of water and gravel, two great charms. I believe that Lord Lyttelton had more genius for poetry (and that not very great) than for improving a country seat.

The house is ill-situated and ill-looking, and is entered by a flight of steps, inconvenient and unsafe in summer and winter. The inside is tawdrily and badly fitted-up with carving, gilding, Chinese paper, etc.; and the hall is very inelegant. With light-coloured paint should I instantly cover the Chinese paper, and in haste throw down the carved work of trumpets, cymbals and windmills.

The ground on the back of the house is pleasingly wooded, and the hills happily sloped; but it is marred by staring temples and obelisks which savour too much of Strombolo[1] gardens.

'Some Daemon whispered, Visto have a taste.'

Mrs B. went round the park in a post-chaise (though there is neither good or safe driving, by which neglect many must lose the beauties of a place they came to see) and from the castle, a well-built and well-understood ruin, was obliged to walk down the hill, it being so steep. The pleasantest spot is about Pope's Urn. The view from the house is very staring, towards the Clee Hills, and the ground in front is confined and very narrow on the stable side. Do not think I bear too hard, or too affectedly, on such proclaimed beauties; but I am resolved to judge for myself and not follow the opinion of every gazer and flatterer.

In Hagley village are some neat houses, all copying the greater example; for wherever a man or garden of taste is established, there are always around them some imitative warts.

[1] Italianate.

At four miles from Hagley we passed through the little town of Halesowen, surrounded by pastoral hills and embellished by a church with a tall spire; and at a short distance arrived at the Leasowes, so noted in poetic story. I will not (dare to) say that either Hagley or the Leasowes (the former residence of rival wits[1]) want poetry to recommend them; but yet I must think that it is from writing they are become so celebrated, for penmanship has the power of puffing inferior places and rendering them visitable by the curious, and admired by the ignorant. Mr Horne, the present possessor, has built a new house; and it is as strange as fortunate that this place, passing lately through the hands of many owners, has not been stripped of the timber and deprived of its rural simplicity; though consisting of only eighty acres, the walk around them is two miles and a half, and guiltless of crossing or tautological twists. The meander is throughout very cool and shady, affording from several spots and benches charming views towards Hagley, the Wrekin Hill, etc.; but the town and church of Halesowen are the pleasing objects, and are well introduced. Rivulets of water ripple by the walks, and can form temporary cascades.

The poet (too often) tells us that his bowers are meant for love; every bench is hung with poetry, and one view is (ridiculously) inscribed to the late Lord Lyttelton. My favourite spot, and verses, are at the Bath of Venus. The place (in my opinion) is not sufficiently *orné*; dirt is not necessary for simplicity, so I could wish that honeysuckles and sweet-smelling shrubs (of which at present there is a total want) were trained around the trees and planted by the walks. Mr Horne however, if he has done no good, has done no harm, and perhaps he is right in not attempting alterations; though I have a second wish, to have the walk widened to admit small chaises that the weak and aged might enjoy its charms. In all this tour I have been counsel for the ladies and bad walkers, thinking that no one should suffer his place to be visited but with intention to make those visitors

[1] The 1st Lord Lyttleton and William Shenstone.

happy, and should likewise equip his servants with attention and civility. At Hagley there is a particular want of these articles; the gates are locked and an hour is lost in seeking for a key.

4 July   The approach to Birmingham is very populous and crowded with citizens' boxes; the old church of St Martin's is a distant landmark. Birmingham is a large town, and daily increasing. We arrived at the hotel last night (Tuesday July 3rd) at 8 o'clock. I, who remembered the bad inns in the old town, was anxious to see what the new hotel would furnish, and was therein much pleased with our entertainment.

The Church of St Philip's forms the centre of a new square. We spent this morning in visiting Clay's and Boulton's manufactories, the latter at Soho, two miles from the town. The works are common in every hand, but an inspection of their different professions (to which Mr P. and I sedulously attended) affords great pleasure, and a happy idea of the improvements of my countrymen.

Bolton employs 500 workmen; before the war he had 700. Women and children contribute to the wonderful skill and cheapness of his wares.

At Clay's I am most tempted, but at Bolton's most amused; the button is now the most flourishing trade at both.

By seven o'clock we were at the Playhouse, which has been lately built and become Royal, and is both within and without very commodious, with one gallery and one row of upper boxes, which give a snug and comfortable look. This front should be much admired for its neatness and elegance.

The play was *The Belles' Stratagem*, and was almost as well performed as in London, the principal characters being represented by Mr Lewis, Mr Parsons and Mrs Bulkley.

We returned home before the farce began, very melancholy, as Mr P. intends to leave us tomorrow morning.

Mr P.'s character rises every day, and fixes him, in my mind, the worthy friend, the well-bred gentleman, ever in harmony, or at least never out of tune. His pleasures he participates and his pains he conceals; the latter should be discovered and not communicated, then pity is sure to follow.

5 *July*   We arose early on Thursday morning to shake hands and settle our bills, which were very reasonable, and the people of the house very civil; so we left the hotel in better temper than the inn at Worcester. Mr P. was prevailed upon to proceed two more stages with us.

The road to Henley-in-Arden is well wooded, but very flat to Leveret Hill, which affords a pleasing and diversified view. Henley is an ill-built, mean town. From Henley (where Mrs Byng changed horses) we passed through Wooton [Wawen], a pretty village in which stands a forlorn house of Mr Holford's, in a shabby condition, with a dry cascade and not one tree around.

The White Lion at Stratford-upon-Avon is notorious as a good inn, and we found a ready-dressed good dinner to sit down to; the well-adapted names of Shakespeare's plays on the room doors are removed because, forsooth, people would choose particular rooms, so The Tempest is alone left, being a name of deterring sound. We drove to the great church, to visit the monument and tombstone of that great ornament of our country, and human nature, Shakespeare; I had e'er now looked up with reverence to his bust, which has been repainted (defaced) by some strolling players. The church (formerly collegiate) contains some good old monuments of the Clopton family (now extinct) in whose park did this Mr Shakespeare divert himself by stealing venison and also in that of Sir Thomas Lucy, at Charlecote near Stratford, and on being prosecuted by that gentleman wrote a ballad which, as I shall quote from an old manuscript in my possession, was then sung, and for many subsequent years at Stratford.

About the year 1690, Mr Joshua Barnes, Greek Professor of the University of Cambridge, baiting at an inn in Stratford, and hearing an old woman singing part of the above said song, such was his respect for Mr Shakespeare's genius, that he gave her a new go, for the two following stanzas in it; and could she have said it all, he would (as he hath often said in company, when any discourse had casually arose about him) have given her ten guineas.

> Sir Thomas was too covetous
> To covet so much deer;
> When horns enough upon his head
> Most plainly did appear.

> Had not his worship one deer left,
> What then, he had a wife
> Took pains enough to find him horns
> Should hold him during life.

This curiosity, taken from my manuscript, Mr Malone intends to insert in his new edition of Shakespeare.

Now arrived the painful moment of parting with Mr P., which left us to melancholy reflections; and awakened in my mind thoughts of other partings that must take place, of a much more serious nature. From Stratford we crossed the old, long, narrow bridge over the Avon, built by Sir Hugh Clopton, Lord Mayor of London, and soon passed by a little park of Mrs West's, and next by the houses of Lady Parker and Mr Shirley, which standing opposite form pleasing views over the meadows.

The spire of Treddington is tall and well-built; and one mile further is the charming seat of Mr Townshend, surrounded by a good belt of wood and watered by a well managed stream. I will, should I retravel this road, take a closer inspection of it. This day and evening were remarkably gay and mild, with soft breezes from the sweet south. We stopped for the night at a small civil inn, the George at Shipston; and whilst the mutton and pullet were killing and dressing for our supper, I made my usual roam about the churchyard which contained nothing curious. Part of the only epitaph I remember was to the memory of Mrs Sarah Edkins, who 'was compassionate to the afflicted, kind to her relations, and very skilful in midwifery'.

6 July   After passing Long Compton, I rode a mile out of the way to see Rollright Stones, a druidical antiquity, which are placed in a circular form and probably have sunk much, being not above four or five feet from the surface, and are now by late enclosures concealed at one corner of a field. Chapel House Inn (where Mrs Byng again changed horses) seems very neat and by standing alone becomes, in my opinion, more eligible; as all town inns are so noisy by low company and intemperance. On the left is the seat of Lord Shrewsbury, in not a pleasing and now a newly-enclosed country. We dined at the Bear Inn at Woodstock, and were wise enough not to dissipate the small remains of our purse in the purchase of steel and leather wares (which are to be had as cheap in London) because the expense of seeing Blenheim is very great, the servants of the poor Duke of Marlborough being very attentive in gleaning money from the rich travellers. We drove the round of the park (attended by a keeper) which is very beautiful and well-kept. Some of the apartments of the house are newly-furnished and abound with the paintings of Rubens, not a favourite master of mine, as all his male figures are coarse and his women wet-nurses.

We fared ill at Woodstock, and were not displeased to find ourselves at Oxford after an absence of five weeks which, however, in general proved agreeable and the weather fine, affording us the sight of many lovely counties and of many places worthy observation; though my frequent thoughts have been that home is the happiest place; and I often sighed (as most people do during such journeys, and even in that of life) for the conclusion. The imposition in travelling is abominable: the innkeepers are insolent, the ostlers are sulky, the chambermaids are pert and the waiters are impertinent; the meat is tough, the wine is foul, the beer is hard, the sheets are wet, the linen is dirty and the knives are never cleaned!! Every home is better than this?

7 July   On Saturday morning after breakfasting on the good bread and butter that Oxford always produces, I walked to see

Mr Reynolds and family and to say that, as Messrs Berties were expected from Buckinghamshire at dinner, he and his daughter must meet them. Messrs Berties arrived at two o'clock. We dined at four. I made weak brandy punch and salad, and Mrs Byng and Mr Reynolds manufactured a cider cup.

As we sat late after dinner, there was only time for a short walk in Christ Church meadow before supper. Mr H—t and Mr B—n dined and supped with us. Grand dinners and suppers must be ordered at inns; bad wine must be called for, and all chickens and scotched collops[1], unceasingly placed upon the table. Our rooms were good, but the Angel Inn must get rid of the old casements, or it will be dreadfully cold in winter.

8 July   This morning, after a charming rain had cooled and refreshed the air, we rode to Pulleins Oak, a favourite tree at a mile's distance from the town, from which spot is the pleasantest view of the University. Thence we went to see a house called Woodperry, formerly belonging to Mr Bertie but sold by him ten years since. It is a neat snug box, commanding an extensive prospect and resembling (in miniature) the Queen's palace. The rain here was so smart as to drive us into a barn off the farmhouse for shelter, the people of which seemed very shy of our company, and by their manners must have supposed us gypsies who came to plunder their hen-roosts. Near this place, on the Islip road, is a public house, at whose door was put up by the late Mr B. (at some expense) the real head (as he imagined) of the ship *Centurion*, which carried Commodore Anson round the world. Old Mr B. at this alehouse built a bow-windowed smoking room, where with joy and safety he could see the terror and danger occasioned by the lion to fearful riders, on startlish horses. The wet weather made us return back faster than we went; and with a good appetite for the fowls and scotch collops again. The chapel service at the colleges begins so early that we hurried away from our dinner in hopes of hearing an

[1] Minced meat.

anthem sung by a famous singing boy of New College. In summer time much of the show and grandeur is lost by the want of illumination, and we were baulked of our intention, as the anthem was very ill-sung, and the service most idly performed, by such persons as I should suppose had never learnt to sing or read, though the Warden himself attended and I thought might have ordered a better anthem for the strangers; but good breeding is scarcer here than elsewhere.

The new windows of this chapel are at present the admiration of travellers, by being the University boast. Now I am sorry to dissent from this run of fine taste, and would hate to think myself peevish or fastidious, yet I must own I preferred the old high-coloured paintings, and their strong steady shade, to these new and elegant-esteemed compositions; and to speak my mind, these twisting emblematical figures appear to me half-dressed, languishing harlots; no doubt but that men of skill have been consulted, who determined them to be of the collegiate and Gothic taste, else they had never been introduced into this beautiful old chapel. My bolt is shot! Remarks will be made by travellers, and people should judge for themselves; my opinions may seldom convince, but yet I hope they will seldom mislead. After chapel we went to tea at Mr R.'s, where we had been invited to hear an infant in petticoats play tunes upon the violin, taught him by his father, a watchmaker. Indeed it was highly entertaining and wonderful to see the mixture in this infant of childishness and of skill in music; on being asked if he could play by note: 'Why aye,' says he, 'give me the book, and then you'll see.' Mr R. laughed at his forwardness, declaring he knew only the few tunes his father had taught him; but his surprise exceeded ours when he found that Master Cobham (aged 5 years, 3 months) knew all his notes perfectly well, and could play anything at sight with a tolerable grace; sometimes for a minute labouring at difficult passages, and in the next pulling the cat's tail. He retired highly pleased with a golden sixpence we gave him. At present he is a greater curiosity than Dr Crotch, and more likely hereafter to shine as a musician; though being puny, it is probable that great attention to music may destroy him. Miss R. afterwards gave us several fine pieces of music in a very grand and superior style; her finger and execution being both inimitable. But on these solemn occasions I feel myself like Mr Western in *Tom Jones*, and wish for an ordinary tune to relieve my vulgar ears, which soon get tired of difficult lessons and hard concertos. From Mr R.'s we adjourned to Exeter College, to the chambers of Mr Brown, who gave us a pleasant greeting and a good conversation. Mr Brown is a young man of modest manners and easy deportment; and I never saw anyone with less embarrassment at his own table. I remark this more particularly as I suffer so much, and am always (in spite of inward remonstrances) constrained, unhappy and flustered at my own table. Mrs Byng's ill state of health made us break up early; and we were at home by 12 o'clock.

9 July   Monday, the day fixed for our departure; and sorry I was to be obliged to attend *a punctilio*, else we had attended the Messrs Berties to a farmer's at 7 miles distance (an old acquaintance of mine) who would have given us a hearty and welcome dinner. Before we parted I took a look at Merton College Library, little-known to travellers but recommended to my notice for its great antiquity, which fully answered my hopes. It is in a tottering state, very gloomy, and the books appear to be as old as the library; the flaring is of Roman tile. We made also a visit to a senior fellow of Magdalen College, and with him surveyed their park, great tree, and the walk around the meadows. Students long shut up in a college have little idea of taste or improvement; so when one party proposes planting, etc. another party opposes, and their alterations in general are as mean as consequential.

I left Oxford at 12 o'clock, attending on horseback Mrs Byng's chaise to Wallingford; where we dined (at the Bear Inn) on mutton and lamb chops, cut from the same loin; the maid endeavouring to persuade us that the larger steaks were mutton and the smaller lamb. The turnpike road to Reading is deservedly admired for its beauty. We had the satisfaction of finding all our friends at Caversham well, except Mr Loveday who had bruised his shin, which sometimes brings ugly consequences.

We sat in the old gallery by moonlight till their early supper hour, which and prayers being finished we retired to a whole-some-houred repose. In the happy gloom of this old gallery the mind becomes placid, easy of impression and willing to afford or imbibe conversation.

The gallery gloom may do very well for a few summer evenings and for lovers, but would soon overcome the spirits of a nervous man wishing for cards and candles. As other old galleries are, so is this reported to be haunted, and that at midnight a coach and six horses, without heads, scour through the gallery, terrifying those that are awake but never awakening the sleepers; as I can well testify. Of this coach history the family are ignorant. Pulleyn, a carpenter, was supposed to have been (in former times) resident in this house, and therein to have killed himself; he also alarms the family nightly by working and making all kinds of hammering noises: one room is called Pulleyn's room. (In Mr Windham's house in Norfolk[1], where we passed some weeks of last winter, is a similar story, of an old woman who spins throughout the night with much noise.)

10 July   Next morning, after breakfast, I walked to Reading to see my horse, left at the Bear Inn: here I had a glimpse of a dragoon roll-calling (for I yet retain a military liking, and hurry away to the sound of a drum); but most dragoon business is in that style of lounge and indifference as gives me much displeasure; the men and officers dressed as they please, and paying the same inattention to their superiors; the commanding officer was hand in glove with his brother officers.

In the evening I walked over the adjacent hills alone, as Mr

[1] Felbrigg.

Loveday, from his hurt, could not accompany me in this, his favourite round.

The next forenoon I passed in Mr Loveday's study and in the garden; and soon after dinner, and parting compliments, walked my horse to Sonning where I overtook Mrs Byng at Miss Rich's house. At seven o'clock we left Sonning, and going through Twyford and across a beautiful old forest scenery in Ashridge Wood, arrived at half-past eight at Binfield. Having to attend my horse to the inn one mile distant, and thence walk back, I did not return to Mrs Forrest's house till half-past nine o'clock; and then met Mrs Forrest[1] ready-dressed and the cloth laid (as I thought) for supper, and so it proved to us, though but dinner to them. Happy change of hours! If they go on with progressive wrong, a few years will bring all right. At present it is wrong for the sake of wrong, and militates against reason, health, economy, good breeding and every other good that can be named. As I was only to make a short stay (for I never sacrifice but one day of the year here), I behaved with acquiescence of temper. When orders at midnight were issued for tea, I retired to bed; two hours later than the Caversham time. Changing from one of these places to the other forms a happy contrast.

12 July On Thursday, after picking up a breakfast, alone, I went to my horse, and then rode by the house famous for the residence of Mr Pope and his therein-written *Windsor Forest*; it has been lately modernized and the old oaks have given place to young larches. Three miles further is the house of Mr Palmer, one of my oldest acquaintance, whom I never neglect to visit when I pass through this county. I met him at the door, going out to visit his hay people, and so I accompanied him and Mrs Palmer on horseback to their hay field. As they wished me to stay to dinner, I could not refuse, knowing I should be in time for that at Binfield six hours afterwards.

Mr Palmer is a humourist of a pleasant cast, good sense and

---

[1] Byng's mother-in-law, a well-known eccentric lady.

a benevolent temper; he lives very comfortably, is well served and his wines are excellent. At our return from haymaking, we were employed for some time in justice business; for to his honour, be it said, he executes this most laudable office in the most upright manner, beaming benefit on all around him. Would all country gentlemen act in this way, as in duty bound, the poor would have cause to bless them; and the parish officers would soon forego their tyrannies. I meant, in the evening, to have visited at Billingbear Park (Mr Neville's), but when I reached the park gate, I found that Mr Palmer had taken too much of my company; so I bore away to the stables, and returned to Binfield before dinner was ready.

On the morrow I took leave of Binfield and in my way near Waltham met Mr R.N. and held a long discourse with him about horses, hunting and the militia.

In crossing Bray Common I found my horse's shoes to be very loose, so dismounted and took one from his foot, which was nearly off, then stopped near Maidenhead to have it replaced and the others fastened; but he was so restive that it became a business of an hour, and not till he was blindfolded and barnacled would he submit. I arrived at Mr Bertie's at Wooburn at two o'clock; he and his brother returned from their ride at three. We dined at four, and passed the evening in sauntering about the garden and in the stables. We had promised to meet Mrs Byng next day at dinner at Hounslow. It rained very fast all the morning, which delayed us for some time, and afterwards gave us a good sousing to Hounslow; where Mrs B. and her sister joined us at 3 o'clock and together we arrived in London at 8 o'clock in the evening of *SATURDAY, JULY 14th, 1781.*

Thus ended our CHELTENHAM Tour.

Vivant Rex et Regina.

2

A Tour Into Sussex
1788

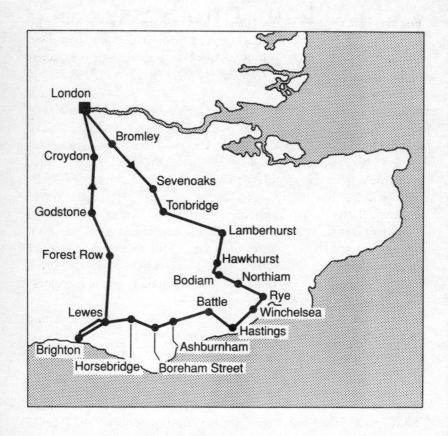

For the last time perhaps (this year) I begin another ride, and with an old friend, whom though a tourist I have never yet accompanied; he is a famous pedestrian, has visited most parts of England, and is more equal on foot to my movements on horseback.

At 7 o'clock on Friday morning, *August 15th, 1788* (for I date with as much particularity as if my writings were to be read, or quoted hereafter), I mounted this famous Poney at Westminster Bridge; Mrs Byng having exerted herself to walk thither with me which practice, could she continue, would prove of infinite service to her health. The sky, and wind, were all sweetness and serenity. Long, lazy, Lewisham might have been well named formerly, but now it is a smart village and the stream is turned out of the road. At South End, farther on, there is a such a pretty assemblage of water and view as might well employ a painter's time. I arrived at Bromley at half past nine o'clock, passing by the College at the town's end.

I.D. had arrived, some time before, at the Bell Inn and had breakfasted; so I betook myself instantly to the same spot.

Though I have known Mr D. for a quarter of a century, this is the first expedition we ever joined in.

Mr D. after breakfast, took to the hoof. How I envy such a glorious independence as this capacity of walking gives him! That he possesses more than most people is certain; but I am of opinion that few people try their capacities in this way, else they would do much, to their surprise. I enquired of the ostler about the harvest (the first Cockney question) and he answered with complete ignorance; strange this to me, who abound with curiosity, or else I should stay in London. Having given Mr D. 30 minutes law[1], I rode briskly after him; but having put up for some time by the way, to avoid a short shower, I did not overtake him and his dog till he had reached the summit of Madams Court Hill.

At Pratts Bottom there seems to be a nice public house, the Bull's Head; from Richmore Hill a fine prospect to the north, but from Madams Court Hill it is of wonderful extent and beauty. On one side towards London with St Paul's in sight, over the southern vale, and towards the south villages, woods and villas, all greeting and gratifying the sight; to the right, Lord Stanhope's at Chevening, beyond that Combe Bank and the town of Westerham; in front, Riverhead village, Montreal, Lord Amherst's; Sevenoaks town and Knole Park. Being now joined, horse and foot, we marched together, 2 miles, into Riverhead at the foot of this long hill, in a lovely vale, where Lord Amherst has built a new house which, with the surrounding grounds, does not seem abundant of taste or comfort. Fearing that my walking delayed D. I pushed forward, and quickly, as I foresaw a storm, which descended just as I entered the Royal Oak Inn at Sevenoaks; and here in a clean parlour was an excellent cold chicken pie served up, against Mr D.'s arrival, who was kept back by the weather.

Our dinner was comfortable, and the two quarts of ale good, but not so our pint of port wine; and I could have wished to have sat still, but we must rise and look about, however fatiguing it is, being on the intent of touring. (With these lazy, sentimental ideas, it were well to stay at home.)

A short walk at the back of our inn showed us the grounds and house of Sir Charles Farnaby at Kippington; the former are green and gay, and the latter new and of red brick, which I abominate; besides, there is plenty of stone at hand, as the house of Mr Lambert near this inn, shows (which commands a fine

[1] Head start.

view over the opposite park of Knole) as well as the grand hospital founded by Sir William Sevenoaks.

The church is of no account, but a good object from Farnaby's. We next entered Knole Park and took a detour, by a sanded walk, of the outside of the walled, old-fashioned gardens surrounding this grand and ancient seat, which has an awful, collegiate magnificence. The apartments, which are numerous and noble, I have formerly seen. At the end of this walk D. took his way across the park, leaving me to return to the inn and pay the score, which was of an easy nature, and nothing to complain of but the puckering port. All the stables on this road seem to be in good order, for the reception of the horses of the fair traders.

On my evening ride I made a sketch; I had not gone one mile e'er a deluge of rain came down; but luckily the White Hart on Sevenoaks Common was at hand, and into a barn I went, where I abode a very dull half hour whilst the storm continued, hoping that I.D. was as safely lodged. At length, tired of my station and the rain somewhat abating, I rode forward, but only into a heavier storm from a sky perfectly black; so I forced Poney along to the turnpike. Can you receive me? No, but there is a public house half a mile further on; onward I spurred, and into a blacksmith's shop at the Cock alehouse.

From Sevenoaks, all the way down hill, through a lovely country of wood, but the road was very stony.

Here fell a grievous deluge of rain, and here was I pent up for almost an hour, with a sight of two, together, of the most perfect rainbows; an ugly prognostication! At last I pursued my way, and in two miles overtook my pedestrian friend, who had sheltered at a wheelwright and was not very wet.

We were soon at Tonbridge, at the Rose and Crown Inn, where we were ill at ease, it being filled by a company of all sorts belonging to the Medway navigation, who here held their annual dinner, and whom the ostler said were 'prieters'.

Our baggage was not to be found, nor arrived; or, perhaps, gone to the Wells; our parlour was shabby; our bedrooms dark and mean; and no appearance of civility. After much enquiry, I discovered my little portmanteau; at a corner of the hall there lay my portmanteau, but I. D.'s was not to be found.

Mr I. D. now desired me never, in my writing, to use the word Mr, but only I. D.; why then, said I, readers may think your name ideal!

A man was detached to the Wells for I. D.'s parcel; and then after ordering beds, and supper, we walked to enter the castle limits, but they were locked up. Thence we tried the church, which has been newly repaired, and within these few days organed by a legacy, and therein were listeners, whom we joined; but I was sorry to think that the old melody, so much better for country work, would be done away, and here they were rich in having all kinds of sweet instruments.

Mopingly we returned to our sorry inn, hoping, however, that supper might make us happier, but everything was wretched and ill served; so tired of the time, and of ourselves, and consequently barren of conversation, we crawled upstairs and parted to our separate wards.

When I was a boy, I can remember hearing a song sung in Kent, in praise of their county, which I never could find in print, and of which I am now glad to recollect the two following stanzas:

> When Harold was invaded,
> And falling lost his crown;
> And Norman William waded
> Through gore to pull him down:

> When counties round,
> With fear profound,
> To help their sad condition,
> And lands to save,
> Base homage gave,
> Bold Kent made no submission, etc.

In this neighbourhood our family, of long standing in the county, had formerly large possessions, which were not entirely alienated till the year 1674; for having being settled at Wrotham, 12 miles distant, they had served for several Parliaments, for the Boroughs of Maidstone, Rochester and Dover, and the office of High Sheriff in the 22nd year of Queen Elizabeth.

Thus ancestry, when risen to a height,
Falls, oft unnoticed, by its useless weight,
Till happy genius with benignant smile,
Again shines forth, restores each shaken pile;
So, Tunbridge manors buried, in their stead,
Fair Southill mansion reared a noble head,
There flourished for a time, in easy state,
Till sad reverse became the will of fate.[1]
But coming changes may again resume,
And plant, on distant heirs, a lucky doom;
Returning seasons bring enlivening rays
Gliding with prosp'rous beams, their happy days.
     Should someone ask, Why did not you aspire
Of these old honours to arouse the fire;
Why have not you, so full of Kentish pride,
Not sought the paths of study, or e'er tried
By putting forth the active pow'rs of mind,
Old heritage to gain, or new to find?
     The answer that I've to such wild talk,
And every question of rude wit to balk,
     Is, that an open mind is rarely bent,
To stoop o'er any avaricious scent,
Trained up to glory (seek no more to ask),
I only studied honour's rougher task;
That's not the source of profit, but of fame,
Despising fortune to uprear a name:
Careless of management, some prudence lost,
A mind in flurry of possession tost,
Pleasure, its lustre all around me threw,
And held Arabia Faelix to my view.

[1] Byng's elder brother, the Fourth Earl, had had to let out his Bedfordshire home, Southill, as a result of his financial disgrace, and the property passed into the hands of the Whitbreads.

No genius ready at an early call,
Will guide your onset, or avert your fall;
'Tis only guardian influence, most kind,
Must stay the passions of an youthful mind.

But I, soon sent abroad, to range at large,
By death divested of a parent's charge.
That parent so beloved, so truly dear,
Whose recollection ever calls a tear;
An uncle lived, like Hamlet's uncle he,
'Meet that I set it down', such this to me!
To my faults open, to my merits blind,
'A little more than kin, and less than kind'.

'Tis lucky season that make truth appear,
Give talents being, show the reason clear;
As the die pleases, as the hours conform,
Eat us heroes, or make man a worm.
What gave to Sunderland unbounded skill.
'Twas, that the time upheld his cunning will.
What brought to Marlbro' such deserved renown?
The happy struggles for each dubious crown;
These formed the statesman, gave the swordsman scope,
Lent every scheme and prospered every hope.
'Twas thus Old Noll, the glory of this land,
Could guide by artful zeal a martial band;
Each jarring schism to one interest brought,
His ready arm obeyed his ready thought:
With boastful wonder let our histories trace
All Europe's terror in his swollen face;
The tightgirt sword, the low'ring broad-brimmed hat,
His rustic habit, and blood-stained cravat:
'Nor born of princes, or to kings allied',
Indulged his own, maintained a nation's pride;
Courage unrivalled, skill but rarely shown,
His humble chair made mightier than the throne.

Not that I doubt such genius or its bent;
But 'twas the age that fostered each intent.

Nor would I dare the inference to draw,
That e'er I hoped to give the meanest, law;
But thrown on happy banks, in lucky climes,

Of turbid fortune, amidst bustling times,
The man is made; these spur him on, to taste
Fair profits beauty, on foul dangers waste.
Then might I move, to active reason dare,
Pluck forth my mind, produce reflection there;
Defend opinion; use each active press;
Urge all the soul to combat, or redress.
 Thus of myself – But, now, I feel a strain,
Inspiring, starts from a prophetic brain,
And bids me future happiness foretell
Will crown another (which I sought unwell),
When fortune shall a graceful garland fling
Of freshest laurels, round the brow of Byng.
 Still on that name my warm ideas trace,
Extent of honour, with extent of race;
And fondly viewing Frederick, deem that he
Will shine that north star, which I hoped to be;
That he, the readiest path, in earliest youth,
Will find of honour, probity, and truth;
That he, reviewing of his father's life,
Replete with hurry, poverty, and strife,
Will quick observe, that thoughtful, prudent ways,
Alone can lead to calm, and length of days.
Let thy bright honour never suffer scar,
Or tendence of reproach; and stick i' th' wars
Like a great sea-mark, standing every flaw,
And saving those that eye thee, to the law
Yielding; thy thoughts with nobleness inform,
Living to shame invulnerable; warm
To each fine feeling; and may every thought,
To highest luxury of truth be brought.
Then, sometimes thinking on that fondling sire,
Who reared his youth, and fanned the rising fire
(Like Cromwell framed by Wolsey's sober way,
Who taught him truly 'How to find the way,
Out of his fall to rise in',) drop a tear,
And from marked knowledge, on his father's bier,
Thus to inscribe;
Known by some friends, and by those friends beloved,

Here lies my father: why not then approved
By all? To my answer's quick and clear,
Known to a few, by few he was held dear.
Born Feby. 18th 1743.*

16 August   At seven o'clock I awoke my neighbour; and when
we had shaved at the same glass, we again tried the castle limits
which we now surveyed. The old turret of approach is in fine
perfection, and so strongly built as to prevent intended demolition. Below it is a bowling green (which for ages was a vineyard),
surrounded by the old walls covered by fruit trees, and washed
by the River Medway; the ditches are filled with copse wood
and the keep is planted with shrubs, to the top of which is a
twining walk, and within it several caverns, one of whom is
entered by steps and glazed with stained glass. This spot
commanding fine prospects, and the beauty of a bold river,
might be rendered very enchanting; but at present it is in
possession of some demolishing Goth!

When returned to the inn, I breakfasted in haste, because the
room was just washed; and then (I. D. being gone forward) paid
an extravagant and insolent charge.

As our intention was to see Summerhill, I took the first road to
the left leading thither, and soon mounted the hill on which
stands this seat (heretofore a place of much extent and grandeur),
commanding the most noble prospect of the vale, through which
the Medway flows to Maidstone, enriched by woods, hopgrounds
and whatever can gratify the sight; but to what I particularly bent
my attention was to the haunts of my youth about Mereworth.

Mr Woodgate, the present possessor, coming forth with his
company, did deign, with some no very high breeding, to answer
some of my enquiries; viz. Did not General Lambert reside in
this house? Not that I know of. Did King Charles ever come
here? Yes. He kept his court here for one summer, during his
taking the Tunbridge water.

* This inspiration was written on December 4th, 1788; being my Frederick's
4th birthday.

This was doing enough alone, and I. D. was not to be found, so I rode down the avenue to the Rye road, where D. had awaited me; and then I prevailed upon him to return back to view the prospect, which he much admired, but thought with me that we should disturb the house by a visit, though for this I was afterwards, upon recollection, sorry, as we came to see, and not to shrink from idleness or imaginary civility.

The way through the grounds, formerly a great park, restored us to the Rye road; and here we travelled deeply buried in woods, only disagreeable as adding to the heat of the day.

Three miles brought us to Pembury, a village of lofty and pleasant situation, with a good-looking public house. (I sometimes dismounted, and in vain attempted to maintain, on foot, the pace of my friend.) Here I stopped to drink brandy and water. The toll of trees at Pembury is a great object from Yotes (my uncle's seat) 15 miles distant. In 3 more miles we quitted the turnpike road, and by a long descending lane came into the valley where stands Bayham Abbey, a noble ruin, in lovely meadows, surrounded by a rapid stream and hills clothed with wood. Adjoining is a neat house of Mr P., the owner, built out of the ruins; we saw him and may presume him to be, from his manner, as deficient in good breeding as does everything around prove a want of taste.

The ruins, though sadly dilapidated and disfigured from being used as a garden, are yet of great beauty, with many arches, remains of chapels and some fragments of tombs. A proprietor of Gothic taste would render it solemn and pleasing, whereas at present it is glaring and fantastic.

I always wonder that an owner of a real antiquity does not print a short account of his possession, which all visitors would purchase with grateful avidity.

After a sufficient examination, we returned by the old gate of approach; near to which stands a pollard ash tree of wonderful girth and age.

A long lane of ascent (whence we had fine views of the vale and the abbey, and on which I cast many a lingering, longing look behind), brought us into the old road at the village of Lamberhurst; where finding a desire to stop and a strong wish for dinner, we put up at an excellent public house, the Chequers, and had instantly spread before us, in a clean sanded parlour, a cold fillet of veal and a cold quarter of lamb, upon which we laid aboard most manfully, pouring down liberations of ale and porter. I also almost finished a pint of port wine; for I. D. drinks little but beer. After the insolence and noise of our inn at Tonbridge, civility and quiet afforded additional pleasure; but judge of my surprise, when after I. D.'s walking foward and I had the bill to pay, our charge for the good dinner with cheese, pint of port wine, porter and ale, with my horse's hay and corn, was only 3 shillings; which could not be at more than 6d. per head for eating!

This inspired us in our evening's way.

We turned off the road to an old mansion called Camberwell, now much shrunk in dimensions, one end being in ruins and the other the residence of a farmer.

Here we observed several deep-tongued southern hounds, only known in the counties of Kent and Sussex, and well adapted by their shape and note for these woody counties.

> Oft list'ning how the hounds and horn
> Clearly rouse the slumb'ring morn,
> From the side of some hoar hill,
> Through the high wood echoing shrill.
> Milton, 1645.

Around the turnpike of Newbridge, there is much wild and pleasant scenery. The whole country is an amphitheatre of woods, their space being equal to the arable ground; though from the over cheapness of coals in other counties, the cannon foundries are now disused here. Flimwell is a small village, where the road divides; and here, on a bench at the Fox and Hounds alehouse, we sat the drinking of a pint of beer, whilst I was pondering on the former usage of this road, as supposing the town of Rye to have been a great inlet into this kingdom formerly – from the journal of that most entertaining traveller, Hentzner, in the year 1598:

> We arrived at Rye, a small English sea-port. Here, as soon as we came on shore, we gave in our names to the notary of the place, but not till he had demanded our business; and being answered, that we had none but to see England, we were conducted to an inn, where we were well entertained; as one generally is in this country.
>
> We took post horses for London. It is surprising how swiftly they run! Their bridles are very light, and their saddles little more than a span over. Flimwell, a village; here we returned our first horse and mounted fresh ones. We passed through Tonbridge, another village. Chepsted, another village; here for the second time we changed horses . . .

From Flimwell continues a ridge called Highgate, commanding rich prospects, and adorned by neat cottages and genteel houses; the church of Hawkhurst happily placed to the right. In this row of pleasant houses, with some good slopes, stood our inn the Queen's Head, of nice aspect; nor did it deceive us, for everything was neat and comfortable. Our baggage had been brought here from Tonbridge by a footman, whom we met on his return. After tea and that I had purchased, at an elegant shop, a pocket comb and some ferret[1] for shoe-strings, we walked a mile to the green and to the church-quarter; upon the former was a well played single wicket cricket match, for the gamesters were expert, one man bowled excellently, and a young man of gigantic stature was an excellent fieldsman.

The church is a large and handsome building, and the church yard filled with lofty tombs; and there are many smart seats adjoining the common, as Mr Boys', Mr Jennings's etc. etc. It was near dusk when we returned, the evening then becoming cold and the moon wearing a hazy countenance. In this inn has been lately built a new large room for quarterly assemblies, and at the back of it, a neat and pleasant bowling-green maintained by subscription about which we walked with our conversable

[1] Ribbon.

67

landlord. We supped on mutton chops and apple tart, and I drank somewhat more than enough of port wine to dispell a snuffling, acquired by the damp room in the morning.

17 August   A dark day with a howling wind unpleasant for tourists; nor were we in haste for departure. At nine o'clock, I. D. walked on, whilst I stayed for some time to pay the bill and to await the coming of the post-boy, who was to carry our luggage forward.

He brought a newspaper with him, which I read through, and then wrote one letter. So that I could not get away till ten o'clock. The road continues of the same beauty, on a light, loamy soil, just admitting the print of a horse's foot and exactly adapted for a walker. It did seem most strange to me that I.D. should choose to keep the beaten track, and not feel curiosity sufficient to walk somewhat out of the strait road to see an old castle; to which I bent my steps from the first turnpike, for 2 miles to Sandhurst and in another short mile to Bodiam, villages of charming situation. Just below the village of Bodiam, and near the banks of the River Rother, stand the noble remains of the square castle of Bodiam.

This castle belongs to Sir Godfrey Webster, who has locked up the gate leading into the interior of the square, and from a narrowness of possession does not allow a key to any neighbour; though surely a proper inhabitant would secure and preserve it, and get a livelihood (or at least much support) from us castle hunters. So I could only walk around the little lake which washes the walls, and adds much to the curiosity and safety of the building. A small extent of surrounding plantation, on the banks of the water, would produce a sweet effect. Something of this, but very meanly, has been attempted. My guides led me back to the Red Lion alehouse, at the foot of the bridge which crosses the River Rother, where my horse had been left; hence I had trotted half a mile when, meeting a heavy rain, I galloped back. Here, after tying up Poney in an outhouse, I journalized for a long time in a clean white-washed parlour, and often conversed with the kitchen company; at every five minutes looking out at the weather, which continued a pelting storm, very gloomy and unseasonable. At our last inn, and in this part of the county, they used a wood kitchen fire, as most of the Kingdom did formerly when wood was plenty; and a common cook here would not know how to manage a coal fire. I felt rather angry, both for his sake and my own, that I.D. was not with me, for he may walk many a day e'er he see a greater curiosity than Bodiam Castle (viz. if his wish be to see castles); and if together now, how comfortably we might have enjoyed a roasted shoulder of mutton and a pudding that were in preparation.

The rain somewhat abating, and my eagerness for departure increasing, I sallied forth, paying sixpence for mine and my horse's reception. After crossing the bridge I turned to the left, and then to the village of Ewhurst, often casting my eyes on the castle of Bodiam, in the meadows below. At Ewhurst the rain returned with violence, but there seemed to be no public house and I was advised to proceed; so I drove forward as fast as possible, in a November souser[1] up hill and down, by wood and through wood, to the village of Northiam, which was distant what was called two miles. Here was a necessity of stopping to dry my greatcoat; besides, both myself and Poney wanted provender.

I rode through the village, a village of cleanliness and beauty, intermixed with shade. Disliking one public house, I put on to another at the further end of the village, the Bells, where the landlord, after putting my horse into a good stable, carried me in to his family dinner, and I readily sat down with him, his wife, two children and a young man to a boiled leg of mutton, turnips and an apple pie. My landlord was very civil and communicative; and to the young man (a fine fellow, six feet high) I talked about the cricket party I saw yesterday evening

[1] A heavy rain.

on Hawkhurst Green, when he spake, as I have before related, of the merits of the players.

This inn, a nice stop, is of the sort with that of Lamberhurst, only improved. I should have mentioned before, with delight, two of the finest babes I ever beheld at Bodiam Bridge; the youngest, 3 quarters old, named Richard, was a lovely creature, quite the prodigious son. We fathers take notice of these things. As the rain continued, I was forced to abide here the reading of two country papers; and from my landlord, on my enquiry, the history of an old mansion house at the village end, on which subject he was very prolix[1] and pathetic, as he had lived many years in that family when the house flourished. He walked with me around the house, wherein one poor family resides; about the garden wherein, however neglected, was much fruit, and I ate many peaches and plums. The house is of the wretched sort, with scarcely any furniture but in two rooms, where I and some ladies would like to pilfer, viz. a library of old books and a closet of old china.

My charge here was very cheap, the house clean, the landlord civil and the stables good. My evening ride was of much beauty, through the villages of Beckley and Peasmarsh, and so descended, by a sea view all at once, into the picturesque town of Rye, by an ancient gateway; which is built upon a rock, clustered with houses, having the appearance of a fortified place.

Like other maritime towns, it smells of fish and punch. By a bad pavement I came to the George, a dirty, sea-port inn with a wretched stable, where, in a back parlour, sat I.D., hardly glad to see me so discontented was he with his treatment at this house. Said, that we must go on, and that a man was ready with our baggage.

This was a blow upon me, who thought my day's work done, that there might be of curiosity here, and that it was better to swallow one's bile sometimes for convenience. During my Poney's feeding, and after ordering tea, we walked about the

---

[1] Extremely verbose.

town. The church is very old but, modernly, defaced by most of the windows being blocked up. Below the churchyard, towards the marsh, is a battery of cannon, close to the very ancient tower built by William de Ypres, now used as a gaol and in most mouldering ruin.

As we were on such ill terms with our inn, the sooner we were gone the better, though sorely against my will was this refitting for an unexpected march; but our baggage was gone and my sheets I must follow. On quitting Rye, I had to observe the curious old walls and part of a ruined gateway. Crossing a drawbridge into the marsh, with the sea to my left, I continued a causeway road feeling heartily grieved to have left Rye (however uncivil) for the chance of a worse situation; for the rain beat against me and I repeatedly thought, 'Never quarrel with your bread and butter'. I.D. crossed the marsh by a footway of much nearer journey. Having passed near the old castle of Winchelsea, and recrossed the stream by another drawbridge, I approached the hill on which stands the town of Winchelsea; and even, then, surveyed with pleasure (though the evening was so bad, and almost dusk) the two towns: the one, Rye, upon a bare rock, the other Winchelsea, on a wooded point, both springing out of the flat and looking like two cities in Chinese paintings.

The steep hill of Winchelsea leads to an old gateway of entrance, of great antiquity, and commanding beautiful land and sea prospects.

This little quiet town seems to have been laid out on a regular plan, the new but few houses remain, dependent on a small manufactory and their Cinque Port establishment. The New Inn I passed by, enquiring for the Bear, but the landlord said, 'This is the only inn, for my Bear is run away.' So I searched in haste for bedrooms, and found two excellent ones, and a good parlour, and was much at home before I.D. arrived, who was surprised at my being there before him and much pleased at the good appearance of things. We now ordered supper, and shutting close the shutters, waited the coming of a roasted fowl, on which, and some excellent cold beef, we made a noble meal. We never sit late; for I.D. is very hasty for bed.

18 August   I walked early to a barber's shop, bought a pound of powder, had my razor set and did hope for some intelligence from him; but he was deaf! After our hot rolls, we surveyed with much satisfaction and leisure the church, standing in a spacious piece of ground. It is a large building, of great antiquity and most venerable look, as the western front is clothed with ivy, as well as many ruins and remaining arches of a cross aisle on that side. Within it is lightsome, though many windows are blocked up. There are on one side three fine recumbent figures of Knights Templar, and equipped in ancient military attire, with curious swords. These, as well as three other opposite figures (of ladies, I should think) are formed of a stone composition. But few brasses are remaining; on one plate in the centre aisle is this description:

> MARGARET JORDEN 1636.
> T'is not deare not a stone can deck thy hearse,
> Or on thy worth lodge in a narrow verse;
> No, pious matron, this ingraven breath
> Is not to speake thy life, but weepe thy death,
> And is here laid by the ingenuous trust
> Of a sad husband in honour to thy dust.

At a small distance is the old friary, now fitted up as a smart villa, with a beautiful sea view, still in parts showing much antiquity, and on one side of the garden remains the shell of their chapel whose inner walls are weakened and disfigured by the nailing of fruit trees upon them. On the eastern and semicircular end, towards the sea, and where the altar stood was an eagle chained (to distress by his misery, dirt and clamour) and at the western end is a noble arch, well shaded by ash trees, which the gardener is for removing, and has also recommended to his master the pulling down one side of the chapel and fitting up the other as a greenhouse, which glorious

72

advice will probably be followed; as the general wish of all possessors of old buildings is to put them to some gardening or farming use, or else to pull down the materials for the repairing of pig-stys or the roads. The tower has been a stand for custom house officers. We now walked the Hastings road, and in half a mile came to another old gateway of approach which was the boundary of the fortifications on the side; (a strong post it must have been, and well chosen by the Conqueror for the defence of his conquest and the wafting over of his Norman subjects). Thence, we made to the left the detour of the town, around which are the traces of the old ditches; and on the north-east side another old gateway of entrance. To the north, the ramparts and ditches are very visible, and on a high knoll is one great wall of building which they call, here, part of an old church; and near the next rising ground (all the works of art) where now stands a windmill, is a circular tower, part of the ancient battlements. This was inspection enough for the morning, and now, having ordered an early dinner, we were glad of so good an excuse to return.

A large cockney party dined here; it appeared that they were stationed at Hastings. We, after a comfortable meal on a loin of mutton and potatoes and finishing a bottle of port, walked down to the sea-marsh and, by the same winding detour that led me here, crawled to Winchelsea Castle[1], one of King Henry VIII's humbug blockhouses; a specious safeguard to the nation he had so plundered! As the door was open, we entered, and sat upon a battlement for half an hour in a very yawning way. However, the views, the evening, the sea breeze and the sight of the haymakers were truly gratifying. It consists of one large, inward, circular tower, with four half-moon bastions, all deprived of their coping and fronting stone. At present it only serves to save many a hare from the greyhounds.

We had now to waddle back our walk, which was finished just as the moon arose; at the hill top, near our inn, is a prospect

[1] Camber Castle.

seat, where we sat for sometime in the morning, enjoying by two borrowed telescopes the views over Romney Marsh and of the Kentish coast almost as far as Hythe.

19 August   How tiresome does a place like this appear after observation! The money goes and the delight is gone! We did right, however, in staying here yesterday, as few places can equal Winchelsea for its views, situation and antiquities. For exclusive of the grand prospects of Rye, Romney, Lydd, Dungeness Lighthouse and the white cliffs of Kent, and a beautiful back inland view, there are three of the most ancient gateways of entrance existing; one fine old priory church; a prison, formerly part of the priory; the monastery, with its remaining chapel, besides the ramparts of defence to the north; and on the sea-marsh, the blockhouse Castle.

The morning opened heavily and threatened bad weather, but soon clearing up, we prepared for our march, but the removal of our baggage was as great a plague to us as was the grand train of artillery to General Burgoyne[1]. At last a carrier was found, and then we could move contentedly.

Our charge was reasonable, considering the tough fowls we had eaten; that of yesterday, the landlord assured us, was just killed to tempt us by its freshness. He recommended us an inn at Battle, kept by his uncle. In a mile from Winchelsea I came to the small church of Nicholsham; and whilst on survey Poney as usual, being tied to the rails, I.D. passed me. Here was nothing to observe but an old hollow yew-tree, wherein was a bench commanding a pleasant view of the vale, closing with the town of Rye. At the mile stone, we passed by the seat of Sir William Ashburnham at Griestland (for we had kept company together, and like children plucked the nuts and blackberries).

And here did I, upon sad recollection, vent an heart-felt sigh to the memory of his youngest son, my beloved friend, a youth of the sweetest manners and whom no one ever saw but to love

[1] He had been forced to surrender to the Americans at Saratoga in 1782.

and esteem. He died at the Hotwells, Bristol 1768; regretted, at this day, by the mistress of the lodging house where he died, though in the constant habit of viewing scenes of death, and of thus monthly losing her lodgers.

On the rising of the hill, to the left, is a charming cottage belonging to Mr Emmet, with views of the best description. Near the hill top stands a good public house, the White Hart.

During our ride we have seen to our left, at the top of the high country, near the sea, the church of Fairlight, which must be a great sea mark.

The descent into Hastings is very pleasant, but the Hastings town is narrow streeted and ill-paved. At the farther end of the main street, and near the sea, is the Swan, the principal inn. Here we orderd for our dinner the old fare, for no fish is to be had, of which I had hoped much at Winchelsea, and more here, but there is always some excuse of wind, or idleness, to prevent the fishermen.

This town stands between two hills, and immediately upon the sea; but it is a bad shore for bathing, though there is always a summer company there. After walking the beach we ascended the steep hill to the right, on whose summit are the poor remains of the castle built by William the Conqueror. In our way, and about its limits, searching many turf-traps set for wheatears, when the custom is to leave a penny for every caught bird you take away. Within the castle we seated ourselves for some time, delighted with the weather, the freshness of the sea breeze and the cheerfulness of the scenery, till the shepherd came to survey his traps, when we paid him sevenpence for his capture of seven birds, whom we sat instantly to pluck in preparation for our dinner spit; and it would have made others laugh to have seen us at our poulterers' work, which being finished, we hastened back to the inn, but were delayed by going into a circulating library where I.D. recognised in the master an old shipmate.

In the lower churchyard I saw this inscription to the memory of William Cramp – a name sufficient to drown the owner. On the top of the stone is carved the figure of an angel lifting a man out of the water.

> WILLIAM CRAMP   Drowned 1785.
> Think not on earth secuier to be
> Though from the bousterous sea are free
> One earth or sea it matters not
> All must die where ears there lot.

We had for dinner a roasted duck, cold beef and plum pie, with three wheatears and a half each; five that came to us afterwards were left behind. The upper church is well placed, and seems large; above it are steep dry walks, proper for invalids and to avoid different winds. Here did the cavalry and infantry assemble for the evening's march, for we are very regular in our orders; so for a mile up the hill we counter-marched, and at the summit took the road to the left, the column of infantry keeping steadily forward, whilst the Grey Hussar skitted about for information.

To the right, glorious views of wood and cultivation, with the sea to our left, whence we gradually declined. We soon came to the seat of General Murray, through whose domain I rode, whilst I.D. kept the high road by the park pale. This Scottish *haro*[1] is ill-placed amidst the woods and enclosures of Sussex; as with the rest of his countrymen he would feel more at home on a bleak heath, but the General is trying what pleasing alterations he can make, by grubbing up hedges and oaks, and introducing the fir, 'The Scotch fir that's never out of place'. Near it is Crowhurst, the seat of Mr Pelham. The town of Battle is well placed on a hillside, but only known from the famous abbey (founded by the Conqueror, upon the place where Harold was slain), the grand approach to which, by a noble gateway, forms the end of the town, but shows a sad want of taste as in the centre are two mean modern sash windows with white shutters. The inside the late Sir John Webster meant to have rendered

[1] Exile.

habitable, but now half is in ruins, as well as the adjoining almonry[1] now called the Armoury.

Having been recommended by a family combination, we disdained putting up at the new inn of decent appearance and thought ourselves bound to follow our parcels into the Half Moon, a miserable alehouse where horses are never received, or company for a night. I.D. made good his landing in a small room, taken off the kitchen, whilst I lodged Poney in a kind of brewing-outhouse, where horses seldom enter. This was bad work! But we were in the habit of alehouses, and might soon become downright trampers. Not that any place, when changing about, signifies in a fine season; but however we could not help grumbling at thus being sent by our last landlord to an inn without even a wine licence or a stall for a horse. We walked to the churchyard, of high and pleasant situation, with brick pathways. The gravestones are all sinking, so that most of their tops only appear above ground. We had for supper a cleanly service of lamb chops, ham and eggs, and a plum tart; and then having said little to each other, we mounted to our sleeping apartments.

20 August   Our hour of rising is regularly at seven o'clock. Before breakfast I walked up the town, where searching a bookseller's shop I turned over a large collection of pamphlets; but they were all theological. After breakfast we entered the abbey domains, which lay high (and that is unusual). The gateway is of gloomy authority, and the abbey commands pleasing views, but there is no care, no taste, no cleanliness! All the habitable part of the building is meanly and modernly glazed. The stables are under old arches, and above them is a prodigious grand hall in shameful rubbish, with a ruinous modern roof falling down; and the sooner that happens the better. Underneath this building are a variety of vaults, which serve for cellarings and the holding of mortar, etc.

[1] Place for the distribution of alms.

We were guided by a servant of Lady Webster's (who was now here with much company, so we were confined as to time and inspection), a forward, ignorant fellow who talked the old folly about Queen Elizabeth's apartments, said that the bishop could not, without the Dean's leave, infirm here, and that the old house near the gateway was the Armoury.

We were permitted, till the family assemblage, to run into the house, catching a glimpse of the lofty old hall and one old chamber; and saw yet a greater curiosity, the family butler, Mr Ingall, 103 years of age, who had been a post-boy in York in Queen Anne's reign, and now frequently, in a passion, gives warnings and threatens to quit his place. He was very deaf, else I would have spoken to him; but we both bowed to him, and his age bowed him to us!

The southern side of the building is in fine ruins, and in fine dirty neglect too! The two remaining towers are of great height and beauty. The walls from and betwixt them have not been long pulled down, and our guide said, 'That Sir Godfrey Webster longs to succeed the old lady, that he may entirely pull it all down.' And then there will be an end to Battle Abbey!!!

When we returned to our inn, we had to undergo our daily dispute about a baggage carrier, all of whom are insolent from a knowledge of their being necessary. The first after much altercation I sent off (viz. in quest of other rogueries), and then was as badly served by the second, a cobbler, whom at last we were obliged to submit to.

In three miles from Battle I came to the white gate leading to Ashburnham Park, and passing through a handsome ride of lofty evergreens, entered by the new lodge the park, a lofty extent of ground, of much gaiety and prettily interspersed by plantations, with the whole in good keeping. But I saw not I.D., so supposed him before me.

By a twining wood drive, and over a wooden bridge, the house is approached; which is now under the masons' hands, to be entirely new-cased, and there were plenty of workmen. I rode by the water and around the house, but would not proceed alone on inspection, so returned over the bridge and laid myself (like a knight in romance) under a tree, left to meditation; but my comrade appeared not! After an hour's ponderation *sub tegmine fagi*[1], I delivered my horse to a mason, and was then shown the house, which is of elegant and useful accommodation, with handsome furniture; but there are few old family pictures, or of good masters.

The offices, the stables, the safe and all the etc's bespeak the nobleman of taste and splendour. Another maidservant showed me the church, wherein are some large marble monuments of the Ashburnham family; whilst the sculpture will repose the deceased on their backs I am content, but cannot endure to see figures (as some here are) in ridiculous animation, in full-bottomed wigs. In a chest are preserved, in this church, a watch with a curiously enamelled dial plate, given by King Charles I, in his last moments, to his friend John Ashburnham (in this name both Charles and I agree) as also the shirt worn by that unfortunate monarch at the block, which is very long, highly wrought on the wristbands and neck, and on one sleeve much stained with blood.

After all my survey finished, I.D. came up, having awaited me at another gate of the park. As he expressed no wish to see the house or church, I proposed to view the kitchen garden from the hope of getting fruit; but here we were most uncivilly disappointed, for though in abundance the gardener made no offer, nor would even permit us a handful from the profusion of Morello cherries. So we turned out in dudgeon!

At the park gate we enquired our road, which they said led to Boreham; but staying rather behind I.D. I turned to the left, as directed, and soon coming into the Lewes road, walked my horse quietly to Boreham. Here was a most tempting public house, and it was now the right hour of appetite, so I ordered the cold beef to be laid forth in a clean bow-windowed room, and then I awaited at a place of wide view for my companion,

[1] In the shade of a beech tree.

who in half an hour came not; so I galloped forward and soon heard of him on the road before me, which he had entered by a distant roundabout path. When overtaken, I stated to him the comforts of my past inn, and so strongly, that he returned; and did not then think the mile of return ill taken when it brought him to such a neat quarter, long and comfortable – all neatness within, all beauty without, our bow-windowed room commanding a fine expanse of country and the woods of Ashburnham, and to the right, views of the sea.

Three miles hence, leaving the high road to the right, we entered Hurstmonceux Park (a name pronounced with such variety of wrong by the natives as scarcely to be found out), a place once glorious, within a park of four miles extent and abundant of lofty timber. Mr Hare Naylor, the owner, having built a paltry citizen-looking house at the edge of the park, and having cut down most of the timber (nothing being left but some Spanish chestnuts near the house and a small grove on the opposite hill), has within these few years stripped, destroyed and pulled down all the interior parts of this grand old mansion of Hurstmonceux; which was probably, eight years ago, one of the largest habitable seats of antiquity in this kingdom. Nothing now remains but the great shell and the kitchen gardens, into neither of which, being locked up, could we enter, or by any noise bring anyone to assist us. On two sides have been pent up water, and to the eastward I should suppose a large lake, filling up the valley. As we had some miles to our evening inn, D. was eager for departure, so I had not the heart to search for the gardener, or any information which might have been of small account. That all the interior was in ruins I could see through the many windows. Surely at the destruction there might have been much plunder for the antiquary, of paintings, carved work, wainscoting, magnificent chimney-pieces, tapestry, etc. etc. All sold as lumber and long since burnt! Though sometimes a curiosity is to be found in a neighbouring cottage, as a bedstead or an old panel painting nailed over a hole. Most luckily the prints, from the pencil of Mr Grose, explain the grandeur, elegance and architecture of these ancient magnificences; which when formerly warmed by good living, cheered by hospitality and crowded by attendants, must have afforded a wonderful display of riches and power.

There have been two great halls, the first of which must have been lighted from the top; the second, the hall of entrance, with the old buttery hatch, is wonderfully grand and light; the beams, carving and ceiling must have inspired admiration and astonishment.

From the castle to the church was an avenue, and much wood upon the hill, which is now a waste, the last trees being just felled. The place is upon sale; and an unavailing auction took place a few days since.

I.D. returned through the park whilst I rode up to the church, whence is a view to the sea, over the level and to the town of Pevensey. No doubt but there are old monuments in this church, but I cannot take a survey of a church alone and in an evening.

By lanes I soon rejoined the turnpike road, which was as pleasant as the evening (for the country is rich in woods, culture and population), so I walked a foot's pace, often conversing by the way and once stopping to drink a pint of warm cow's milk. By seven o'clock I was, first, at Horsebridge, where seemed to be a very good public house, the King's Head; my horse being put up and a double-bedded room put into preparation (our baggage was arrived), I walked to meet I.D. The evening now closing, we were soon at supper, almost the same as of our former evening, mutton chops and broiled ham; in a sitting room of most spacious extent, being 36 feet by 21. Our bedroom, too, was of noble dimensions.

21 August Our host's name at Winchelsea was Bray, the same at Battle, and so is our host at Horsebridge; all relations. We like asses have been braying about for these four days.

We have never been in much haste, nor has it been necessary for our intentions or suitable to our equipments. Today we have but a very short way in idea. Soon after our departure from

Horsebridge (where vast droves of cattle pass to the London market, as I suppose from the marshes) we turned up the Uckfield road, and when arrived at park pale, got a key of admission into Halland Park. Halland was one of the many grand old seats of the (minister) Duke of Newcastle, who here, at times, displayed his folly and prodigal hospitality to the freeholders of Sussex.

The park of great extent was till lately a forest of wood, which is nearly felled, so that now it exhibits a scene of wildness and waste; the old house has been pulling down all the summer, but a part remains, which will soon come down with the yet-standing avenue trees.

Nothing can look more dreary, or be put to less use, than this park, though there are deer in it. Lawton Common on the park edge is very wooded and foresty.

We were soon again in the turnpike road; then our distance was too short, and the day too early, for a stop.

In five more miles, with the steep downy hills to our left, we arrived at Lewes, and went by direction to the Lewes White Hart Inn at the top of the town, after passing the Bear where, I believe, we should have stopped.

The only good thing, or of novelty to us, at the White Hart was some brill fish; which being ordered for dinner, we made some small movements, and returned to be much displeased at the difficulty of getting an eating room, and a double-bedded sleeping room up two pair of stairs.

Our fish at dinner was a treat, and we ate of it with pleasure; good port, that is port that should be swallowed, we have not met with, and the beer everywhere has been very indifferent. And though I have sometimes seen wholesome comfortable-looking brown bread under a cottager's arm, yet I have been obliged to eat of tough, white, tasteless bread.

I do not believe that in the county of Sussex there are any such excellent inns as the Haycock at Wansford Bridge, where on a late tour I made some abode! Nor do I think there is so cheap an inn in England as the White Hart at South Mimms,

14 miles from the capital, on a great road. Our evening ramble (after a purchase of peaches, my walking over to a bookseller's shop, and an enquiry for letters at the post office) was to inspect what exists of the old castle; where remain an entire gateway, blocked up by houses, and two towers with a wall at the top of the keep, to which we were shown by winding steps. It is neatly kept; the two towers form rooms, and to the summit of one is an ascent, whence is an extensive view and to the sea.

The priory ruins are on the other side of the town, in the meadows, and still cover much space with many old walls and arches, a brook running beside them.

In an adjacent meadow is a prodigious, large, stone pigeon-house, which they say was in use to the priory. As the evening was very fine, our stay was very long; and whilst I was exploring every old corner I.D., like another Dorothea, laved his feet in the brook.

At the town end there was a busy display of harvest; the country around was abundant of good crops.

We now walked to the downs and on the race course, and did not return till dusk, when we had for supper some small soles that had been reserved for us.

I.D. expressing a wish to return instantly to London, I could but instantly assent.

22 August   Up at 8 o'clock; a dark rainy morning. I was some time in dressing, longer at breakfast; and then to procure a change of dining and bedrooms for the reception of Mrs Byng and our son Henry, whom I expected to dinner, he, poor little fellow, to be placed here at school for the first time. I did contrive (by not quarrelling with the house) to get a better dining room, and the promise of succession to a goodish bed.

So my morning passed till 10 o'clock, when I grew restless to be abroad, as the weather cleared up after a deluge of rain.

I first saw some exercise of the Light Dragoons, and then climbed a keep or bastion, at some little distance from the castle, where remains a piece of old wall.

The ancient church of St John has lately undergone a destructive reparation (destructive I mean to the antiquary) for then all the brasses, stained glass, and anything moveable, fall a prey to the masons and glaziers.

The key not being to be found, I saved sixpence, nor was the inside worth seeing; on the outside are placed, as the stoppers-up of an archway, two old stone coffin lids, around one of which is a curious inscription to the memory of a Danish warrior. Antiquity can go no further back.

Then I crossed the river to where resides Mr Sergeant Kemp ('in a shady, cool, retreat') opposite to the old small church of St Morland, when the returning rain drove me for shelter into a venerable looking cottage, with an arched stone entrance and an iron-guarded door, wherein were a woman and her two children. She said she was the wife of Mr Kemp's huntsman, was very civil, brought me pen and ink for my journalizing, and told me that her house was supposed to belong to the friars; and probably it might have been a cell belonging to the priory, and the large house a residence of the priors. How wretched do the miseries of a cottage appear (and this was only of comparative distress) – want of food, want of fuel, want of clothing! Children perishing of an ague! And an unhappy mother unable to attend to or relieve their wants, or assuage their pains, nor to allow time sufficient even for the reparation of their rags; whilst the worn-down melancholy father (perhaps a shepherd), pinched by cold and pining with despair, returns at evening close to a hut devoid of comfort or the smallest renovation of hope. For no longer are left the fostering, forgiving hand of his landlord, or the once bountiful buttery of the manor house, to apply to!

(All the rich and gay world huddled together in London, on turkey carpets, before register stoves, can but little conceive the pangs of poverty; and what mischiefs they inflict, what benefits they withhold, and what true grandeur and felicities they forego, by thus sacrificing their lives and fortunes in the company of vicious women of quality and rascally politicians!)

I made an abode of novelty and necessity here for an hour,

when I resumed my walk, and into the Cuckfield road; here the rain, recommencing, obliged me to shelter myself at a turner's and again at a saddler's. At last I worked my way home without being much wetted. I thought myself lucky in being able to get this walk, and that this day, the only day of intended idleness, should prove the only bad day of this tour.

I.D. did not appear, during our being together, to be in right health, for he neither ate nor drank; which indeed curbed me (as one person always stimulates or prevents the other), and from this cause we have kept too early hours, and have been longer in bed than even in London. Whereas in my last trip, I never retired till half-past eleven or 12 o'clock, after having well talked over the occurrences of the past and the intentions of the coming day.

Mrs Byng and our son Henry, and – to my great surprise – my late companion in touring, Mr Windham, who kindly came as escort. Dinner was now to be hastened, and their journey related, which had been rendered agreeable by the pleasant company of Mr and Mrs Harben, who live opposite to this inn; he is a banker, and his eldest son is distributor of stamps[1] for part of this county.

Hearing that I was here, an invitation to tea was sent to us. After dinner we took our son Henry to the school, seemingly very fit for little fellows (kept by Mr Raymond, a Swiss, and his wife, who are very careful people and competent of such charge), where I hope he will improve in strength by the goodness of the air. We drank tea with Mr Harben and family, and then walked in their garden and, at my desire, into the rooms at the castle top to see the view there. From Mr Harben we received a flow of compliments and civilities, and an offer which we accepted of his phaeton[2] to carry Mr Windham and Mrs Byng to Brighthelmstone tomorrow.

[1] Byng himself, of course, worked in the Stamp Tax office.
[2] A type of carriage.

There was no appetite at supper at our inn, or a liking for the potted wheatears[1] or a desire for late house.

When we had been some time in bed, our room door was forced upon by drunkards, which alarmed Mrs Byng exceedingly.

23 August   Mr Harben furnished us this morning with his phaeton driven by a postillion, to take Mrs Byng and Mr Windham (at Windham's desire) to see Brighton, and I rode by their side.

The road leads by Falmer, a small village which would afford a pleasant situation to a shooter, a walker or a harehunter, who might here during a long autumn enjoy these sports rationally, with the comforts of a sea view and breeze; or if frisky, and eager to be unhappy and expensive, step down to Shergold's for his claret and all the wicked etceteras!!

Brighton appeared in a fashionable, unhappy bustle, with such a harpy set of painted harlots as to appear to me as bad as Bond Street in the spring, at three o'clock p.m.

The Castle is reckoned a good tavern, and so we found it completely; and most comfortably too, after our walking the Steyne, entering the booksellers' shops, sitting by the seaside and endeavouring to look like old residents. But not till we had been equipped by the masterly comb of Mr Stiles.

Nothing could be better than our dinner and the two bottles of claret and port that Windham and I soon sucked down, and then sighed for more wheatears after the many we had eaten dressed to perfection. We then saw the magnificent assembly room here; and though we would not stay to see the play (*Henry IV*, Falstaff by Mr Ryder) we had a peep into the Playhouse. In our morning's drive poor little Wowski (Mr Windham's little dog, bought at Wansford Bridge) was run over by the phaeton, and her leg much hurt.

We did not leave Brighton till past seven o'clock, where is

[1] Little birds, much prized for eating.

plenty of bad company, for elegant and modest people will not abide such a place! As for the Castle Tavern, it seemed excellent, and much money might be tolerably spent in it.

Our drive home was almost in the dark, meeting many chaises by the way, as we had pointer trainers[1] in the morning.

It was but decent to wait upon Mr Harben at our return, with our best thanks, and to express our happiness in leaving our son Henry under the eye of such civility.

The old blockhouse at Brighthelmstone, by the encroachment of the sea has been gradually undermined, and is now quite fallen into the sea.

[A paragraph has been cut out from the manuscript here, ending '. . . and Divisions.']

24 August   There cannot be an inn of a worse description than is this White Hart, and the Star looks as badly; so if ever I should come this way again, the Bear must be my trial. In this inn yard, as in many others, are verses over the horse trough for the benefit of wit or the ostler.

> Whoever dips or washes here
> He aught and shall pay a pot of beer
> And if he refuses the beer to pay
> He shall he dry burnt without delay.

At half-past nine o'clock, having again paid my compliments to Mr Harben and begged a holiday at the school, I left Lewes by the upper road. To the village of Offham two miles, at the foot of the South Downs, near to which Sir James Bridges has a pleasant sporting seat; through a wooded country, and by Mr D'Oyleys park pales to Challey, a small church, where divine service was beginning. In Kent, Sussex and wooded counties, the churches are low and mean; whereas in Huntingdonshire, Cambridgeshire and other open counties, the churches are large and lofty. Soon after Challey, I was overtaken by Col. D'Oyley

[1] Hunting dogs.

in a post-chaise, coming from his brother's, who pressed me to come in to him and to have his servant mount my horse; but no, that could not be, for various reasons. To change my free situation on horseback for a corner of an hackney post-chaise, and to let a servant ride my friend's horse, will never do! I kept up with him till I came under Lord Sheffield's park pales, when I rode through his grounds and around the house, which is placed pleasantly, and surrounded greenly and by some good trees, and with lakish ponds in front.

Returning by the lodge, of good Gothic taste, I passed by the large new inn on Sheffield Green, where Col. D'Oyley, changing horses, renewed his invitation. The country here is rich in wood, much of which is consumed in the burning of lime; which in my mind (ignorant in farming I profess myself) does that sort of good to land that dram-drinking does to the constitution – as momentary assistance!

When I had mounted the summit of Dane Hill the Forest of Ashdown begins, healthy and wild, having been stripped of its remaining timber by the late Duke of Dorset, of mean memory, mentioned before at Knole. After passing Kidbrook, Lord Abergavenny's, which shows nothing extraordinary, I came to Forest Row and put up at the Swan, the right kind of house and at the right hour too.

A leg of mutton and turnips just boiled, added to a plum pie, with good cheese and half a pint of brandy, made me feel as full as an alderman. This, a clean cloth and civility was a facsimile of my last dinner at Northiam. In this garden stands a most noble and reverend yew tree.

I believe that I stayed loitering here two hours, for I had plenty of time, though I meant to go further than at first I proposed; for my baggage was to be left at the Crown Inn at Grinstead, which would have been too short a distance, and besides Mr Harben advised me, if possible, to get on to Godstone, an excellent house, and avoid the bad inns of Grinstead. So I had desired Col. D'Oyley to forward my cloak-bag to Godstone. A gentleman intent on touring may be able, by making much enquiry in London, to find out about half the curiosities in any county; and then in a second trip he will discover the third quarter. But as for country enquiry it is almost in vain, from the ignorance and want of curiosity in the natives! So of today; and I was pleased to find something – by myself. In half a mile from Forest Row I saw a building, to my left, with spires, and yet not a church. So I enquired and got the regular answer, 'That it was an ancient old place.'

Turning to the left down a woody lane, I soon came to Brambletye, a venerable, deserted mansion in its latest ruins, with two most solid stone lodges, coped with stone to the top and difficult to demolish. A gateway and all the stone window partitions remain, but the inside is entirely plucked out. A neighbouring cottager told me that it had been abandoned about forty years. Over and about these ruins I scrambled, and meditated for ten minutes; bethinking me of the great improvement of the roads, which have introduced learning and arts into the country and removed the (formerly wretched) families, who buried themselves in mud and ignorance, to the gay participation of wit and gallantry in the parishes of Marylebone and St James's!! How wretched and dull, and unimproving, must have been the life of these sequestered females, miserably employed in reading, working, walking, obliged to rise early, go to bed early, sometimes to receive their neighbours and relations; but never tasting (in those Gothic days) the dear and eternal delights of flirtation, the midnight supper, the dance till daylight. Fashion opposed to fashion; dress compared with dress. Eating ices in January, and wearing roses in February. With modern hands that never work, and limbs that never move but in a dance!!

Three miles brought me to East Grinstead, pleasantly situated upon a hill; over the country to the left I bent my eyes in vain, to find out Mr C.'s (our solicitor's) now-building seat.

When at Grinstead, I walked into the churchyard to survey what was left of the church that fell down and which the clerk said would be soon rebuilt by Mr Wyatt, and that Mr Gibbs-

Crawford was at the head of the rebuilding committee, adding that he (Mr Gibbs-Crawford) was himself building a grand house, and was the greatest man in their parish or neighbourhood!

Happy I was to find that my baggage was gone forward from the Crown Inn, and that I was not to sleep in any of the vile-looking inns here. Soon after Grinstead I passed by the house and parkish grounds of Mr Evelyn, wherein is erected an extraordinary monumental obelisk; he, like all other modern planners and according to that general taste now prevalent, must stock up hedges and lay wide and waste; and then these lawns, ill-suiting the business of farming, are obliged to be divided again by filthy rails and hurdles.

Our ancestors were happy to ride from field to field, from wood to wood; but now all is to be lawned, to be clumped. All to be seen at once! Surely modest nature should make but partial discoveries, to eager the eye, to indulge the imagination, and not start all her charms at one display. Below Mr Evelyn's, at Felbridge, were I to write in the language of my predecessor, Leland[1], I should say, 'Their was muche wodi and morische grounde.'

There is on the rise of Godstone Hill a transcendent view to the south, over woodlands to Ashdown Forest; to the north, opener enclosures backed by the ridge of hills that pass through Surrey and Kent. Altogether a prospect that would delight a Dutchman, as not showing a drop of water! The White Hart Inn at Godstone proved perfectly to my wishes as to situation, reception and entertainment; the mistress was civil, the servants attentive, and my supper (which I took after seeing my horse eat up every corn) was of the best service; viz. a fine boiled fowl, whose parentage and education I learned of the landlady, with a fresh morello cherry pie and good port wine.

However, but for writing I should have been very melancholy. Journalizing, when alone, is always a solace.

[1] John Leland (c. 1503–52), the earliest English antiquary.

Today, I have been lucky in inns, at Forest Row for a noon stop, and at Godstone for the night.

The bed here was as good as my other entertainment; a hard smooth bed was a treat! I was waked, as all travellers should be, by the sun, and in a few minutes downstairs; for I now leave all dressing till I get home. My bill was very reasonable and the people civil and contented. The roads were in fine order, dust just laid, everything smelling of freshness; and perhaps I had gone along too idly but from being overtaken by a heavy farmer upon a smaller horse than mine, so we forced each other along, and quickly too, for we were at Croydon in an hour and a quarter, and a steep hill by the way. Here we parted, and I went into the Greyhound Inn for breakfast, feeling very hungry; my companion the farmer, an elderly-looking man, talked of times long past, and then proved to be six years younger than myself. I can see others' ages in their looks, and shall be almost ready to 'break my faithful looking glass'.

After breakfast, at a small bookseller's shop I found, if no old books, a great treat in the master, Mr Hawes, a bewildered Methodistical poet who has been abused by the reviewers. He would force upon me, gratis, his poem, this crust, etc., etc., all smelling strongly of Bedlam; and these was I obliged to promise to peruse.

The old archiepiscopal palace (which I had seen before) I again walked about to take my leave of; as being lately sold, it is now abandoned to the uses of a calico printer. The casements are taken out of the old hall, the gardens are demolished etc. etc.

> Imperial Caesar dead, and turned to clay.

From Croydon – which I quitted at ten o'clock – at an easy pace, passing by the Duke of Bedford's shabby seat at Streatham, to the left by Streatham Church, I returned to my household gods by twelve o'clock – on *Monday August 26th, 1788.*

3
Tour to the North
1792

Barnard Castle
Richmond
Askrigg
Middleham
Masham
Ingleton
Ripon
Settle
Skipton
Knaresborough
Clitheroe
York
Wetherby
Haslingdon
Ferrybridge
Rochdale
Manchester
Doncaster

Macclesfield
Leek
Tuxford
Newcastle
–under–Lyme
Newark
Trentham
Grantham
Stafford
Stone
Shifnal
Greetham
Brewood
Wolverhampton
Wansford
Dudley
Birmingham
Alconbury
Henley–in–Arden
Huntingdon
Stratford–on–Avon
Biggleswade

Woodstock
Welwyn
Oxford
Abingdon
Benson
Henley
Slough
London

I am happy (vain perhaps) in thinking that I enjoy the pleasure of touring as much if not more than most men, and each tour three times over: viz. by anticipation, by the present enjoyment and by a record of the past.

Those who wonder at my anticipating pleasures seem, in my opinion, to be wanting in judgment and desires. Anticipation is a preparation of the mind, as necessary as that a lawyer should study his brief, or that any man should fit himself for an event he hopes, or knows, must arrive.

Men who have held the steadiest course through life have adhered to this doctrine; whilst dashing speculators have, from want of foresight, lost their way and bewildered their talents. Before I set forward upon this new progress, let me well examine Dr C.'s collection of topographical prints, that I may not trot by a place which I shall afterwards learn was an object of admiration. Let me consider my time and consult my abilities. Let me rummage myself forth to observe, and decant upon, my own country; and not sink into that sloth and want of curiosity that, with wonder I observe, men of great fortunes yield to:

> To me more dear, congenial to my heart,
> One native charm, than all the gloss of art;
> Spontaneous joys where Nature has its play
> The soul adopts, and owns their first-born sway;
> Lightly they frolic o'er the vast mind,
> Unenvied, unmolted, unconfined.
>
> Goldsmith

A relation of mine died a few days since at the very advanced age of 87 – a long life! But what charity did he bestow, or what indigence relieved with his great fortune? What friends did he acquire, or whom did he make happy?

To these questions I answer: of charity he was ignorant; and as for friends – why these to acquire, and to continue and, if necessary, to assist, is the first delight in life, the honour and comfort of a noble heart; but this dawdling fool neither deserved nor gained one friend. The riches that blind fortune threw into his lap procured him houses, victuals and drink and, what he wished for, idleness, stupid idleness; which is reckoned by most mortals the chief of earthly blessings, to have the mind and body in perfect stagnation, to observe upon just what passes before them, to rise to eat, and to loiter through the day.

If this is life, let people live to 87 years of age and brag of longevity. For my own part, I will brag to have already lived to that period by having employed myself, and my time, in doing something; by rising early, by taking exercise, by reading, and writing much; and then at, and after, dinner I can enjoy the good things of this life as well as any man. My own disposition is correspondent with Sir Thomas Wyatt's, whose poetry is very pleasant.

I had promises from Mr and Mrs Colman of accompanying me and Mrs Byng to Biggleswade, for the first days of my outset; but their promises 'melted into air, thin air'; not from a want of civility or of wishes, but from business to which he must now particularly attend.

My chestnut mare, Spot, who is in fine order, I shall ride from town; and when at Biggleswade shall take up my bay gelding Bumper (now at straw-yard) for the carriage of Garwood and our baggage.

> Tired with the town and all its noisy sway,
> With eager haste I make the northern way,
> Leave pomp and vanity, fatigue and care,
> For sweet tranquillity with rural fare.*

* I shall insert some of these (laughably written) scraps of poetry, from one of the publications of a vain pedant (Mr Maude) who will make his appearance in the course of this tour.

A long London winter bends me to earth; my nerves are terribly weak and my chest is alarmingly sore; I feel in London like the enraged musician, stunned by noises, cries and rape, and nearly driven over, every day, by curricles; and if I mount my horse, can hardly escape from a Brentford stage[coach]. The ceaseless account of diversions and fashions make me sick; and I will not accord to the unnatural hours. Nerve-worn, and with reason, I must, though melancholy to go alone, take the field.

At 12 o'clock, *Saturday May 26th 1792*, I had taken the Paddington Road, which the rains of last night had made nice riding and the face of nature gay. This, with tolerable weather, is the season to view her. Beyond Edgeware are what remains of Canons Park and House; a wonderful change from a Dukedom to the present possessor! Then 'each parterre a lawn', now each parterre a potato ground! Trade and gambling overset all distinctions. I turned round upon Elstree Hill to admire the prospect! What view finer? What village pleasanter? The all-around so rich, so verdant.

Mr Phillimore's seat at —— is a well-wooded, retired spot; and the lane by it continues, for some distance, as shaded and sequestered as possible; too much for me at present, and at my onset. Some hasty showers made me skulk under the hedges. In melancholy mood, in this sweet but gloomy country, I continued by Park Street hamlet to the pretty village of St Stephens, just above St Albans, where I put up at the White Hart at half past 3 o'clock; and such an inn is scarcely to be found (though perhaps the best here) of filth, inattention and charge; though I did not afford them much scope by only taking some cold beef (such stuff!) on my return from the walk round this once-famous abbey.

I am very low, and wearied; but will hope that from country air and fresh scenery I may revive. The wretchedness of the inn made me hurry off. A laney, stony road of 7 miles, passing through the village of Sandridge, brought me into the North Road at the 22nd mile stone (so I have gone three miles about);

and in 3 more miles I arrived at Welwyn, where the White Hart appeared magnificent after that of St Albans.

> Thy shades, O Welling! for they never tire,
> Deep from my soul I cease not to admire.
> Here, there sleeps Young, whose well-spread mental feast
> Draws the wise lore, and marvels of the East.
> He lives! perennial lives! With awe attend!
> Drink at his fount, and be to all a friend.

I prowled about the pretty environs of this village till half-past eight o'clock, when I was summoned to eat of an eel, etc; and from that time sat in stupid despondency till I crawled up to bed.

27 May   Glad to quit my blankets, 'caught up in the alarm of fear' (no sprinkled sheets for me), for so active and eager was I as to wake every hour from 4 to 7; and then in haste to breakfast and away. Here they are building a new, large meeting house, sad omen of the downfall of the churches! For the dissenters will soon choose the parliament; and then look to yourselves, my Lord the Bishop, Mr Dean, ye fat prebends and ye idle, absent rectors.

What a lovely day! Such as the poets have written about and we wish in vain for. The (few remaining) birds were in full song; and the air was perfumed by the hawthorn bush, who now powders the earth with blossoms.

My way, though so well known, seemed short; by half-past eleven o'clock (thinking of nothing at all, what a blessing?) I arrived at my country seat, the Sun Inn at Biggleswade. (Let us now refer to my poet.)

> Thy road, my Biggleswade, deserving draws
> From the pleased traveller his just applause;
> Nor less the lucid stream that laves thy side,
> Decked in the flowing pomp of ready pride.
> Whether for gain, or in the finny line,
> For on thy eels, good gods, how we did dine!

> Alike the merits of thy placid flood,
> To near and distant wants dispensing good.

Sent instantly for Bumper from grass; unlocked my chest of drawers; and made arrangements for my campaign with as much alacrity as Rochambeau can do for his.

> (Votaries of fame and worshippers of power,
> Suspend the pleasing phantoms for an hour.)

Thus would I speak to the herd, the silly, the vain, the vicious herd of fashions in London to endeavour to make them see, feel and taste the healthy delights of the country: for to what a pitch must folly and fashion have arrived when they have changed day into night, summer into winter, and will suffer no gentility to quit London till August.

I had for dinner at 2 o'clock (the hour of rational and useful appetite), a boiled fowl, greens, roast beef, Yorkshire pudding, asparagus, tarts and custards! (Let us look to the charge hereafter.) I ate like a parson or a farmer (Swift could not decide who was the better eater), and so greedily at first that I only eyed and threatened the tarts and custards. Mark the effect of the country air upon one who was formed for a quiet country gentleman; to be idly busied in farming, planting and gardening, and not to be worried every morning by revenue prosecutions, and every evening by sights and relations of follies and fashions.

My wishes would be to form a curious rosary; to observe the growth of curious grasses and of new trees; not to be obliged to listen to the malignity of faction and the accounts of the pleasures of a faro table. I leave negative pleasures to the gay world; when I can smell a rose and eat a slice of old, well-kept mutton. I know that two senses have been gratified; but does the old coquette receive much satisfaction from the continuance of her tight stays, and the adornment of her head with false flowers?

At half-past 2 o'clock Garwood arrived by the coach, with my (*heavy*) travelling baggage under his arm. You may think (whoever you are that read this) that I did not lose the fine evening (no, indeed I did not; nor do I intend to lose an hour of my holidays) for I walked 2 miles before tea, and almost as much afterwards, when the evening grew cold and I ordered a fire. This season, I know, is too early for touring; but another month in London had destroyed me.

About nine o'clock the rain commenced, and continued smartly when I retired, to sheets my own, at eleven o'clock.

28 May   A brilliant though windy morning. It should seem that I had much to do from seven (my hour of rising) till nine o'clock, my hour of breakfast, as shaving, arranging saddles, fixing straps, etc, and attending to the shoeing of Bumper, a most material and much neglected inspection, for a lame horse ruins us and defeats my plan. At 10 o'clock I intended my ride (Garwood to go alone, and prove his horse and his horseman-ship) but Mr Repton, the now noted landscape gardener, came in and delayed me for half an hour. He is a gentleman I have long known, and of so many words that he is not easily shaken off; he asserts so much, and assumes so much, as to make me irritable, for he is one (on the many) who is never wrong; and therefore why debate with him?

I wondered that he should not keep his own post-chaise, and he wondered at my riding; so wonders never cease! I left him at breakfast, and took my ride to Gastling's and More Hall Farms, but both the Mr W.s were gone to our fair. I had left word at the inn that I hoped they would dine with me.

The country looked gay from the red cloaks flocking to the fair. My dinner (I love to repeat good ones) consisted of spatchcocked eel, roasted pigeons, a loin of pork roasted, with tarts, jellies and custards. Enough for one gentleman? Garwood gave a good account of his horse's going—a horse I bought cheaply, as being untractable and furious; but quietness brings them steady. He probably has been whipped into vice. My mare last year could not be dressed, and now she is as tame as a sow.

In the evening the weather, after much wind, turned into heavy rain; so I had only to write, to tea and to stable, and to wish for some quiet society, wondering where I saw chaise travellers, masters of their time, not put up in such weather and be comfortable, instead of forcing through the storms and seeing poor post-boys wet to the skin! Why, there is a good inn, with good coffee and good wine? Stay then, and play at cards and backgammon; and depart when the wind does not blow a hurricane and the rain fall a deluge.

> Yet the trembling year is unconfirmed,
> And winter oft at eve resumes the breeze,
> Chills the pale morn, and bids the driving sleets
> Deform the day delightless; so that scarce
> The bittern knows his time, with bill
> To shade the sounding marsh, or from the shore
> The plovers when to scatter o'er the heath,
> And sing their wild notes to the list'ning waste.

This will beat down my favourite May blossoms. At 7 o'clock, the weather clearing up, I achieved a walk of an hour, although I have caught a fresh cold and the pains and soreness of my chest have returned. The foul weather has damped the delights of the fair and driven the company like wheatears into shelter, so the men must be fuddled and the women ruined.

There is a kind of fisherman (alias porter) – Mr Holdstock, of whom much more in subsequent tours – who has taken up his abode near this inn, and makes artificial baits etc. As I love an oddity, I sent for him and conversed with him upon piscatory subjects. He said, 'that London did not agree with him' (probably not), 'that he subsisted upon making false flies etc. for the London shops; and should be happy to angle with me at any time; that the Colonel's dog Ranger had lived with him, and that he intended to paint his picture' (being a kind of Jack of-all-trades). I asked him if he had read Walton? 'Oh yes; every book upon the science.' He would have presented me with a false minnow,[1] as not being selfish, and I presented him with a

---

[1] A fishing fly.

real shilling. Considering Ranger's situation (though this may be a very honest man), I have determined to take him with me.

At 9 o'clock Mr Repton returned from his visitation in this neighbourhood, to draw his plans and to relate his journeys, his consequence and his correspondence. Scarcely any man who acquires a hasty fortune but becomes vain and consequential; though Mr Repton being now sought for, has a professional right to dictate and control, and being Nature's physician, to tap, bleed and scarify[1] her. But he is very wrong (in my opinion) in not being well-mounted, and in not building a comfortable travelling chaise with a good cave for Madeira wine. But to all this Repton is a stranger; and piques himself upon sleeping in *fresh* sheets every night (!) which hereafter he will dolefully repent.

Having much discourse (for Repton is an everlasting talker), we did not part till midnight.

29 May   A most blustering morn; and if the wind subsides, the rain will fall, for the clouds seem full. I arose at 7 o'clock; Repton was up at 8, and then went off to Mr T.'s in this neighbourhood, where he is to plan and oversee.

My letters from town being answered, I felt an uncertainty of stay or go; but should I yield to every cloud, or feel dislike to quit an inn, I had better in staying at home.

So 'To horse, my brave boys, and away.' Let us compare these charges ten years hence. Nowhere shall I find a cheaper charge.

A 'wind tempestuous' bore me to Sutton where I called upon Mr D., an agent of Lady B.'s, with enquiries after Mr Osborn's mare, at grass in the park. He civilly walked with me into the park; but seeing her hopelessly lame, I forebore any traffic. Thence I pursued my way through Potton; in two more miles to Gamlingay, a village in Cambridgeshire; and so by Waresley Park (one of those to be improved by Mr Repton). This road, for my call and as more novel, I preferred (the round about) to the pleasanter

---

[1] Tiny cuts in the skin for bleeding.

North Road. To escape many storms of rain, I sheltered under hedges; luckily the wind was south and at my back. A dreary open road to the miserable village of Eltisley, of mud houses and aguish inhabitants. I had not long entered the old North Road when a severe storm came on. I backed my mare into a hedge, and wished for a friend; then an old story had been delectable and the storm a trifle, but shivering alone, and wilfully, won't do. I stayed in the hedge 20 minutes, and then trotted away to Godmanchester where, overtaking Mr Speed's hounds returning from airing, I entered Huntingdon like a sportsman. The rain falling very hard, I entered in haste the first inn, the Crown: a bad one it is, for no fire was lighted and the stable is most dismal.

There are players here, who perform tonight; and with a companion I might have been eager to have stayed the play, but they do not begin till the genteel hour of seven, so I shall hurry off to be at mine ease, I hope, at Alconbury Hill. The season is yet too cold for common inns; but I repeat my necessity of going from London.

My dinner, room and attendance were all as bad as could be. I walked my mare to Alconbury Hill (G. had arrived an hour before me). There took my tea, and then a sauntering walk. All the country around is newly enclosed; which Capability Repton at Biggleswade said 'was a fine invention and a noble thing, for in Norfolk they allotted to each cottager an acre of land'. 'Noble, and useful indeed,' answered I, 'to give to a man an acre of land, which he may sell away in an hour, in lieu of that permanency which our ancestors (under the guidance of Providence) allotted for a perpetuity.' I saw an advertisement, in the Cambridge paper, which proved how a country may be depopulated; and daring treason to the prosperity of the land is such an advertisement, 1,000 acres without a farmer, or a cottager! The living a certain sinecure!

> Space for his lake, his park's extended bounds
> Space for his horses, equipage and hounds.
> Goldsmith

Two houses yet hang out oaken boughs, in memory of the day. Alconbury Hill is not calculated for windy weather, for wind searches every corner thereof; as for the weather, it feels tonight like Christmas, and they hope for peas in 3 weeks' time! Either I was warmer, or the weather was warmer at this season, when I was younger. I now keep a double journal by writing long daily letters to my home. I had a large fire, for it is a bleak spot, and a good supper in a good room, with much huntable discourse with the waiter, the landlord's brother, a happy removal from Huntingdon quarters.

I was contented with my supper, and highly gratified with my bed which was excellent, with a thick, smooth mattress (for here come hunting gentlemen to instruct them) and curtains pleated like a paper lantern; but notwithstanding this, I left it at six o'clock to enjoy a fine morning.

Mr W., who was once forced to a tour by Mr O., exclaimed at the first inn where they were well treated, 'Why go on; are not we very comfortable here?' And so I said at every good stop. I now took a most happy and refreshing walk to the top of Stonegate Hill, where passing under Monk's Wood, fronting the morning sun, listening to the birds and observing the many labourers altering the road, I revelled in the delights of the country and of an early morn. Who can but enjoy a fine early morn? And yet how few will! None in London, that nest of folly, fashion.

The waiter, smelling out my taste, told me that the labourers found coins, old iron, etc, at Stingall Hill; so, I stopped in my way to enquire, and found that the coins were halfpence and the old iron, horseshoe.

To the right of the road, opposite to the turnpike, at the bottom of the hill stood Sawtrey Abbey; of which no memorial exists but the field on which it stood, being called Abbey Field and abounding with mounds of foundation. The day was most charming, a south-west wind with flying showers, all which I escaped. About Stilton much rain had fallen last night; as I approached Wansford Bridge, I appeared to be coming home, and found a good Bridge accommodation, and reception there as formerly, though the old waiter is gone, which to the traveller is a loss. The comparative state of my inns is: Biggleswade, good, all but beds; Alconbury Hill, good, all but stabling; Wansford Bridge, good, all but wine.

I begin now to rise unwillingly after dinner, and shall soon prefer a nap to a ride. However, I feel myself in better health from exercise and the country air; but health at my age is only negative: not producing activity or spirits, but an abstinence from malady or racking pains, that's health at 50. I often wish for the gout, as a consolidation stamp for the several taxes upon life, if a stamp is necessary; and I believe it is. And who should know better? May the weather continue warm, else inns in general cannot be inhabited.

I left Wansford Bridge at 3 o'clock; and when at the turnpike opposite Burleigh Park stood for some time, in terror of a thunderstorm that passed beyond Stamford. After I had got through Stamford another storm came on, and I rode with all my speed to avoid it to the village of Brigg Casterton; and just got under a gateway when it came down, horse, foot and dragoons, hail, rain and thunder.

(When upon the hill above Stamford encouraging Ranger, he started a hare and had a fine view. Our Bedfordshire Militia, upon a march, used to say that the sight of a hare coursed was to them as enticing as a pint of beer per man.)

After the storm I crawled forth (where Garwood sheltered, I know not), and left the high road of a mile to my right, to view Tickencote church, when behold, it was almost pulled down! And what is more strange is now rebuilding with stone, from the old model exact, at the expense of Mrs Whitfield of Stamford (a woman of much taste she must be, and a staunch church-woman I warrant ye). The old nobly-roofed chancel with its beautifully painted stone arch is remaining, and to be preserved, together with, I hope, a cross-legged knight carved in oak. When finished, which this summer will complete, it will exist (ages after all others of this style are gone) a model of Saxon architecture; and to the honour of this lady. Now if a nobleman wants to rebuild a church (none do but for a removal), why not build one after this model? My horse being held by one of the masons, I stayed some time in the inside, and when I came out, 'Presented my compliments, a tourist's compliments, by the master workman, to the lady, begging her to perfect her magnificence by glazing the church with stained glass.' The mason agreed with me and promised to deliver my message.

Two miles further, upon the North Road, I turned left over a foresty common to Exton park gate (Lord Gainsborough); the outskirts are farmed off, but it is not a very large park, without beauty or keeping; the house is at the further end, near the church. Of these strange buildings and absurd inventions, some remain, which should be pulled down. The pools are handsome, but their banks are not planted. I wandered about this park for a long hour, not meeting one creature! And then returned into the North Road within a mile to Greetham Inn, the Royal Oak, where Garwood (who manages very well) had prepared for me. This is a raw, cold house, too much of the windmill sort, and I believe I had done better to have gone on to Witham Common; but we must live and *larn*, and a road to be known must be often travelled.

The waiter is one of those old donkey, drunken, conceited fools, that would drive Colonel Bertie wild; now could I totally abstain from him. My evening walk, very wet and dirty, became very short.

In the adjacent woods, Sir W.L. has been permitted to cut ridings! That he should not do in the woods, as it much assists the poacher, chills the timber, and gives a very unfair advantage over the fox, who is to be viewed and hallooed at every turning; but I suppose it is right, being the high fashion. My parlour, supper and wine were so unpleasant that I could not (in my usual way) build a castle, but only thought of the morrow and of a departure. In one instance I am right as to early time, being before other travellers, or the bagmen, from London. The stabling here is good.

31 May   I hurried to bed early last night; one of the miseries of being alone. My bed was good, and my *own* sheets are dry. I shall see Repton laid up by the rheumatism, wondering at the cause. The morning sun shone so brightly into my chamber as to drive me from bed at past six o'clock, and I was at breakfast by 8 o'clock though the waiter was very slow and tiresome; and then most glad was I to leave Greetham Inn, where everything is bad and they are dirty, tedious, ignorant, etc., etc. It was a gloomy agreeable morning, the roads bad and greasy. Streeton church and small village, to the right, stand pleasantly. I am certain I had done right in stopping last night at the Bull Inn, Witham Common.

The day was so sweet that I walked down all the hills, which are frequent. The George Inn at Colsterworth is now shut up. To the left, upon the hill, is the hamlet of Woolsthorpe, the birthplace of Sir Isaac Newton, but why mention this again? Or about this road whereon I have travelled before.

Ponton Steeple is worthy of admiration; so is Grantham Vale. Now the stone buildings begin to give way to brick; I wish the roads would change into gravel, or sand. I put up at the Angel (the old house) in Grantham, which is a very tolerable inn, with good stabling, and then paraded about the town. The Old Conduit in the Market Place was built in 1597, and repaired 1773. Surely Mr Manners's house is a strange uncouth place, fit only for a public building, but not for the residence of a gentleman of fortune, and to be cribbed up in a small enclosure. I have met Colonel M. and one of his daughters. Hard this upon me, who hoped that my acquaintance were dying off.

Garwood is very attentive; but he is gloomy and does not exhilarate me, for he always seems as if he were coming with a complaint, or to relate a misfortune. T. Bush was not like this; he inspired and urged me along. Now Garwood is despondent, and draws me back: the one would have made an active soldier, the other a passive one.

> Or yet in turn the weary limb refresh,
> And in thy visions magic scenes address.

107

Seize yonder spot, where lofty domes arise,
And Grantham's soaring spire salutes the skies.
Grantham, the nurt'ring school of Newton's mind,
That dealt a general harvest to Mankind.
Now in my turn the weary limb refresh
And, not in vision, solid food address;
Seize yonder fowl, whilst smoking steams arise,
And Grantham's soaring spire salutes the skies.
Grantham, the nurt'ring school of Newton's mind
That deals out good Oporto to Mankind.

Which was, luckily, my lot, by the assistance of the waiter from Wansford Bridge who now lives here – and, no doubt, enhanced my pedigree and character. (I must never think of Mr W. and his desire to stay.) Zeal, hope and activity if possible, must urge me on; and my motto, 'Let Fiery Expedition be my Shield'. I saw a bill in the parlour, with a charge of two bottles of claret! This is money thrown into the sea; as well call for champagne in Wapping. At 3 o'clock I left Grantham, to mount the hill to Gonerby village, where appeared something like a feast, which I love to see, or to hear the squeak of a fiddle, and always look about for a cricket match, or fives playing, for little recreation have the poor, and but a short summer.

The view from Gonerby Hill is very extensive but not of beauty, all wide views are horrors to me; like an embarkment into Eternity. Sir J. Thorold's new house upon a hill top commands all this vale, staring around in vain for beauties!

Descending into the flat, the road becomes of a gravelly amendment. So both man and horse jog on at their ease. The mile-posts, made like way-posts, are both expensive and ill-looking. Forston village stands high and makes a show; and Long Bennington is a very long and large village indeed. Thence a pleasant flat of four miles of excellent road leads into Newark. Here I put up (alone, or 'first is always wrong'), at the Kingston Arms; and made some kind of quarters good, as getting stalls and a baddish parlour.

Then for a walk to gaze at the remaining front of the Old

Castle (screening a bowling green) and by the Trent side, who appeared most serene, nor was her brow ruffled but by the small fishes who scarred the surface.

> Till Newark's verdant plain the hour beguiles,
> Where lucid Trent in pliant progress smiles.
> Say, what is Royalty? Descend to scan
> The thorny, devious paths inverted ran,
> Ill-fated Charles! There seats of fable woe,
> Where ruins nod, and weed lethiferous grow,
> Proclaim aloud, in fighting accents tell
> How Cromwell ruled, how regal fortunes fell.

It was an evening for love, for contemplation, for gratitude, for hope, for every good feeling; nor could I return till 8 o'clock, to feed the nag and order supper. This eternally ordering meals tires exceedingly; besides, inn cookery in general is wretched work.

I supped till past ten o'clock, when the moon, shining bright, tempted me to take a turn upon the Market Place, a very showy grand place. I wish there had been soldiers to set it off; unluckily I never meet any, and the uselessly called-forth Militia make me sick. I hoped likewise for a play here. Newark church is a noble building, with a noble spire, but must be too much lighted within, now that stained glass is abolished. I ride away from peas and strawberries, which I suppose are now in appearance in London. Sat up late, to make me sleep well. The Old Cross has been tolerably well repaired within these last few years by Mr Mellish, as a copper plate upon it announceth.

1 June   Arose at half-past six for the first intention, this year, of going forward; and as the morning was lovely lost not a minute, that I might reach the first stage to breakfast, and there 'study fashions to adorn my person'. Taking with me clean stockings, neckcloth and shirt, I had crossed the bridge and was already in the meadows when the Newark clocks struck seven.

This is like a workman? But impossible in company; at least I never met company who would do it.

The ride from Newark, through frequent villages and upon an excellent road, with the freshness of the morn, gave me life and spirits. Through the two villages the Muskhams; thence to Cromwell, with a pretty church and churchyard: and to Carlton-upon-Trent where Mr Pocklington, at and about his lace, has shown more vile taste than can well be imagined.

So to Sutton. All this Vale of Newark is rich and populous; the country now rising presents a fine view of Lincoln Cathedral and of the Lincolnshire hills. I seemed to be soon at Tuxford, 2 miles short of which is Scarthing Moor Inn, a single house and seemingly a good stop. Tuxford is a mean, dirty place, though the inn, the Red Lion, proved a clean and civil house, where I breakfasted in great content at half-past nine o'clock (before the windows in London are unbarred) after the pleasant operations of shaving and shirting; heating everything well before the kitchen fire (for I die under damp).

I then walked about the town and the churchyard, wherein are but few epitaphs (I am afraid I am not keen, but train off). This was the best, upon

> MISS MAY CHAMBERS.
> In my fifteenth year God thought it fit
> I must Obey, and did submit;
> God thought it fit that I should have
> In my fifteenth year a silent grave.

A reluctant quitter of life, and likewise very fond of talking, we may conjecture.

I breakfasted completely, upon coffee, and found a cheap charge 8d; during my breakfast I saw my lackey pass by. From the hill above Tuxford, Lincoln Cathedral shows grandly, and recalled all my last progress. But to the north, the prospect becomes very rich and beautiful, with a great show of population, to which show the red houses contributed.

There lies by the roadside much spar stone, whence I should

think that lead might be found. Descend the hill to Markham Moor, where there seems to be a tolerable inn; to the left is seen the deserted Haughton Park, the noble house they pulled down, once a grand domain belonging to the Duke of Newcastle, whose seat at Clumber, to which there is a stone of direction upon the common, has swallowed up the others.

The road of beautiful features continues to Gamstone and Idleton villages, with a view of the Forest to the left and of Mr Eyre's seat, The Grove, to the right. The vale towards the Retfords is rich and verdant, and the two churches appear to advantage; I always judge well of a town when I observe a good footpath of distance to it. Retford tasting of a navigation, and of manufactories, shows in gaiety! I walked my horse over the stones.

There is a new-built town hall in West Retford, for both East and West Retford joining together a great place. I walked around the great churchyard, below which is a worsted manufactory. At the end of Retford stands the house of Mr E—(an officer of our office), a neat well-built box; adorned and planked in the true Cockney taste. Leaving Retford I soon came upon moory ground, which is now generally enclosed, some very lately, and this brought me at one o'clock to Barnby Moor where, of the two inns, I was uncertain at which my valet-de-voyaging had put up; but I found him at the Bell and there ordered dinner. As I entered, the rain seemed in rapid advance (after this very fine day); but I was 'at mine ease in this inn'. A civil landlord and a good parlour; so foreseeing the weather, I said, 'Garwood, we must abide here. Look to my bed.' For as I am forward in my march, and the country is all novel, what does it signify where my stop is; I only wished to have reached Doncaster as the gayer place.

Of eating and drinking, a true taste is lost in travelling; and soon one cannot distinguish, for down goes the tough chop and the puckering port; but then it is carried off by exercise. May poles are adorned in this county; I wish that the females were not so much, for the veils *prevail* . . . I eat rye bread, and eye *awry* with a cold eye, the ladies; and so they do me, and see the wrinkles. I must shave every day, and scrape away. The port wines here and at Grantham were good. At 5 o'clock in a fine, wet growing evening, I ordered coffee; and had then only to scribble, and to attempt a sketch of the view of the road from my window. Though I should not forget an excellent map of Yorkshire by Tuke which hung in the parlour, and afforded me many hints of my near and distant progress.

Then walked to the stables, to prevent that slumbering inclination which comes on certainly at a certain time of life, but which must be fought against, as well as all other approaches of our grand conqueror Mors[1], who by every sly scalade steals in, or mines, or storms. But when we can, let us oppose the monster and say, 'I won't come yet, keep off, you fearful rascal.'

My evening, long by myself, passed in quiet hope, and that fine weather might ensue. At eleven o'clock I retired to a good bed and a good bed chamber.

2 June   I looked frequently out of my windows at early morn; and finding the rain to continue, did not rise till 8 o'clock. I drank snail tea for breakfast, for my chest is very sore, as every cold or damp flies to that quarter. How difficult to meet our touring wishes; for if we go to a solitary inn, our spirits flag! If we come to a town inn, it is all noise and confusion. In the lone inn, there is a damp; in the town inn, heat and stinks.

The ostler, here, only knew the next stages, but a very scientific post-boy directed me quite wrong; at last the landlord (slow in coming) did point out my course. At nine o'clock, the day mended and I mounted Spot who is, as likewise Bumper, in very fine order.

Quitting Barnby Moor Bell Inn, a very good one, I turned to the left out of the main road, and by a very pleasant, light country came in three miles to Blyth, a small and now disused market town. (There were formerly, at short distances, small

[1] Death.

market towns to which, on a stated day in every week, the corn and every produce of the country was brought, and it made a little holiday; but now all these little markets are disused, as the corn is engrossed and all other product bought up by higglers[1] so these towns are decaying, nor are their fairs better-attended, as the horse dealers go round and purchase all the nags.) This is a pleasant soil; and I think that this part of Notts is very pleasant. During my ride, I started the old topic in my mind, 'How happy would society be in touring, and how wretched the single person becomes, who cannot communicate; and wants a companion in pleasure and pains. But I believe this must be a solitary pleasure, and that a man had better be saved simply from a wreck (like Robinson Crusoe) than with a companion; for assuredly they would disagree, and go to different parts of their island.'

The approach to Blyth is very bonny, from the beauties of the mill, the enlarged water and the backing woods. I got the key of the church, which is old, with a very handsome steeple; and in it a white-wigged recumbent monument of a Mellish, whose seat is close adjoining; it seems to be a bad house, and the taste around is execrable. The new-built stables appear to most advantage; the water is of quantity and transparency, but it wants shade; so does the bridge, and the whole place; and the town and stables should be planted off. Before the stables I sat for some time, whilst a boy held my mare at the church gate. I was glad to hear of the good psalm singing and music, and that they were not all gone to the meeting.

I was here near an hour, and rode away with tolerable direction over the same kind of light country to the village of Harrow; to the left is a view of the approach to Lord Scarborough's park at Sandbeck. (That country, and the about it[2] I have seen, as also the town of Tickhill, which I now entered.) In Tickhill it became necessary to gain information of my road;

[1] Middlemen in the corn trade.
[2] i.e., the countryside round about.

and of several grave-looking people I enquired, when all advised me to 'ask further on, at the town's end'. But I was principally directed to the blacksmith's shop whence the Old Vulcan came out, as grey and as hairy as any badger.

He ordered me to turn to the left, to turn to the right, and to turn so often that he forgot himself. However, I obeyed his first turn and then found a better guide, a direction post, whence I came in 3 miles of Stoney Lane to Mr Lydiard's, and by an intricate road and over a common, another 3 miles to Edlington, and by Mr — to Conisborough, a village on the road from Rotherham to Doncaster; of good looks and charming situation; but to the right stood the object of my visitation, Conisborough Castle, upon a hill embowered by wood. After much hunt and some vexation, I did find the castle key at a public house; but the publican did not deign to accompany me, and with difficulty I got an old man to hold my horse: so I went up to it alone, and only lost some foolish prate.[1]

An old castle in a wood; and through the grove frequent peeps at the stream. What can be finer? It belongs to the Duke of Leeds, who has done more than most Dukes would do, for he has secured by a strong door the lofty castle and has repaired the steps and railway leading to it, of which I had the key. But as I often say, and must repeat, Why not build a guardian cottage, print a book for them, and let them make their fortune? In the tower is seemingly a deep well, and upon the walls some old stone chimneypieces.

Around the outer walls I crawled through the wood, where charming walks might be made at the expense of £2.2.0. Returning to my horse (having saved the expense of a guide), I rode by the wood boundary to Mr Walker's Iron Mill upon the river (Mr Walker is with his Iron Works in this neighbourhood, what Sir Richard Arkwright is with his Cotton Works in Derbyshire), and there saw the boring of a large howitzer. From a rocky hill above, I viewed Conisborough Castle to the greatest

[1] Prattle.

advantage with the church of Conisborough to the left, over the wood, and a sweep through the vale of the River Don. And at a short distance from this hill there is a view of the same river, to the right, in a vale between Loft Woods. Of this scenery, so very beautiful and romantic, I sat myself down, several times, in the pleasing contemplation. The road also, upon the hill, is as rich and gay as possible, passing through the villages of Warnsworth and Balby, with Mr Bradford's White House to the right, backed by woods.

Doncaster looks well in approach, and is a well-built, well paved, wide-streeted town. The Angel, where I expected everything comfortable, I found to be nasty, insolent and with city stabling. In a sad room, after my long ride, I could not eat of what they brought (I am not often so nice, but, 'There's matter in't indeed, if he be angry'), which was a dirty bit of salmon, that had been dressed before, with two lumps of boiled beef. I sent them both out; and then could not get a waiter near me. I longed to be able to kick the landlord, to whom I complained in vain. At last I made a peevish dinner upon some cold meat.

It was market day, though that had nothing to do with this house. The Market Place, the Butchery, and all about it, is in good style. Nearly opposite to this inn is the house wherein Mr Bonce resided: Why would he not stay there and be quiet, and belong to the town clubs?

In the evening I wandered about every quarter of the town, and to where the cross stands at the entrance of the road from London.

Here were no players nor any show! The church is large (the only one); and now that stained glass is removed (which was intended for obstruction of the sun, and for meditation) must be like a greenhouse.

My evening was very dull; my only pleasure and employ was from the receipt and answering of a letter. I believe that I slumbered after supper; recovering from that, I hastened to bed.

Eager to leave Doncaster, I breakfasted in haste and before nine o'clock was leading my mare over the bridge and long causeway, crossing the River Don, and the meadows, which are beautifully bounded and must form fine objects to Mr Wrightson's seat at Cusworth; which house appears to much advantage from the hill to the left, but its modernity offered no temptation to me.

The road being novel to me, extremely good and affording fine views, gave me ample satisfaction. I felt all the pleasure of a hopeful tourist, with every delight and feel of health that I derive from the country air. Above Robin Hood's Well Judge Peiryn has a seat by the roadside, and a paddock with much deer. I walked my horse in hand, down all the hills, which relieves both man and horse. (Garwood pursues his way by himself.) The descent to and vale about Wentbridge is very picturesque. There I saw many clean-dressed homespun people walking towards their church at Darrington when I left the high road; and passing by the church, whose bells were chiming for service and assembling the devout. (All would go to church if churches were well served.) I came in another mile to Catton village, where are several smart houses; and in a mile further to the town of Pontefract, built upon a dry soil, showing handsomely and of much greater extent than I expected. It is a town of a good aspect, surrounded by garden grounds producing liquorice, a plant I never saw before, looking like young ash. The new steeple to their new church is not to my taste, being a hall of Grecian fancies. At the end of the town are the poor remains of the castle, so famed in old story, and in the Civil War. In this survey I was attended by the labourers, who worked in the garden ground within the walls, who explained or invented History very well.

From the top of the keep there is a magnificent prospect as far, I believe, as to York Minster. The remaining walls are very thick; and under the garden ground of the centre is a long vault, entered by stairs, called the magazine, where they now keep the liquorice roots. (Of all the former grandeur, now only these poor ruins remain.)

I liked the survey much, and my attendants were very communicative. Below the hill stands the old church with a much handsomer steeple than the new one; but the body is a ruin, a fine one where, and in the chancel, are many tombs, for now they bury therein.

Near the town is an old deserted mansion called New Hall (mentioned in Captain Paulden's narrative), purchased by Lord Harewood from the Duke of Kingston, but being quite blocked up I could not get into it.

Two short miles, and to Ferrybridge. Crossing the bridge, I was met by Garwood on foot. (Then I expect something solemn: the horse dead; or . . .) 'The inn I have been at won't do, Sir; the stabling is too bad; and the people are very insolent.' 'Well, then, I'll go back and put up at the Angel; and do you come over to me.' Here I was well-placed and found a good stable, a good parlour and an intelligent landlord. Having ordered dinner, I made a great toilette; then dined cleanly and comfortably, and drank (a little) of a good bottle of port. After dinner I achieved an evening ride upon Bumper, who carried me safely but very uneasily. I took the high road to the hilltop; then turned to the right into Byram Park, Sir John Ransden's, about which, and around the pleasure ground, I rode at my leisure. It is a verdant, well-wooded place, with a goodish house and an extent of made water. But the timber and the shade are the beauties; and rare ones they soon will be.

I then rode through Brotherton village, and home to tea. My latter evening was, likewise, well passed in walking by the river-side, admiring the country and the well-built bridge (and when at the church, endeavouring at a sketch); and then in the other quarter to the ferry, where is a good fall of the river – a day not ill spent? And finished comfortably in writing, after the cold beef and tarts had been seen and well considered. The evening stable inspection I never omit. My landlord gave me some hints and plans; and I think I shall enlarge mine by my route of tomorrow.

4 June   Long live the King and may his children prove a comfort to him. So must every father and good citizen wish; for as the parents are patterns of conjugal fidelity, so ought their children to be of duty. This is a large inn of two parts, the old and new; the new contains some good rooms; both house and stable seem to be of infinitely better accommodation than that over the water, and mine host, Mr Denton, is a great sportsman and talks vehemently about hunting. At nine o'clock I left Ferrybridge; as the weather is cold, so things strike me in a cold manner, else I may say that I was disappointed at the looks of Ferrybridge, of which I had heard so much; for it appeared to me only as a wharf, without shade or feature. Indeed I have seen no grand features upon the road: the pleasantest country is about Newark and Retford. To like home, one should travel. Then it becomes wholesome physic; where can I drink wine, and find a bed, but at home? Or what view have I seen like that from Highgate Hill? Nor have I realised the ideas (of a visionist, perhaps) of passing through groves, or walking by purling brooks. This road is not half so pleasant as the Dover Road, or Western Road, when at a distance from London.

I held a conversation of information this morning with my landlord, Mr D. (a scientific man), whether I should follow the straight road or take that of the left to Leeds; or that of the right to York? The fall of my switch determined me: but upon my asking mine intelligent host if The Players were at York and his answering yes, and my never having seen that city, determine me that way. In three miles I came to the village of Milford, and soon after to Sherburn, once a market town (nay within these twenty years), but now every stage coach is a pretty market, galloping away with the produce of the country. My opinion hold, that the labourer has quitted the country, and that Enclosing Acts have in a great measure been the cause. But I shall be answered by, 'Think you not that our population is as great as formerly?' 'Why, aye, in many counties where manufactures flourish, I think it is, but they have sucked up the villages and single cottages; Birmingham, Manchester and Sheffield swarm with inhabitants, but look at them, what a set of mean, drunken wretches! Are they of the make, of honesty, or the use of the husbandmen?[1] Ask of the Army what they are?'

[1] Small farmers.

118

The less intercourse, the more virtue: coalition and collision bring us every vice. The business of agriculture is as permanent, and moves as regularly, as the globe. But is that the case with manufactures? May not some event overturn them? And who is to maintain the mechanic? The husbandman works regularly, is sober and industrious, and poorly paid, but the artisan will work (from high wages) but four days in a week, and wallow in drink the other three, and if unemployed will be ripe for and active in any mischief. Then in gallop the dragoons, and ride over them!

I dread trade, I hate its clamour. As a gentleman born, I scowl at their (over-)advantages. It is in trading towns, only, where rioting and discords begin. And yet they want representatives; why, of all places they are the last that should be represented, for their members will be most falsely and violently chosen and their towns for ever convulsed by faction. Look at Leicester: house against house! Think of the last election at Liverpool! Old Sarum is a better and honester representation than any great manufacturing town could produce.

The church of Sherburn stands so high and looks so grandly that I could not but go out of my way to look at it. The view from the churchyard is good; within the church there is nothing to observe upon but that psalm singing is given up. An old portal stone carved, of Our Lord crucified betwixt two thieves, has been lately dug up, which the Sexton said an antiquarian had offered £40 for. 'What a pity it was not sold for the benefit of the poor, for its worth is but 40d.'

Returning into the road, I passed near Lord Hawke's seat at Scarthingwell; on the left, the famous and bloody Field of Towton.

> No laurel here shall emblematic grow,
> Nor verdant wreath bedeck the victor's brow.
> Erase, ye Daemons foul, the tragic page;
> Hide from the Muse's ken your hostile rage,
> Where Horror vaunts each character of Death,
> In all the attitudes of parting breath,
> And grimly dreadful skulks the mourning ground.

Promiscuous dealing havoc wide around;
Bids Cock's pure stream with civil gore to glide,
And Wharfe, a Peeress of the liquid tribe.

Passing Towton village, where is a long extent of wide, new-made road, for the benefit of the hasty passenger but not for the satisfaction of a quiet traveller who loves the twine, and the shade, and the view sometimes caught, but not the great staring endless road. This new road now leads magnificently into Tadcaster: a market town with a handsome old stone bridge over the River Wharfe, navigable to this town. This is the first rapid stream I have seen and it falls above the bridge in a wide and bold sheet of water. Hence a flat country continues, and a very uninteresting one till York Minster appeared; which did not rise before me as I expected.

Approaching York I left the Race Course, Knavesmire, to the right where the opposite object to the Great Stand is the Gallows!!! Which may be a view of improvement and a good hint for such a station, but yet surely it might be concealed, or else removed; and why not a gallows portable?

I here found that I was getting into gay life, from the address of a young lady – 'How do you do, my dear?' And also met two sedan chairs. With admiration I entered York Micklegate.

Leading my mare over the stones, and over Ouse Bridge, I soon came to the George in Coney Street, which inn is one of these very old houses whose front is adorned by stuccoed imagery, and in it is a very grand apartment with much carved work, and stained glass in the windows. My landlord said that our house was formerly a mansion of the Duke of Buckingham, and was built upon the site of the Priory of St Leonard's. In two hopes here I was baulked, for instead of soldiery there were only the militia assembled (debauching themselves and disgracing their country); and the players were gone to Leeds! Should not Mr Denton have known this? Dinner ordered, I went to the bookseller's shop (Mr Todd's) where was a catalogue of the very eve of publication; looked at, and in, the Minster, and then sat down for two hours to a comfortable dinner and a bottle of good port wine. Then walked around and through the Cathedral, and on Clifford's Tower to the Public Walk, which is of great length by the bank of the Ouse, but it wants gravel and fronts the western sun. It was 9 o'clock when I returned from this ramble and walking about the streets; a brilliant moon, but a cold air. Some boys were throwing squibs, and I saw the company issue from the Mayor's Dinner in the Town Hall though this is a Whiggish town. Read the London and York newspapers; and sat up till eleven o'clock.

5 June   Coming here, I have gained a city and a Cathedral; but have missed a large manufacturing town, a play, Kirkstall Abbey and Harewood House, and Castle; so that I believe the balance is weighty against me. After breakfast, and having seen the militia soldiery march out to a field day on Knavesmire, I went to the Minster and was well and warmly seated. The service was decently performed, but unlike to that of Southwell or of Lincoln; some voices were good; the Anthem was tiresome. There would be no disputing the dimensions of the several Cathedrals; but to me, Lincoln seems far superior to York, from situation, perhaps, and not being cooped up. The glazing in windows in York Minster is very grand; but I cannot forget the transept window of Lincoln. I was shown in the Vestry two curious rings, as well as Culphus's Horn. The pavement pattern was the invention of (that great architect) Lord Burlington; and might be invented by a schoolboy for his kite. For me to mention the monuments were ridiculous (they are described in print), and out of my intention; who only want to remember the petty occurrences of my travel, to mark the weather and recall the charges. The Chapter House is very fine and gave me much pleasure. Whenever I build a library, it shall be from the model of a Chapter House.

Now to the Castle, the pompous receptacle of the felons and debtors of the County of York. Bad symptom of a County, this? When gaols are magnificently built, and where every felon and any debtor that can afford it are to live in state. All the instruments that have been used in murder, and all the chains which were used to hold felons, were shown to me by the surly pompous gaoler (as great and as disagreeable in his deportment as was the sexton in the Cathedral).

How noble are our gaols! How comfortably do the confined live therein! Quite a temptation? And yet how quickly we condemn; and how barbarous is our transportation?

I surveyed all the buildings; saw the debtors' room and the felons' yard. Thence I went to view the Assembly Room built from a plan of Lord Burlington's, who was surely the most tasteless Vitruvius?[1] and has left the *saddest* Egyptian Halls and *woeful* walls to record his invention!

6 June   This Angel Inn at Wetherby I should highly recommend for its civility, cheapness and good cookery. They take in both the morning and evening papers, which become a wonderful treat at this distance from London. At 7 o'clock, mounting Bumper, I rode to Mr Thompson's, Wetherby Grange, whose grand beauty is the (concealed) Wharfe. The grounds are idly neglected. All these rivers should be lifted up by masses of rocks thrown in, which would deepen and show the stream, increase the murmur and preserve the fish; now they glide away, unheard and unperceived.

Returned through the Paddock and by the high road at nine o'clock, with nice appetite to my breakfast. Bumper is a bone setter. (I have since learned that I ought to have gone to Thorpe Arch, a small public water-drinking place, and abundant of much beautiful scenery.)

Garwood rode with me for the first time; but Bumper was too hot to follow so he kept ahead. To my left was Stocked House and the old park, wherein near Spofforth toll bar stands a wonderfully large pyramidical stone. A pleasant, light, wild

[1] Lord Burlington was the patron of the manifesto of the Palladian movement in eighteenth century architecture, *Vitruvius Britannicus* (1717).

country to Spofforth village, with a pretty church and parsonage whose minister, hearing my enquiries, directed me to the ruins of the Old Manor House; where, the day being delightful, I took my pencil for the first time in this journey.

But, surely, this could not have been the old, demolished house, but one of a much later date.

After some short stay here for my drawing (which are all rendered worse by my usage of a coarse pen at the first inn), I had a most pleasant ride over the hill whereon Breamer Hall, an old deserted manor, now a farm house, stands. And there to view Plompton Gardens, belonging to Lord Harewood; which the gardener ushered me and Garwood about whilst the horses were led round to the gate of going out. This, being only four miles distant from Harrogate, must be a delightful saunter of love or retirement from that place; for it is a charming spot and of much simplicity, where the water and rocks are drawn into the happiest alliance.

This was a pleasant half hour. By the high road three miles (I should have gone through the woods and grounds) leaving Harrogate to the left, which I had no wish to see, I came to Knaresborough, a town of most romantic approach – a long crawl over a bad pavement and through a crowded Market to the Crown, a small inn; where securing rooms and ordering dinner (some trout), I took my wander through the Market Place, and to the hill upon which totter the remaining ruins of Knaresborough Castle.

The Old Castle, the river beneath, the opposite wood, the church with a view of the bridge and of Coghill Hall beyond, form one of the richest and most comprehensive landscapes that can be seen! Part of the old Tower (the King's) is a prison for debtors. Descending the hill, by the church, to the bridge (of which there are many, and good ones, in this country, and this is very neat and well-built), I walked up to Coghill Hall, apparently a good house, with surrounding picturesque scenery, and in front the River Nidd, wide, shallow and brawling. This would be a sweet place if quietly situated; but as it is placed close to a town, and in everlasting gape from Harrogate, I do not envy the possessor; besides, the water should be much impeded, the buildings to the right of the house removed, and much of the town of Knaresborough thickly planted off. In hunger I returned to my inn, but my appetite was baulked by the greasy frying of the trout. Why go into trouble to make nastiness? At all times frying is a difficult and unwholesome cookery.

The port was not bad. (Wine and beds have been generally good; or have I forgot the taste and feel of my own?) At four o'clock, attended by a boy to direct and by Garwood, I went first to view the Crag House, hewn out of the rock without either taste or design, then to Sir Robert's Cave (of this curious description), scooped out of the rock, with this figure of a Knight Templar guarding the door.

The only thing in character here is an old ivy tree covering much of the front. Within it is filthy, and without there is a little dirty flower garden instead of a gloomy thicket of trees!

Disappointed with these objects, I hastened down the hill to the dropping well, at the back of the Mother Shipton's Public House; the distillation is in an ample round, a magnification of what is frequently to be seen, and would wet anyone beneath quickly to the skin.

Garwood, who has curiosity and investigation, made many enquiries and got several petrefactions; of which there is a continual supply from things lodged below the dripping, as birds' nests, old wigs, etc, etc. One year will dress a wig in stone. The woman who shows the well was very foolish, and offensive.

Garwood now retired and I continued my walk through the wood beyond, of good timber, and of lovely views of the river and of the overhanging ruins of the Castle.

Next for a ride (I go through my exercises?) to Scriven Hall, the ancient residence of the Slingsbys, a rare old family who have (idly) sold the borough to the Dukes of Devonshire and the living to Lord Loughborough. This is a green, well-planted place, with a good house which to the left commands a noble view; infinitely preferable to a stare in front. I then took the Harrogate Road and back; and not satiated of survey, I entered the church wherein are several handsome monuments of the Slingsbys. (I enquired of the Clerk if the preaching was good? 'Aye,' said he, 'from our Curate.' 'But where is your Rector'? 'He never comes but once't a year, at election of the parish officers. Our old Minister was very gentle; but this bears very hard upon the poor. His name is Cheap. He was put in by Lord Loughborough.' 'Why, then, he is a Scotsman?' 'Aye, certainly; why Loughborough is Scotch, too.' This non-residence will be the ground work of a reform, and will form the main hinge.

I returned to my inn before 9 o'clock; at the back of which, from my stable door, is one of the finest views that can be seen, even unto I believe York Minster. In the small garden adjoining have been lodging rooms built, which are commonly occupied by those who prefer a short distance from Harrogate! They are now engaged for the Duchess of Buccleuch. The men of the town diverted both me and themselves by playing leap-frog. The young ladies have not benefited by their vicinity to Harrogate. From innkeepers, whence you expect information, none is ever to be had; nor will they stand still to hear your questions but are endeavouring to steal away with 'Anon, anon, Sir.'

My supper consisted of a boiled Jack and a cold pigeon pie; when I anxiously expected the company of (this inexplicable genius) John Metcalf* who, for me unluckily, did not come

---

* John Metcalf, born at Knaresborough in the year 1717, lost his sight when only four years old, soon after which he became unconscious of light and its various effects; being instructed to play on the violin he attended as a musician at the Queen's Head, High Harrogate, for many years, and was the first person who set up a wheel carriage for the conveyance of company to and from the places of public resort in that neighbourhood. In the year 1745, he was engaged to serve as musician in Colonel Thornton's volunteers, and was taken prisoner at the Battle of Falkirk. Being soon released, he returned to Knaresborough, and commenced common carrier between that town and York, and often served as a guide to intricate roads during the night or when the tracks were covered with snow; nor was any person more eager of the chase, which he would follow either on foot or horseback with the greatest avidity. Strange as this may appear to those who can see, the employment he

home this night but was gone to Spofford. I should not have lost the sight of such a phenomenon – whom they said added, to his other wonders, the power of card-playing and was a dab at put.

7 June   My yesterday was fully employed; perhaps too fully, more than even a tourist's eyes or thought could digest. The question then may arise of, Why not tarry? or take these observations more leisurely? That will not do alone; a simple tourist must hurry that he may not recoil upon himself: he must from economy of time, money and temper be ever upon the move and tire himself, that he may not tire himself. But as these former do not fall to my lot, I must undergo the latter in my annual trips, whilst I am able; and then record them, for the pleasure of my age.

> *Cui dormus est, victusque decens, et patria dulcis*
> *Sunt satis haec vitae, caetera, cura, labor.*[1]

Leaving Knaresborough, I walked forward by Scriven Hall park till overtaken by the horses; from the road, rather stony, are many fine views with some sweet snatches, to the left of the River Nidd. In five miles we came to Ripley, a small market town where is an old seat, the Hall of Sir John Ingleby's, which did not seem to be worth the stopping at.

---

has found for more than twenty years past is still more extraordinary, and one of the last to which we could suppose a blind man would ever turn his attention – that of projecting and contracting for the making of highroads, building bridges, houses, etc. With no other assistance than a large staff in his hand, he will ascend the precipice and explore the valley and investigate the extent of its form and situation. The plans which he designs and the estimates he makes are done in a method peculiar to himself and which he cannot well convey the meaning of to others.

  This extraordinary man was at Knaresborough, his native place, in June 1788, being just returned from finishing a piece of road and constructing a river over a rivulet at Marsden, near Huddersfield in Yorkshire, being then in the 71st year of his age, healthy and strong.

[1] Sleep, to be alive and well, and a sweet country
Are enough for this life, for the rest is care and toil.

The road hence much mends; and passing by the village of South Stainley soon brought within sight the venerable and black-looking Minster of Ripon. Meeting many cows and calves driven along I dreaded a Fair at Ripon, and my fears were soon confirmed for when I entered Ripon, the market place was crowded by cattle and holiday folk. I got a good stable, and a good parlour wherein I could see the tedious fun; after parading the Fair and staring at the booths, the misses and the Scotch cattle, I sat down to a good dinner – trout, and roast fowl.

At 3 o'clock I went to the Minster to evening service where my landlady Mrs H. told me, 'Here was a good Corps' (choir!). The church was filled by all the holiday people, whooping and hallooing; nor was one in the Choir but myself, a reader and a clerk. So being quickly scandalized at this irreverence, and at the ill-judgment of opening the Church on this evening, I departed.

I received many letters from home, but nothing more satisfactory or fuller of devotion than this one from Frek:

My dear father,
    Now I am well, thank God, and my mother too thanks.

Though it was a gloomy threatening evening, yet not to lose time and to escape the Fair (being alone) I determined upon a survey of Studley Gardens, three miles distant. The Park is pleasant, with famous hawthorns, good trees and fine views towards Ripon and its old black Minster. The house seems to be of no particular account.

At the garden gate we left our horses; where, strange to tell, there is no cover built for them! (I suppose that Mr Aislabie[1] never rode, or possessed a good horse.) Nature has here been very bountiful in furnishing hill, vale and wood of fine growth, with a charming stream; but Mr Aislabie did not, I think, well consult the genius of the grounds, which are tricked out with

---

[1] John Aislabie, who laid out the landscape garden in the first half of the eighteenth century at Studley Royal.

temples, statues, etc. and the water is carved with various shapes and nowhere fully enlarged! From a paltry Gothic temple with sashed windows is first given, below you, a view of the noble remains of Fountains Abbey.

The rain now falling fast drove us under trees for shelter, whence we hastened to the Abbey (there overtaking and conversing with a party of gentlemen and ladies who went from the inn at Ripon some time before me). Oh! What a beauty and perfection of ruin!! The steeple is complete, and every part in proper keeping, except the cloister garden which is infinitely too spruce; the ground of rubbish, of great depth, has been cleared away (as it should be done but never is, in similar ruins) to the flooring, or that level. Here, from such trouble, has been discovered much mosaic pavement of the Chapter House, with several inscriptions upon the abbots' gravestones. There has been much wonderfully done by the late Mr Aislabie, but there is yet much to do, as proper planting around it – and for the small river, which runs beneath the Abbey, to be greatly enlarged.

Here is enough left to explain where stood the refectory, the dormitory, the out offices and the abbot's apartments; but most of all to be admired are the magnificent double cloisters, whose roof has been admirably screwed up. In these I made a long walk of pious, melancholy reflection.

I crawled about here in the rain till almost wetted through (whilst the chaise company skulked under arches), regretting the bad and ill-chosen time, and hoping that a further day might arrive when I could dedicate the whole of it to this unique survey. The hollies and fir trees in these gardens are superb; indeed all the trees are very noble.

I was two hours in my survey; a miserable time for the poor horses, but luckily the saddles were not wetted. I trotted back the way we should have come, and instantly sought for dry stockings, and for brandy to make an ablution. I also heated myself with coffee and toast.

The Fair was quite discomfited by the rain, which sent the poor damsels draggled home, and left me nothing to do but write and read (luckily the many) newspapers till the stable hour. Then for a good cold supper and, as usual, an early bed.

8 June   It had rained *successfully* all the night, and continued when I arose at the late hour of eight this morning, after enjoying a happy rest; which has not been the case in my tour, and especially the night before, at Knaresborough, where I never slept but to dream horrors.

The chaise tourists (with whom I held some discourse) now took their departure in two chaises. Hence they go to view (the late) Mr Weddel's seat at Newby; and they civilly offered me a seat in their chaises; but I do not envy chaise tourists, who are to be hurried and jolted along, in danger of bad roads and without ever seeing a county to such a rainy morning, when everything must appear to disadvantage?

At 10 o'clock I repaired to the Minster where (their) service was going to begin; but as there was no chanting today, I fancied it too damp, so only walked around the inside, where I saw some few old defaced monuments. They are going, they say, to glaze the eastern windows with stained glass. It is all in dirty decay, and must have shown in another light before the year of destruction 1539, or before the downfall of the two steeples in 16[64]. There is a small vault near a pillar called (very properly perhaps) a confessional chapel.

I enquired much about the Horn by which the Charter is held, but in vain. At last I found out the Worshipful the Mayor's house; his old wife (in manners and words a Mrs Trulliber) bawled out to his worship that a stranger wanted to speak to him. Down came Mr Mayor and sent for the Horn which is nightly blown before the Mayor's house. He then entered into a *larned* and most elaborate discourse about the country, Fountains Abbey, etc, to the wonder of his wife, but to my questions could give no answer – viz. as to the meeting of the English and Scotch Commissioners here in 1639, etc, etc, etc.

At last the maid returned with the Horn, a common cowherd's horn. 'I'll be hanged,' cries Mrs Trulliber, 'if the gentleman does not want to see our fine horn upstairs, which is always worn on grand days.' 'Why, to be sure, that must be it,' exclaimed Mr Mayor. So down it was brought, richly ornamented with silver and cased in velvet; appendant to it hangs a silver cross-bow, and a spur (for the making of which this town was formerly famous) with several silver plates of some of the Mayor's Arms fixed upon a blue velvet shoulder belt. 'Your arms, my dear,' cried Mrs T., 'should be upon't.' 'Hold thy tongue,' answered Mr Mayor; 'the woman's a *fule*.' Having seen this, I was contented and bowed away.

The day was brightening. I took a roundabout survey of the Minster and returned to order dinner.

There is a keep of an old castle at the back of the Minster. I repeat, often I am afraid that a tourist (and if alone too) requires vigour of mind and of body else he droops. By society he refreshes, and is encouraged; but alone, he must be spurred on by himself, commune with himself and repose upon himself – I would not now tour alone if an active, agreeable companion could be found, but the recollection will be most pleasingly painful hereafter; with ('about this time of year I was 30 years since, at Ripon; then I saw Fountains Abbey. Then there was yet left some country manners, and civility; a good dinner was to be had for 1s. or 1s. 6d. Oaks were to be seen in hedgerows, ostlers smiled for 3d. And waiters bowed for six pence. Oh! How often did I attend the solemn, chanting Cathedral service – now put down with the bishoprics – and found where I was known respect paid to a gentleman of birth and situation. But, alas! Since the levelling system prevailed and overturned all distinction, the strongest brute prevails and the weak fly, or die').

When I think of my own touring about, and the eternal racket of the whole Kingdom, I exclaim, 'How different, how sensible were the lives of our forefathers.' and revert to what Lord Clarendon has written of his ancestor H. Hyde.

From the death of Queen Elizabeth he never was in London, though he lived about 30 years after; and his wife, who was married to him about 40 years, never was in London in her life.

(Hear this, ye modern married dames, the wisdom and frugality of that time being such that few gentlemen made journeys to London, or any other expensive journeys, but upon important business, and their wives never; by which Providence they enjoyed and improved their estates in the country and kept good hospitality in their houses, brought up the children well and were beloved by their neighbours.)

I left Ripon at three o'clock – and the good inn, where I fared cheaply and well. The road stony and disagreeable through an enclosed country of no particular observation to the village of Grewelthorpe, at the end of which we dismounted at the house of the gardener, who has the superintendence and showing of Hackfall Woods and Walks.

Here, thinking myself weatherwise, I held a council with Garwood and the gardener. 'The weather is coming up wet' (spake the foreman). 'Had I not better pass on, and return tomorrow?' 'No,' answered the gardener (fearful, perhaps of my never-return), 'the weather will be fine.' So we put up our horses (for here are places for horses; though to the shame of Studley, all horses there must stand exposed!).

There is so much to admire, so much to celebrate, that I know not how to proceed in description, or speak half in praise due to Hackfall. Strange that no account, nor prints of this place, have been published; at least I never saw any! Entering the wood by a small gate, the path, which though wild is sufficiently well-kept, passes by a rattling rivulet, forming many natural cascades, and from the hilltops the rills are so collected as to flow in narrow silver currents through the wood.

But here, as well as at Studley, the walks should be widened and small carriages admitted. At Studley, art is not too predominant; here Nature is consulted and in abundant beauty she revels.

A day (if an Italian day) should be devoted to this inspection. Wine and provisions might be brought in a cart; and then music and love, to fill the scene, Hackfall would appear an Eden. If mine, I should build in or enclose it, for I could not be distant from such a mistress. There are many rural buildings and seats; and a castle, called Mowbray's Castle, has been erected upon a woody summit, and without offence to the character and scenery of the place.

Overhung by steep, wooded hills, the rapid and romantic River Ure frames its broad and rapid course (nobly swelled by the late rains), wherein the angler will find abundant pastime from the numbers of salmon and trout. Nothing can be more grandly wild and pastoral than the unexpected view of this river! From the hilltops, at various spots, are transcendent views, even as far as York Minster. Let those who possess steep, wooded hills, of spongy summits with streams beneath, learn from Hackfall how easy and cheap it is to form enchanting walks and to guide the ripple down the hill. At one point several of these rills are to be seen, gliding through the wood like streaks of liquid silver.

Hackfall, being in shade and softness, requires hot summer days for its visitations; unluckily my evening (an evening inspection is wrong) was in gloom, and it felt damp and cold. Two hours did I employ in my walk (four miles I should reckon it), and when I approached the last mile the rain began to rattle upon the leaves! 'Now, gardener, we must hurry.' I should have deferred my visit till the morning; but I hope, charming Hackfall, to see thee once again.

We re-entered the gardener's house, a nice cottage it is, and therein sheltering myself in a snug parlour (for the rain fell in buckets) I discoursed with the gardener about these two gardens; about old Mr Aislabie, his taste and works; of the gardener's own age and family; and much about J. Metcalf, whom the gardener supposed to be dead. Thus the time jogged on till a long stay, or to escape wetting, were impossible. 'So ride away, Garwood, and prepare.'

Then I loitered for some time, through fear, but go I must, so I held down my head, but dared not to ride very fast over the pebbles; however I spread what canvas I could, and turning to the right crossed the River Ure by horse bridge and soon arrived at Masham. Here Garwood had wisely prepared a blazing hearth, before which were spread my linen and second breeches, and to work I went to strip off my lower wet garments (my upper ones were dry); this done, after a grand ablution of brandy I attended the stable, which was of the summerish sort, and then pored over an excellent map of Yorkshire till supper time. With my landlord, a civil, hearty fellow, I held much discourse concerning the country: trout-fishing, cockshooting and such like topics. What I view of Masham town from my windows seems to be curiously built, for it looks like a huge square of barracks with esplanades for the troops.

It feels November, and the wind sounds as if from a sea beach instead of soft zephyrs, smiling suns and plaintive nightingales; so in an outlandish place I must creep to bed and pray for summer.

9 June   And I have quitted home a fortnight? There is much wood about Hackfall and Masham; and much that was felled I passed by last night.

I kept my bed this morning until 8 o'clock, for bad weather prevents alacrity and crushes hope; in me, too, to whom every minute is precious and must be paid for. Masham church is a very handsome building, in a spacious churchyard, with a tall spire upon the side of which is the clock. Before the church porch remains (for the stand of a dial now) one of the most beautifully carved shafts of an old cross. The inside of the church is well and regularly pewed, and the windows are modernly glazed. Therein are several monuments of a late date; some of the Danbys whose seat is a mile distant; and a very ancient one of a recumbent warrior with his lady, of fine workmanship, which has been lately repaired by Mr D., who has given what becomes not so large a church, a small hand-organ. Though this district is called Mashamshire, and this church would contain a very large congregation, yet there is only a curate to perform divine service!!

Prenez garde, mes amis. The milkmaids here yet retain some

133

commemoration of Maia, by decking their milk pails with garlands; but much of this devotion to Ceres was transferred to Charles the Second, as what remains of festival is kept upon Restoration Day. Wales is certainly the country of most curiosity to a traveller, for by retaining language it retains many customs and much purity. My landlord seems to be a quiet inoffensive man, but yoked to a tigress, if I may judge from her high-pitched voice and the horrid noise in the kitchen. Peas are now in blossom; strawberries, I suppose, are unknown here. Before ten o'clock I had left Masham; the country is green and pleasant, but the roads are so sharp and pebbly that I move but slowly.

All timber must diminish as enclosures enlarge; six fields are everywhere laying into one! Is this good for the cattle and the land? Certainly not. And the loss of wood is usually prejudicial to the landlord, and to the tenant. In a few miles, to the right of the road at a short distance, appear the remains of Jervaulx pronounced Jervis Abbey, in the vale below High Jervaulx; to these I walked through some meadows, sending my horses round; a great extent of building is to be seen, though difficult of access. I got an honest Yorkshire tyke to walk about with me, who knew nothing, but that 'it was sadly blown up, and emaciated'. He spoke also of the quality of materials taken away, and of several stone coffins being found, but was most intent to show me where the jackdaws built and was delighted at starting an owl; Mary Hewlet, as he called her. Part of some chapels remain, and much for the observation to an antiquary, but all the doorways being stoned up, I had to climb over walls and force my way through nettles and brambles. (The day was very pleasant.) What has ruined this place, with most others, has been the building of a house near the ruins. This mansion has now dwindled into a farmhouse before which is a gateway of approach, an attempt at the Gothic but of no very ancient date. The great old barns are now falling down. The view from the terrace above the farmhouse is very beautiful, affording a large meander of the River Ure. My attendant was truly civil, and at last was going away without any hope of reward! He was a fine, healthy, strapping fellow, who would have caught the eye of a recruiting sergeant, and of more worth to the Army than a dozen of drunken mechanics from Birmingham.

Thence I came to the village of East Witton, above which is Witton Fell (the first appearance of wild country), and from Braithwaite Hall descended into the pleasant Vale of Coverdale. Coverham church is a neat building, and from the churchyard the vale is seen in great perfection. Having with pleasure surveyed this view, and observed the charming little waterfall that tumbles into the road, I walked to the remaining gate of Coverham Priory.

At the back of Mr A.'s house are the ruins. The day was so pleasant, and the country so novel, as to restore my spirits and invigorate my wishes.

We now mounted the hill to Middleham Moor, a fine dry turf, whence is a prospect of the two Vales, of Coverham and of Wensley, and below appeared Middleham Castle. Garwood led the horses down the hill into the town to what seemed a sorry inn; however it yielded well (for they spake of their trout, and of their cold larder, with reason), and I was shown into a clean parlour up one pair of stairs. I not only ordered several trout for dinner, but now dictate their cookery, and prevent the frying and the parsley, and the fennel and butter, and substitute boiling and anchovy sauce. As for cold things, they introduce cold ham, cold beef, cold fowl and gooseberry pie. What more can be found at Wansford Bridge? The port wine and the ale seemed to be equally good (as Dr F—d used to say of his actors and actresses). Indeed, I think I have met with very good port wine in this journey; or may have lost my palate. Hitherto I have not observed the proverb, 'After dinner sit a while', but today I sat quietly, drinking many bumpers[1] to the coming of summer.

Then made a thorough out-and-inside survey of Middleham Castle, which must have been 'a fine, great, large wide thing';

[1] Large glasses of drink.

135

and I walked up the hill, where seemingly has stood a much more ancient castle, whence this *modern young gentleman*, the present castle, is seen to best advantage, as well as the course of the River Ure through Wensleydale.

I next took a stroll round the churchyard, the tourists' stroll, and then another stroll here and another gape there, till I was obliged, for the vanity of the thing, to order tea; when, getting bold, I achieved a long walk upon the banks of the Ure, but the evening was cold and embittered all the views. At eight o'clock I returned, and saw mine host (for the first time) who was as communicative as his little knowledge of the country would permit him to be. I supped comfortably; in such a place no show can be expected, and the only noise is from worrying dogs.

10 June   Old White Rose; but then we old men must think of the eleven days; for this new style[1] has perplexed us like a clock set forward, and no white, or red, roses will yet appear in the north. When I went to bed last night I found my bed unusually heavy, and discovered that the blankets were doubled and that, so, I laid under four, which occasioned a long fatigue of new making. I arose at eight o'clock (now this has been a shockingly late hour in a sultry summer's morn), and took another round of the Castle, whilst my coffee was preparing; at eleven o'clock I was attended to the church, and became there an object of speculation, I suppose, as a stranger and being put into the Dean's pew (the Dean of Middleham). There was a decent, well-dressed, well-behaved congregation, with a singing loft, from which there was too much singing from about a dozen voices, male and female, and two bassoons, of better accompaniment than an organ. One of their attempts was too powerful for them, 'And the trumpet shall sound', the bassoons imitating the trumpet. The service lasted long, but our service is much too long; the Curate, the deputy of Mr Dean, had a good voice and performed tolerably.

[1] The new, Gregorian calender had been introduced in 1752, resulting in the 'loss' of eleven days.

Behind me, in the chancel, were ranged the town schoolboys with their old master (in manners and fire, much resembling an old print), who threatened them very often and with reason.

I now felt a haste for dinner; and this is a description of it:

A Boiled Fowl.
Cold Ham. Yorkshire Pudding. Gooseberry Pie.
Loin of Mutton Roast. Cheesecakes.

A better dinner, and better dressed, I never sat down to; but fear that the charge will be heavy – 1s. 6d. at least. We shall see.

Now for my evening ride: the landlord, a tall, handsome young man (but of the tame, useless breed, not one of those hustling, intelligent fellows who make the best landlords, or guides), accompanied me at my desire to my look into Wensleydale. The landlord recommended our going up the eastern side, and returning by the western side of the vale. Good. So we ride over Middleham Moor, a high ridge and famous for horse-training, to Bolton park wall, at a distance from Bolton Hall which is across the River Ure. This is a poor, miserable dismantled park, for the timber is gone and the few remaining deer seem to be starving. From this point, there is a noble view of the vale, of Bolton Hall woods, of many villages, and of Bolton Castle to the left, to which place my intention lay; but now the landlord, like many other guides, was out of his knowledge and protested that he had never travelled further! We should not have taken this side of the river. We descended to the village of West Witton, a very pretty village, and there sought intelligence; and were directed to a track, which led to the river which they said we might cross. This track soon became so narrow, and so stony, that we dismounted, and over great stones, through bog and water I hobbled for an hour (growling inwardly at guides and innkeepers) till we came to this pass of the river; where the violence of the ripple giddied both myself and my mare so much, and the stones were so large, that unless the landlord had seized my bridle and dragged my mare after him, we should never have crossed it voluntarily.

Now for my justification, and not to appear unseemly fearful, I shall be glad to ask any gentleman of the country, 'What is thought of that ford below Redmire? Is it reckoned a safe and pleasant passage? Or if of sufficient terror to alarm a Cockney?'

We might, indeed, have crossed at Aysgarth Bridge; but that was a future intention, and would have been six miles about.

Being happily landed, we came to the village of Redmire; and by Redmire chapel, whence is a sweet view of Wensleydale. Two miles of good road, and of ascent, brought us to the noble ruins of Bolton Castle.

After a survey of the outer walls, I entered by the staircase into the rooms inhabited by the families of two farmers; and from one, a surly peasant, did get permission to see these miserable chambers, once the residence of the unfortunate Mary [Queen of Scots], and by a long dark climb of stairs to creep upon the battlements, of wild and dangerous observation. The walls are of immense thickness.

A maid servant attended me about the Castle, for the farmer was too great a man to be disturbed; however his wife, of a civiller breed, showed me their parlour and another room which are lighted by the three large windows. The apartments, shown as Mary's, are upon the floor above them. How much more comfortable must the unfortunate captive have afterwards found herself at Hardwick in Derbyshire, in those magnificent apartments, than in this gloomy Castle.

We returned down the hill to Redmire, where we made enquiry for the road, through Bolton Woods, to Bolton Hall – and were directed to a single house where the key was kept, but unluckily there was no place within; the first gate that we found locked we contrived to pass beyond by scrambling over a hedge but the second, leading into the woods, was not to be forced, neither were the pales to be surmounted, so we were obliged to take a roundabout course, through fields, before we could arrive at Bolton Hall. Had I gone by myself, I had gone right and had escaped vexation; but by putting myself under the ignorant guidance of my landlord, we have been five hours in our ramble, for we left Middleham at two o'clock, which my landlord thought too early by an hour for our ride.

Bolton Hall is a gloomy, deserted seat of the Duke of Bolton, all in wild neglect and disorder, which some few years will level with the ground. It was built by Charles Poulet, Marquis of Winchester. Being shown into the house, which we did not know to be inhabited, I was joined by a formal, old gentleman who offered his services of attendance and information, neither of which he was capable of giving, having lately suffered a paralytic attack which had almost deprived him of all his faculties. I had to lead him about; nor could he relate anything but relative to his late attack, except detailing the history of Miss Polly Peachum, of her being here, and showing the bed in which she always modestly slept alone. There is not now a bed in the house – viz. in the best rooms, that could be slept in. There is much carved work and some old tapestry left.

He, my old guide, endeavoured to talk of literature and ask me, 'if I was a connoiseur?' He at last drew me, whilst I led him, into a lower room amidst ladies (probably his wife and daughters) where he puddled about till he had found several books of poetry, which he would have presented to me, and of these I accepted one; and I now discovered the writer of the poems I have so often quoted in this tour, Mr Maude, who having served *under* the Duke of Bolton, in the sea service, was recompensed by being placed his agent *over* his great and extended estates in this county; this gentleman resembles his *principal* in manners, and a light glazed grace.

A short mile to Wensley village, a village that gives name to the dale at the entrance of which to the right stands this (Piscatory) House, lent by the Duke of Bolton to Mr Maude, and a nice summer and piscatory situation it is.

Upon Wensley bridge and about the churchyard I long loitered, in admiration of the view and of the circumjacent country; and here one should loiter an hour in admiration of the sweep and the rattle of the river, of the view on the one side to

Bolton park and to Bolton park woods; and on the other to the church and castle of Middleham. All these with the bridge, and church of Wensley, form the most picturesque scenery. I had yet three miles of return, and the river to ford again; which here, though deeper, was not dangerous like the former ford. After much plenty of observation and a sufficiency of riding, I was notwithstanding at home by nine o'clock, and made my first daylight supper: trout, civility and clean linen. But this is an horrid dull place, through which travellers never pass, so too gloomy for a single passenger.

11 June 	I rose, at early morn, to a bright St Barnabas; and then took a walk around and a long farewell to Middleham Castle! Of the Western Port I tried a sketch, which served to divert myself and to fix an hereafter remembrance in my mind of Middleham Castle, and that in the year 1792 I was tolerably young and active.

Taking leave of Middleham Castle, I came in a mile to Witton Bridge over the Ure; to my left the gay-looking village of Spennithorne, and thence over disagreeable stony country to the moors, there getting a sight of the town Richmond in a distant valley, approaching which the hills and vales appear to much advantage. Richmond stands most romantically: the noble Castle, the bridge, the River Swale, all catch and charm the eye. A sharp ascent leads to the market place, which is spacious and handsomely built; and in it, at the King's Head, I secured my quarters, but in a newly-painted room. In this town are now assembled for their annual exercise the North York Militia, composed of much good stuff: what a pity – to be thus uselessly abandoned to alehouses, and to stand sentry, *Nobody knows why!*

Here I received many letters, and a grand packet of pleasure. At the back of the inn, in a garden, are the ruins of the monastery of Greyfriars, now called The Friarage.

I next made a walk around the Castle, and a noble walk it is, with the hanging bank over the River Swale, and views of the utmost beauty towards the bridge and the backing wood.

Returning from these gratifying sceneries to another of hope –
dinner – I was not so highly gratified with stale salmon and
buttered chops that did not make my chops water; but I feasted
upon my letters. My wine here was good, so I take another
bumper and I speak with sorrow, more than from bravado, that
I have commonly finished (within a glass or two, for my return)
my bottle at dinner.

My evening happy saunter was through the churchyard;
stopping frequently to survey the river, the waterfall and the
Castle, with its lofty tower, reminding me of Ludlow Castle.

The path twining by the river side, under a wood, whereon
two jolly anglers walked with me to their sport, and could I
have spared time I had made a third.

From this vale there is a super-abundant enjoyment for the
sight: the town; the Castle; the churches; the river; and in my
first view, the Abbey of Easby or St Agatha, to which I eagerly
bent my steps and enjoyed it at full stretch.

There cannot be a more complete, a more perfect ruin. About
every part of it did I crawl, and every part could I trace;
adjoining is a small church, sprung from the ruins; an old
gateway, one of the former approaches, is left. Above these fine
ruins has been built (to expose modern architecture) this ugly,
staring brick house, whose owner too has felled most of the wood
about the Abbey, leaving foolishly a few oaks, to prove how
beautiful many must have been.

How romantic now (how shaded formerly) is the situation of
St Agatha. It is viewed by me now, a petty antiquary, in its
great beauty of decay, and hereafter how I shall be envied by
some succeeding antiquaries for such an enjoyment. There
cannot be a nicer ruin (an antiquary's phrase) or one of happier
situation. In my way I observed to my left, insulated by the
River Swale, the remains of St Martin's, of which but little is
standing; and that little I could sufficiently view from the
opposite bank. I returned with a proper fatigue, to renovate for
fresh fatigues and transports. This is Life. That's your sort;

fatigue and leisure, pleasure and fatigue. Thus we struggle through life; and a tourist's is a hard life, but it is a life of choice.

Having tasted (sweetly) of one walk, I was eager after coffee to try a second, when I took another ring (like a hare) over the bridge, and through the wood above the river, and Mr Yorke's seat. Now this wood might be made a little Hackfall, and the views from it are delightful; the river foams at bottom and the bank rivulets might be opened, which should always be done inside steep hills. My wearied legs obeyed my curiosity, and I trailed a long journey here, and then about the market place and to a civil shop thereon, half perfumer, half bookseller, who was really informant. This brought on the hour of nine, the signal for my supper. My landlord is a very civil old man, though perhaps not older than myself; for my looks are all gone! But they lasted long, and then went at once. When I was twenty, I looked twenty; when I was forty, I looked twenty; but during the last year I am all shrunk and withered like an apple, 'The Sere, the Yellow Leaf'. It becomes an old and melancholy turn of life when you are obliged to brag of age, and to *plume* yourself – upon *your* misery.

12 June   Time must not be thrown away; and so to business. I rise now to a moment and, today, to a fresh morning. Then paced about the market place for an hour, till my coffee and hot roll were ready.

The North York Militia is a fine body of men, but ruined here and rendered useless to their country every way, both as soldiers and labourers; whenever I see a fine young fellow I think what a handsome soldier he would make, and yet, when made one, I should pity him as doomed to be sacrificed in some horrid climate: a transportation, for they never return! The adjutant of the Militia one can distinguish at a distance by his red face and old sergeant-like appearance.

After breakfast mount our horses for a ride, I upon Bumper, who is a rough, awkward, intractable brute; the country was high and bleak, so was the wind. Meet numbers of horses with lead from the mines. At the end of some miles, descend into a vale and soon came to the small, romantically-placed village of Marske, where the parsonage, the church, the mill, the bridge and the stream are all severally worthy of admiration; near the bridge is Marske Hall, the seat of Mrs Hutton, which at the small expense of removing the mill, and the surrounding garden walls, might be made a sweet place, and would then command all the meanders of this wild stream.

I did take a ride, and was amply repaid not only by looking at this cool, pretty retirement, but by the rare situation of Clint's (Mr Stapleton's), to which I rode opposite near the bridge, and there for some time ruminated, in rapture at the first view, whether I should like to set myself down for life here; but though a charming place to wonder at, on a summer's day, yet I should want good roads, and gravel and sand, for the winter, and to eat early productions of the garden. Now, here, nothing can come to perfection; and summer lingers, till winter returns with all his frowns and fierceness. The day was windy, with showers; from one of which I sheltered in a blacksmith's shop at Marske, before I went up to the front of Clint House. It was a brisk and cheerful day, and the way home seemed short. Then I resorted to my friend the bookseller, and went over Todd's (York) Catalogue; and glad I was to find that nothing therein would have tempted so choice a collector as myself. He recommended to me to seek a Mr Cuit, a painter of merit who took sketches of this country, and I found him at his house with two young ladies, the scholars, a poor, civil kind of man; but his art did not enchant me so much as the view from his back window over the vale, the River Swale and Easby Abbey. I advised the young ladies, 'Not to stoop over their drawings; but should that pain their bosoms, might it be the only pain they ever felt therein'. Looking into the larder (a good larder it was) at my return, I took thence (that is the right way) a cold shoulder of lamb, etc. and a gooseberry pie. 'Now for your good bottle of port, waiter'; spread quickly, I never dealt better.

But now to set off upon a full stomach that's the hardship.

For I wish now to loll, to meditate, to build castles and to repose upon myself. Butter sells here for 5 pence the pound, and a fowl for 10d; and coals are very cheap, houses good and at easy rent, walks charming and fly-fishing excellent. Richmond becomes one of the best retiring towns in England. I had left Richmond before three o'clock, but was detained at the town's end, by rain, for half an hour under a sawyer's shed.

Then away; pass at the back of Aske grounds, Sir Thomas Dundas's; a stony and hilly road, with a fine view of the vale to the right; and from Kirby a good look-down to the ruins and the meadows of Ravensworth Castle, which were so distinguishable from the hill as to make an observation of descent unnecessary. From Gayles church another sweep of the fine vale, over Leeming Lane, is to be seen. Here a good road brought me into the high Northern Road from London to Port Patrick, when, being unused to level or gravel, I seemed to bound along. The Vale of Greta is well-wooded, and Greta Bridge is of pleasant situation; there are two inns – the farthest is much the best. A well-grown plantation within the park walls of, and on the opposite side of the road to, Rokeby Hall tempted me to ride down to view it. The house is a vile, ill-fashioned tasteless building; but what is modern art if not lent to assist the purposes of noble Nature? For here runs the River Tees, in a wide, rattling stream betwixt two well-wooded banks, and yet no sight of it is caught from the house, nor any of its woods and wilderness introduced into the place! This river flows as neglected by here as does the Wharfe by Mr Thompson's house, Wetherby Grange!

The grand object from the house, and well brought in, is the ruin of Eggleston Abbey; to which (after my full admiration of the river and of its banks, and with equal dislike of the new, nasty, tasteless bridge, and my grief likewise at the building of a noisy paper mill on such a spot) I bent my course. These ruins are entirely neglected and choked up by weeds and nettles! A mean old house is attached to them, and there are some cottages at the back of the orchard. Was it cleaned out, planted about and the ground sloped to the river, it would be a sweet place; at present, it forms a fine object from Rokeby House.

A lane of a mile and a half brought me to the hill top, above the town of Barnard Castle, in the Bishopric of Durham, which thence shows to advantage with a fine view of the bridge and of the Castle. It is a black, shabby town; and well we entered it when we did, as a storm long brewing up then began to fall. Some doubt arose about the inn, and I nearly entered one when I determined upon the other, the Bull, a better sort of alehouse, where I produced a tolerable parlour for myself and tolerable stabling for my horses. The best bedroom was, unluckily, just painted. During the rain I sat over a good fire (for here coals are very cheap) conversing with my landlord, who was very ignorant, about the country; and when it cleared up, took a stroll about the town and around the Castle walls which beautifully overhang the River Tees. Within the walls, I was shown about by a fellow who dealt out all the old stories of Oliver Cromwell, and showed me where, from a dream, they had lately dug for money, but found it not. My supper consisted of a boiled trout and cold beef, with an excellent cheese, made in Teesdale. I sat over the fire till I slumbered; although I had many letters from Mrs Byng to keep me awake!

13 June   This morning I ordered Garwood to call me early, as I proposed a long ride. My bed and bedroom here were not of the first comfort; but the nights are short, and the exercise makes me sleep well.

Breakfast hurried over, I travelled upon the Yorkshire side of the river, on a tolerable road (viz. for this country) to —— where Mr Mayor has a good looking house, but laid open in a modern taste. Thence to Cotherstone, where the excellent cheese is made, and so to Romaldkirk, a goodish village with sash-windowed houses and a well-built church.

Though often complained of, yet I think that I was more harassed in this village by barking curs than ever I remember.

The road now became worse; and in three more miles led to

the bank of the Tees in a wild, bleak country, only inhabited by miners, or visited by grouse shooters who come in parties into this country at this season. At Eggleston, in the Durham side, there is a smart, white house of Mr Hutchinson's; and I observe, with pleasure, the demolition of the heath by the progress of the plough up the hills.

I have had a hydrophobia – since my crossing the River Ure below Witton; and here we were stopped by the Tees, who though not violent nor stony afforded a wide, and no easy, pleasant ford, but through it we must, and did, go, and soon came into Middleton, a small kind of a market town where we had been recommended to Mr Sherlock's, a kind of a public house without a sign. I am here in that sort of wild country and unvisited village that I wish to explore, and wherein to lose the memory of all the midnight follies and extravagant foolish conversation of the capital. From Barnard Castle it is reckoned ten miles to this place, which I rode in three hours and a half (guess the distance?). Trembling for their roads and miles, I had brought a nightcap in my pocket. Having ordered dinner, hired a guide and crammed his and Garwood's pocket with bread, cheese and ale (brandy I idly forgot), we resumed our march, I riding upon Bumper; the vale now becomes barren of corn and trees – the ash tree scarcely produces any leaf, or marks the seasons; miners' cottages are scattered about.

We at length arrived at bottom, when leaving our cattle in the outhouse of a cottage, we became pedestrians and following our guide through many hilly, boggy fields, a mile of walk, till we entered a little birch wood; when, being anxious to stand beneath the fall, we endured a most fatiguing descent and a very dangerous crawl at the river's edge, over great stones and sometimes up to our knees in water, till we arrived at the very bottom of the fall. The sweat running from my brow and a flap of my coat, my only coat, nearly torn off by the bushes – poor Sancho, I thought of thee and of thy green hunting suit. These are noble falls of water, unequalled I suppose in this country, of about 69 feet; and must be yet more wonderful after heavy rains or hard frost.

I re-crawled up the wood, and then to the summit of the cascade as near as possible. The basin at the bottom I should suppose a fine place for fishing; and here the salmon must stop – our distress now was about Ranger, who could not follow us over the bottom rocks and whom we had often heard cry. However, when we had gained the summit he had got round to the opposite side, and now the difficulty was to bring him over. At last the guide offered to wade the water and properly, unequipped, performed this (desperate) undertaking, plunging through a rapid stream, and scrambling up and over great stones, but he returned with the dog in his arms!! We then crept through the boggy wood into the field, where opening our budget[1] like Lord North, or rather like Sancho (all such descriptions in Spanish would make me feel very hungry) we ate and drank voraciously, I walking about for my head was as wet as my feet.

But where is your friend, your companion? One who would have enjoyed with you the observations, the sweatings and the cold meal; else, who cares for travel, or for what you saw and what you did? This is, everlastingly, the burden of my song. I had dragged my servant hither, and hired a clown to conduct me; but where was the participation?

But I am right in this touring, for I expand my mind and limbs, enjoy, though alone, the present, and record it hereafter. As for the fashion of going there, coming here; dining at night, breakfasting at noon; staying in London till October and doing only what is a fashion – why, a fig for it. Fashion imposes heavy taxes; surely I may be exempted?

A tiresome mile of return to our horses. Then I ordered our guide (as being speedier than the cavalry) to push back to Middleton and hasten our dinner. I rode Bumper again; and we returned by a quarter past three o'clock. My dinner was a

[1] Pouch.

roasted fillet of beef and potatoes, with potted trout (a dish they invented); but first I stripped off my wet shoes and stockings, and put on a warm woollen pair of the landlord's, and my head I rubbed with brandy with some of the half pint I quickly finished. These are primitive manners, yet left in such a distant quarter of the Metropolis as this is, only visited by some (*foolish, romantic*) tourists or shooters, else they are shut up in winter, or in snow; for the snow was not wasted till a month ago, and since that the ground has been covered by hailstones!

The market women, upon the road, all addressed me with good morning. My dining room was not ceiled, but was adorned by a chest of drawers and a clock.

> Imagination fondly stops to trace
> The parlour spendours of that festive place;
> The whitewashed wall, the nicely sanded floor,
> The varnished clock that clicked behind the door,
> The chest contrived a doubled debt to pay,
> A bed by night, a chest of drawers by day, etc.

I soon grew anxious to be going; more than Garwood was, who had made an acquaintance with the apothecary of the place (mark the distance from London, and how genteel society is sought for), with whom in the kitchen was a long discourse held about this afrementioned waterfall; which the apothecary told me he had measured, and that from the top of the upper fall it was 63 ft, from the top of the lower fall 56 ft. He, the apothecary, seemed sorry to part with such good company and would have relished our passing the night here. For variety on my return, I chose the upland road on the Durham side of the river, which they said was shorter, but rougher and not so pleasant as that on the Yorkshire side, and so I found it; for it lay over the moors and was very stony and boggy, but I certainly came home in much less time than I went in the morning, for I was returned by half-past seven o'clock, and not a little tired. Which a man may be who is not accustomed to hills and stones, and who has been plunging over rocks and into bogs.

I received another and a long letter from home, that cheered me till my supper came, consisting of a very large trout, as the landlord called it; about which trout we had a long argument, I averring 'that it was no more a trout than he was'; at this he fired, 'Pray, what is it, then'? 'Why, a young salmon, covered with scales, who are bred in this river; and would, in time, get down to the sea.' Upon this excellent fish and Scotch collops I supped, and soon after felt most inclined for bed, wherein I slept like a pig for nine hours, till awakened by Garwood and at 8 o'clock to a fine pleasant day.

14 June   My young landlord, a hearty good-looking young man who talks of nothing but of angling and of grouse-shooting (the two sports of this country), was to ride with me and show me the country. Garwood, my Groom of the Chamber and Gentleman of the Horse, is now taught to teach me; for when I say, 'Feed your horses, and do them up,' he answers. 'But not till they are watered and dressed.' Which reminds me of the examination of H. Random at Surgeon's Hall; asking him how he would treat a patient, if so, and so? 'Why, I would bleed him.' 'What, before you had tied up his arm?'

At ten o'clock, attended by my young landlord, we rode over the North Side Moor, holding much discourse about grouse shooting and of Lord Darlington's and his son's Lord Barnard's foxhounds; who by thus following hunting became country residents (which now, none else are), and by that means of infinite service to this poor neighbourhood. Lord Darlington's farmhouses being whitened gave a cheerful look to the country. He, Lord Darlington, grants no leases to his tenants; which in a great estate I think particularly wrong, for I would have leases most tightly drawn, being an enemy to waste and insolence. My (hunting) suit was, this morning, sent to neighbour Snip, for *corroboration*, for new flap linings and to sew up the wounds of yesterday; and he also attended upon the knees, at my knees, to sew buttons and strings to my old articles, who look deplorably, from such eternal pressure between horse and ass.

Leaving the moor we turned into enclosures and soon passed a rivulet by an old, castellated small house into Raby grounds, to which this house might be made to form an excessive beauty.

We now came into Lord Darlington's farming grounds, which are fenced by clipped hedges and white gates; a sad presage of the taste in Raby park? Wherein are very few single trees; and all the plantations are mean, of ill make and without bold sweeps; the river likewise running through the park, which should form a Thames, is turned to no account! The whitened ill-fancied Gothic buildings in the park are of a most wretched taste, and in full exposition. Behold the grandeur of Raby Castle. *How is the Castle manned?* I was obliged to send my name to Lady Darlington, and ask permission of entrance. I am told that many are refused! Why not a fixed day, or fixed hours? At entrance there is a porter's lodge with a portcullis (of wood) and a vile gate; and this lodge is in a spruced-up taste! In short everything displays the fancy of a citizen, not the grandeur of a northern baron.

I was met by a fat housekeeper and shown into the Great Hall through which carriages drive, passing through the house. This sounds grand – but must chill the house with winds; and it felt so cold, and so resounding with echo, that I hastened into the other apartments which are Frenchified, deal floored and modernly glazed, without pictures. 'Have you any picture gallery?' 'No.' 'Not chapel?' 'No. That was taken with the hall.' 'No library?' 'Yes, one upstairs, kept locked.'

'Now, pray, show me anything ancient'; so she took me into a room above stairs that charmed me, of 90 by 30 feet, with old windows and a lofty wooden roof. There is a plan of ascending this room by a grand staircase from the back of the hall; and a noble thing this would be. Why, I should not sleep till it was executed.

'Lord Darlington, will your lordship permit me, a stranger, to lay out £20,000 for you? And I then think that I could make your house a wonder of beauty; your park should be studded with trees; your hills should be covered with woods; a Thames should flow through your park; the kitchen garden should be removed; and that devilish nuisance the dog kennel carried out of hearing. The hall should be in eternal warmth; I should build a chapel and a Gothic staircase, and I should render that great room, fitted up with cedar and glazed with stained glass, one of the grandest libraries in the universe. The upland ponds near the Castle must be destroyed and in a removal of ground, a view would be obtained of the river in the valley, etc, etc.'

The housekeeper, observing my taste, asked, 'If I would look into the kitchen?' and a curious old kitchen it is – and *tolerably furnished*, for there were two men cooks employed; here is an arched roof 50 feet high, and 26 feet above that to the top of the dome. The family were going to dine out! Why dine out? I would never dine out. People should dine with me at their ease, at my expense, and I would always drink my own wines.

Contented with this sufficient survey, I departed; and near the lodge being met by Lady C. Barnard on horseback, was struck instantly in love by her white teeth and elegant bow! She is reckoned the Diana of the North.

The view from Raby Castle is very rich, towards the church of Staindrop and over a fine country. In all parts of the park, the fawns are just dropped which shows the backwardness of the season here; but did I live in such a place, I would cover an acre of ground with glass and be able to take a summer's walk in every winter day. Adjoining to Raby Park is the small market town of Staindrop, one of the smart towns that can be seen, and largely adapted for a place of retreat, from the cheapness of provisions, and where a good fire (the first of comforts) may be kept up for a penny a day!

Mr Lee's at the town end seems to be a pretty place. We were now in the high road from Barnard Castle to Durham, nineteen miles; and had I no other pursuit in life, I had turned my horse's head that way.

In three miles we quitted the high road and took down some fields to Streatlam Castle, a house of the late Mr Browne's, a place in neglect and wild disorder. There is a rockery on one side and a stream (of great capacity) in front, with a miserable kind of park! '*Thou hast it now, Glamis* etc'. The house appears to be of the worst kind. Returning from this gloomy inspiration into the road, we soon left it again to view a great stone quarry; and thence came to Barnard Castle over the heath, by four o'clock to my ready dinner and to a good fire (though none at Raby Castle). I was very hungry and very comfortable; and had a just-arrived newspaper.

My evening walk was to Toller Hill, by the river, on the Yorkshire side; the evening was as remarkably fine as is the view of the Castle and of the hanging woods over the river. Here I meditated and walked for two hours, and to the top of Toller Hill, through the wood – which walk has been spoiled by opening the road. Some anglers were employed. Altogether, it is a walk and survey of wonderful beauty; worthy of undertaking any difficulty for but that of riding down from London, ALONE, to enjoy.

Coming in, I asked as often I do if any old people were to be seen, and being directed to an old man of 90, who lives in the back street, I received a lesson from his wretchedness of mind and body to round (if possible) my wishes, and to revert to the Struldbrugs of Laputa.[1]

Some light tilted carts passing by, left us a paper which seems to show a grand display, though they do not stop here but are on their way to Newcastle.

After attending to my cavalry at their nightly feeding and littering up (a duty I owe to them and myself), I attended to my supper of a cold fowl, etc, etc.

15 June   I have been a long time stationary at Barnard Castle, which is an unpleasant, black-looking town, very unlike the cheerful appearance of Staindrop! Herein is a manufactory of stuff. Called at 7, breakfast at 8 o'clock, and now I turn my face southwards. Hitherto I think I have not been idle, but have well

[1] The immortals, in Jonathan Swift's *Gulliver's Travels*.

employed every day; never have been prevented by weather, nor detained by it, against my liking. I shall hope soon, in my southern descent, to see and feel some of the operations of summer.

The morning was cloudy but quickly became clear. I left Barnard Castle at 9 o'clock. Soon crossed the high road; and then soon began to have a taste of the moors and of their stony tracks; a sprinkling of cottages and enclosures continued to Rotherford Bridge whose most grand and lofty arch – seemingly never trod – caused me a stay of two minutes attempting a sketch.

Now the country rises into bleak moors (a wildness of country that I came to see), where I felt the air extremely cold and was glad to get within a greatcoat.

The way being so steep and stony, we walked on foot half the way. From the top of the first mountain there is a most wonderful view over Raby Park, towards Stockton, and of the sea, I believe. Ranger will not move; a hunting dog had been a great beguilement by the way, as this part of the country (the New Forest I believe) is very productive of grouse and hares.

At last descended into Arkengarthdale, and there at a public house stopped for directions, and to fortify with bread and cheese and brandy and water; we got but bad intelligence from the publican, who would have guided us to Reeth – whereas our way led over the forward hills.

Over many a wild hill did we work our weary way, passing by several smelting forges (into one of which Garwood entered to view their process). We now from another hill descended in Swaledale – and into the villages of Low Row and Feetham upon the river banks, which is now low water but must be a wild, rapid stream in winter; this is most plentifully supplied by a most romantic rivulet from the opposite hill called Crackpot, to view whose cascades and foaming falls of water I often dismounted from my mare. This charming little beck seems to have been unnoticed by former tourists! The day being fair, and the country so novel, made me endure the length of this tedious ride; and then you are obliged to converse with a servant! For man must communicate.

The next hill appeared steeper than any of the former. At the top are coal pits; and an exceedingly long descent leads to Askrigg, a small town in the valley where, uncertain of the inn, I put up at, I believe, the worst house, the King's Arms; however, the stabling was excellent and the landlord very civil. I was seven hours in coming these computed twenty miles!!

Now, gentler reader, if thou hast only travelled to Hackney or Clapham, you can form but little idea of the country I have traversed, or of the roads I have trodden today; the one all black miserable moor, and the other a sharp pavement, which if quitted you plunge into a bog.

I was heartily glad to seat myself upon a chair, for it was now almost five o'clock, and then I got but a baddish dinner, some fried trout and some tough mutton chops; however, the wine was tolerable and I lighted a great fire. I love not the cold of Raby Castle. This marks the difference between the mean inn and the great mansion: here I order a great fire, and enjoy it; there (if invited) I must freeze in state!

Dinner quickly ended – and radishes served up for a dessert, as they serve up turnips in Scotland – I began my enquiries of mine host, who offered to guide us in our walk; which seemed to be over many stiles and fields (for my help dragged after me) to Whitfield Gill, to which we descend through a small wood (after we had viewed Mill Gill a mile distant) and here after scrambling across the stream, which I did in state, upon great stones laid in my way, and so came under the fall; where I laid myself upon a stone at full length like a deceased Knight Templar. This falls in one stream, and finely arched by rock and wood; and in my mind infinitely preferable to Mill Gill. (I presume that I take as much trouble in my observation as ever tourist took.) All these places are of vile approach; such plungings over stones! Once this evening I slipped and was up to the knees in water. Young feet [are needed] for these surveys, but my mind is yet young and urges my body.

Of Mill Gill, half a mile higher up, I had taken an ample inspection; for here is much to wonder at, much to admire. The river here falls in two columns, which heavy rains reduce into one. Garwood, inspired at Knaresborough, hunts petrefactions[1] and examines all the rocks; I like to observe a mind of investigation and enquiry. I had returned before nine o'clock (through the churchyard, wherein is an excellent epitaph to the memory of an *Honest Attorney*) to the excellent stables, built after a Newmarket model by that famous jockey, Jack Pratt; who being for several years rider to a foolish Marquis, contrived to pick up a pretty penny, and here laid out much money, at his native place, upon these premises. A stone cross in the market place is the only one I ever saw perfect.

People live to a great age here, owing to the fine air and good water, and perhaps owing more to their distance from temptation; all are employed in knitting stockings, worsted, and yarn, an idle work, for the workers go where they like, talk, saunter and sit down. But now the cotton trade is coming in, and a cotton mill is built near the town, as many are in the neighbourhood. I bought a pair of coarse stockings for my wet expeditions, or to put on when wetted; they cost me 8½d. As I came over the hills from Swaledale I saw many pyramids of stones, which are placed as guides for winter travellers in the snow, many of whom have perished upon these hills; people at that season should never travel alone or in pairs, but in parties to assist each other. In the last winter, two persons had nearly perished but for a party; for the instant they are bewildered, they become oppressed by cold or fall into deeps.

The May blossom is now in blow here, June 15th. After stable-view I ate of eggs, cold meat, hung beef etc, with excellent brown bread, and was happily tired when I retired.

16 June   From an oddish hard kind of bed I arose at half-past seven o'clock (all beds are alike to the fatigued tourist) to a fine

[1] Fossils.

morning and a bowl of buttermilk, which was quickly followed by coffee and a brown toast. Breakfast finished I walked forward, and was not overtaken by the cavalry till near Nappa House, which looks like one of the Knights Templars' houses, now all abandoned except one end inhabited by a farmer. The ironwork of the windows, with the beams of the apartments, remain, with 70 stone stairs leading to the battlements covered with lead. About this place is an old grove, and in the grounds several small ones, which might be all enclosed in a paddock; and then if the front wall were taken down, it would be a pleasant place. Were it mine, I should take a pride and pleasure in fitting up the old hall and parlours in the truly ancient taste.

Retired from the world, a man might here enjoy fly-fishing and grouse shooting in the highest perfection.

From Nappa I soon crossed a ford of the river; when passing through the village, I came in half a mile of the church of Aysgarth, the mother church of several dependent chapels in this vale (one of which is Askrigg), and now I descended to the bridge of Aysgarth, there sending back my horses to the public house and ordering Garwood to return with a guide.

During his long absence, I had to admire the delicious scenery around this charmingly-placed whose wildness has been sadly demolished by a late (Adamatic) reparation and the cutting down of the ivy.

But what has completed the destruction of every rural thought had been the erection of a cotton mill on one side, whereby prospect and quiet are destroyed. I now speak as a tourist (as a policeman, a citizen or a statesman, I enter not the field); the people, indeed, are employed, but they are all abandoned to vice from the throng.

If men can thus start into riches, or if riches from trade are too easily procured, woe to us men of middling income and settled revenue; and woe it had been to all the Nappa Halls and the Yeomanry of the land.

At the times when people work not in the mill, they issue out to poaching, profligacy and plunder. Sir Richard Arkwright may have introduced much wealth into his family, and into the country, but as a tourist I execrate his schemes which, having crept into every pastoral vale, have destroyed the course and beauty of Nature; why, here now is a great flaring mill whose back stream has drawn off half the water of the falls above the bridge.

With the bell ringing and the clamour of the mill, all the vale is disturbed; treason and levelling systems are the discourse, and rebellion may be near at hand.

Garwood now returned with a guide and we began our walk through a wood by the riverside, in high admiration of every beauty and of every fall of water (some of which are very charming) till we descended to beneath the High Force. (Heaning Fall, I am ashamed to say I did not see; though no fault of mine, as no information is to be had, or any curiosity to be heard of, on the spot.)

Reviewing the first, I spent some time; and below this second waterfall we seated ourselves upon the stones for half an hour, admiring every different point of every rock, and learning from our intelligent guide the history of the glorious salmon fishing beneath this fall; for here, these fish being stopped, are caught, of an amazing size, by trolling[1], which must be glorious sport. A charming spot this is, for dining or tea-drinking parties – never did I pass a time of happier observation.

Returning to the bridge, I walked up (whilst Garwood and the guide went for our horses) to Aysgarth church – and around the churchyard a pleasant view of the vale and to Bolton Castle. Here I drew out my pencil and happily employed my time in taking this sketch and inscription in the churchyard, till my horses appeared; when I easily found the right road back, returning content and comfortable, and hungry, to an excellent dinner of trout, roast fillet of veal, etc, etc.

But here I must not stay to ruminate, but must hurry to enjoy, so at 4 o'clock I was on horseback again (quite a Duke of

[1] Fishing with a running line.

Brunswick of rapid movements) and by the end of Askrigg where stands the Old Manor House of the Wortleys (now Lady Bute's – for the Scotch have made *some* permanent inroads into this country); below which is a most picturesque fall of water – not indeed of the boldness of Mill or Whitfield Gills, but such a one as a southward traveller would ride twenty miles to see, and would be an ornament to the finest park or garden.

Bainbridge is a pretty village; they are now rebuilding Bain Bridge. In this village there is, also, a pretty fall of water; after climbing the hills and then pursuing a long distance, we came upon the banks of Semer Water, a lake of size and beauty, surrounded by romantic hills, some wild and some cultivated. This is the first piece of water I have seen in my tour, and it should seem to be little visited by tourists, though highly deserving of their notice.

Dismounting upon the bank I walked thereon for some time, discussing with three anglers who complained of their bad sport, from the unfitness of the weather, though the lake abounded with trout; they fished with 3 or 4 flies upon each line!

Hearing a splash (for my ears are now very quick to such sounds) I walked forward till I was led (beyond the farm house at the south-east angle of the lake) to a single spout (called, I believe, Bain Force) which, novel and beautiful, made ample amends for my trouble. At my return to Semer Water a gentleman, one of the anglers, had just taken a trout of a pound weight. A curious tourist, resident here for any time, would discover wonderful beauties and a number of curious water forces. Of Wensleydale and the environs a good guide book might be published.

My ride over the hill was very cold; for summer is not come and seldom does come, I believe, into this country. I entered and walked around Askrigg church, wherein they were practising the psalm singing for the morrow, and remarked the pews, formerly belonging to the Metcalf family. My host is very civil and produced to me a very good supper, tonight, after my pleasant fatigues, which sent me to bed at an early hour.

17 June   An absence of three weeks, and I seem to have rambled far and wide, but with all of the wish for home and conversation. This morning opened loweringly. I hope I may not be detained in these melancholy mountains, for such they become to the eye, after our first curiosity is satisfied. When detained let it be by the side of a high road, where carriages are always passing and newspapers daily are taken in. This place will not produce a plain copy book.

The rain continued too long for me to think of breaking up my camp; so I sat at drawing, writing, with many stable visits till two o'clock. (But why not church? Why, because I had conversed with the minister and had heard an account of the service and preaching.)

My dinner consisted of the trout caught yesterday in Semer Water and sent to me by the gentleman I there addressed (very civil this), with a roasted fowl and a gooseberry pie. The gentleman, Mr Blakey, who is in the cotton business and comes from Manchester to establish it in this country, was standing at my stable door when I was going to my evening ride; and I readily accepted his offer of accompanying me, from growing tired of my own society.

We rode along the vale leading to Sedbergh, leaving the village of Hawes to our left, over the water, till we stopped and put up our horses at a public house, the Green Dragon at Hardraw; whose landlord accompanied us a short distance to Hardraw waterfall, which is a cave of rocks of tolerably easy approach, where the stream flows over the top of the rock in one sheet of about 70 yards in height – making a most rumbling noise in falling, with a fierce foam at bottom. It is possible to stand behind this fall without being wetted. This is different from all the former I have seen, as being so separated from the rock; but I feel – like Canton in the play of the *Clandestine Marriage* – 'De Gazette put out of my head, de advertise – and so away dey all go, l'un apres l'autre.'

The hawks build in the quarries; but they are destroyed as much as possible, from their destruction of the grouse. Our ride here of six miles was pleasant, from a sight of this wild, high country, and our landlord advised me to visit Hell Gill, a famous pass with curious bridges, six miles further on; but I heeded not the adviser, else I should never return to London. (We introduce no husbandry to till these moors, most of which might be rendered fertile in grass, or in grain, or the esculents; here would likewise the inhabiters grow, and with deeper root than in a cotton mill; a man must be born and bred a country gentleman, or a country labourer, for a citizen and an artisan will never make one, or the other.)

From being a riding switch fancier, I cut numbers; and my return of thus using a long riding rod is to strike my horse from under my arm, upon his haunches, and make him throw in his hindquarters, which spurs will not do, nor any short whip to be used on the side, as the horse, seeing your motion, swerves away. I could not but invite Mr Blakey to supper; but he had not long been with me when two fellows of the town, his friends, intruded themselves – as if into a club room! So I went out to my stable attendance, and at my return, luckily, they were gone; when Mr Blakey made many apologies, I seemed contented.

Mr Blakey then stayed supper (a good supper it was), discoursing of manufactories, Manchester archeries, etc; but the best thing I got from him was the account of the best inns on my journey. Amongst the lime rocks I found road stones of six inches in length, regularly marked with circles, called the Fairies' Rolling-pins; some of which, short pieces, I picked up beneath Hardraw Scar.

There are gentlemen who come for the grouse shooting to this house! 'Well,' said I, 'and do they bring their wine.' 'No.' 'Nor their own cook?' 'No.' 'This surprises me, for should I come to any place for a stay, I would have my own regular cellar padlocked up; and should bring my bedding and mattresses to repose upon after my fatigues. Few people understand this!'

Company-keeping is productive of bad hours.

18 June   The weather of this morning was so cold and so rainy that I despaired of quitting Askrigg today, which now becomes a dull place and whose environs I have sufficiently examined. Had the weather been warm, I should certainly have accepted the civil offer of Mr Blakey, who had procured permission from Mr F. of a day's net fishing for me upon Semer Water.

He this morning attended to show me my road and to indulge his own curiosity, but would have endeavoured to delay me from the threatening of the weather.

At eleven o'clock we left Askrigg where the accommodation and wine were tolerably good and the stables (which with the house were built by Mr Pratt, of sporting memory) are excellent. There are no gardens here adjoining to the houses (probably from the coldness of the climate), so garden stuff is a great rarity, as coming from a distance.

In the depths of winter, when the snows have fallen, the roads are almost impassable, nor will poor people venture over the mountains but in companies of five or six; single people or even pairs have frequently perished in the snow. The business of the poor is knitting of worsted hose, a very idle employ; and that I might encourage the manufactory, I purchased a pair for 8d. to put on if well wetted.

The ascent of the mountain Cams is one of the longest, steepest and most stony in Great Britain; for they say it is nine miles to the summit, and the first four are very steep. If the roads are bad, the country barren and the winters long, yet the inhabitants are compensated by the plenty of coal, the trout fishing and the grouse shooting, which is a season ardently wished-for and brings a short harvest to the small inns. Upon the hillside we were encountered by some sharp stones. Mr Blakey (a great dealer in slip-slop language, such as talking of *Putrefactions*, etc) spoke largely about the Manchester trade, now creeping, and which he comes to help forward into this quarter of the country; and of the wonderful importation of children purchased in London at so much the half score (nine sound and one cripple) by those merchants, the most forward against the slave trade.

As I had expressed a wish to see grouse, Mr Blakey took with him a good pointer, who soon by some good points produced my satisfaction, only interrupted by the petulance of Ranger, who caught one young ring ousel.

To spring the grouse, it was necessary for us to quit our horses and clamber over black boggy ground, when we started much game. Round us the curlews shrieked their cry. An extent of this country belongs to Lady Bute, and as her heir is of a land who grasp but never relinquish possessions, great part of this country will be in the hands of those who never could stay, nor hope for conquest. I was much fatigued by the tediousness of the road, whereon we at last met two farming men with whom we conversed about the grouse and their abundance. Crossing a ford, Mr Blakey led me to a public house called Grierstones, the seat of misery, in a desert; and though (unluckily for us) filled with company, yet the Scotch fair held upon the heath (there I go to meet Macbeth) added to the horror of the curious scenery. The ground in front crowded by Scotch cattle and the drovers, and the house crammed by the buyers and sellers, most of whom were in plaids, fillibegs etc. The stable did not afford hay. My friend, who knew the house, forced his way through the lower floor and interned himself in the only wainscotted bedroom upstairs, where at length we procured some boiled slices of stale pork and some fried eggs, with some wretched beer and brandy, to which my hunger was not equal and from which my delicacy revolted. When our room was invaded by companions, he called out, 'This is a private chamber.'

The only custom of this hotel, or rather hovel, is derived from the grouse shooters or from two Scotch Fairs; when at the conclusion of the day's squabble, the two nations agree in mutual drunkeness, the Scotch are always wrapped up in their plaids – as a defence against heat, cold or wet; but they are preventions of speed or activity, so whenever any cattle strayed, they instantly threw down the plaid that they might overtake them. All the Yorkshire around, though black and frightful, seems of small account in the comparison of Ingleborough, at whose base we now travel. Mr Blakey's dog, who was my only diversion on the road, seems thoroughly master of his business and worth four times the sum (three guineas) that Mr Blakey gave for him. I believe he could sell him for five guineas. The reckoning being paid, very genteelly, by me, I proposed to Mr Blakey to ride forward to accelerate our intention.

There fell many storms of rain; and these come upon you in a mist from the mountains, without giving the least warning. Our poor horses were glad to be delivered from their sty; and I then pursued Mr Blakey's steps to a vale called Chapel-en-le-Dale; where from the first house he called to me. This was the habitation of a jolly shoemaker, a fine bold-looking fellow; and his wife, to whom he had not long been married, was an excellent contrast of sweet expression and feminine softness. He is the guide to the neighbouring caves, the noblest of which, Wethercote, is adjoining to his house. Our horses being put up, he took us into his house and presented us with ale in a silver cup! Perhaps there is no corner of this island that can afford wilder scenery; but Jobson[1] thinks it is a paradise (and the winter's roar but binds him to his native valley more).

There is a horrid chasm, just below his house, called Gingle Pot, down which we peeped and threw stones. But how shall I describe the wonders of Wethercote Cave (pronounced Cove)?

From the top of this perpendicular cave are to be seen the falls of water that lose themselves at the bottom, and to which we approached by a most laborious descent. Here the two cascades are to be seen through, upon a small passage leading into a horizontal cave: much wetting is to be encountered and some danger apprehended. These cascades fall with a horrid din, filling the mind with a gloom of horror.

Honest Jobson now assured us that, 'He must guide us to Yordas Cave, which was near at hand, and highly worth seeing'; but from the cold and frequent wettings, my curiosity was

---

[1] Georgian equivalent of Muggins, a country fellow.

quelled. However, Jobson insisted and Mr Blakey appeared anxious to see it.

So off we set, passing by the small chapel and some neighbouring houses, where Jobson bought a pound of candles to carry with him to be lighted at the cave, from the burning turf he took in his hands. Our guide was a merry, hearty fellow, and with much fun defended his county from our abuse, while we were crossing the terrible, stony mountains, called Gragareth – though he called it a short step, and strode away (often renewing his fire with fresh peat), where from bog and stone our horses could not keep pace with him, yet it appeared to me a distance of three miles.

Crossing a nasty, stony brook, we arrived at Yordas Cave; where leaving our horses at the entrance, and lighting our candles, we entered the cavern. It is well worthy of inspection, not too tedious, and beautifully closed by a cascade. Jobson stuck up candles by the way, which gave a most fanciful effect.

On our return a shepherd was found with our horses, glad to see any other living animal but his sheep, and offered to conduct me to mine nightly inn, which Jobson would not decline, so maintained his office.

I had now to take leave of Mr Blakey, who had many dismal miles of return; and we parted with much civility and with great promises, in his part, of sending me grouse, fresh and potted. Our road (how fatigued of the day and myself I felt) was along Kingsdale (why so called I know not), till I came in sight of Lonsdale and of Ingleton, where I was doubly pleased to house at the Bay Horse Inn, of most neat and comfortable appearance without; and so I found it within, for ordinary supper, trout, etc. I tried the uses of my worsted cheap hose, for the first time, and found them very comfortable.

Jobson had seated himself in the kitchen, in full enjoyment, at my expense; and I tasted his happiness. A newspaper, a stable inspection and a comfortable supper in the most cleanly parlour ended a day of much novelty, bustle, fatigue and observation.

19 June   A cold, blustering morn; nor was I in haste to arise. My first early walk was round the churchyard, whence are lovely views of the Vale of Lonsdale, leading to Hornby Castle, nine miles; on the road to Lancaster, eighteen miles; I had some demur whether I should not take the road, but when, then, is my tour to stop? So I will round it here.

The bridge, with the two rivers that pass beneath it, forms a scenery of great beauty. At Buckfast I saw vast droves of Scottish cattle passing to the south. The landlord's little boy then conducted me in my walk of observation, over the bridge, up a rocky, brushy hill to the slate quarries; whence great quantity of slates are exported, and much found beautifully studded with a golden spar (which, with other trifling curiosities are collected by a poor cooper at Ingleton, to whom I paid my shilling).

The wind was so high as almost to blow me from the hills into the river beneath, which at half a mile further up, forms an exceedingly fine fall called Thornton Force, above and below which I took my stand for some time, in high admiration of its beauty. (I think I may now brag of having seen all the grand waterfalls of Yorkshire.)

My walk back was over the hill, to the valley of Thornton, and thence down a lane to the church of pleasant situation by the side of the Kendal road! Nearly opposite to Thornton church stile is a public house of neat appearance, and below it a house of Mrs Foxcroft, upon the Lancaster road, with a view of Lonsdale vale, closed to the right by a distant view of Hornby Castle. Upon Ingleton bridge I met a fellow, sensible I thought, as speaking my sentiments; for to my insidious enquiry, 'If the cotton trade did not benefit the poor?', he answered, 'The worst thing in the world, in my opinion, Sir. For it leave us neither stout husbandmen nor modest girls; for the children bred in a cotton mill never get exercise or air, and all are impudent and saucy.'

Tired of Ingleton, though a sweet situation, as I should be alone of any place in cold, drizzly weather with bleak winds from the mountains, so I hurried on my dinner; which consisted of a large and well-flavoured trout, veal collops and several cold dishes. I was off by three o'clock, and upon an excellent road, which man and heart enjoy, though the rough, stony paths may have been of service to the horses, as rendering them careful.

The country was pleasant, but the weather very cold; luckily, however, Ingleborough served for a screen to keep off the wind. Through Clapham (not near Westminster Bridge) and through —— I rode briskly, and till the long hill descending under Giggleswick Scar, a steep slaty eminence; and then slowly by the well, which formerly ebbed and flowed, and by Giggleswick, the parish church of Settle, a small market town, where after some doubts put up at the Spread Eagle. Settle is a poor gloomy place. After fetching a gratifying parcel of letters from the post office, and procuring a newspaper, I sat myself down quietly for tea (for the weather was too bad for walking) when I saw the half-drunken farmers scamper home from market. There is a rock overhanging the town, where some idle schemers have endeavoured to make walks and to form it into a public garden; but all trouble were thrown away upon it. The landlords in this county are more uncommunicative, and more ignorant of places and of roads, than any I ever met with! Ask them about the next stage or town, and 'They cannot recollect the signs of the best inn, nor the name of the person who keeps it.' 'Stay, I think it is a widow-woman.' One gets wild at their ignorance of the only things they might know, and of their not being able to assist the traveller or tourist. ('Do you know the country well?' 'Oh yes, perfectly.' 'Then what is the name of that bridge?' 'Of such an hill?' – Then they are completely bewildered.) Better ask your dog than them, for his tokens would assist you. I told the minister of Askrigg, 'That I would go for the swallows flew high.' At this he seemed surprised and asked the reason. 'Why, Sir, because the game is not beaten down by the atmosphere.' I am angry when a shepherd asks me the time of the day, and is ignorant about the weather: for what else has he to consult but the sun, and the signs upon the hills or in the sky? My landlord tells me, for my comfort, that we shall hear the snow upon the

166

hills. I had a trout for supper (with other things) of the same size as that at dinner; *Venienti occurrite trouto*, which means, Get what is best in every county. A dismal, black, raining evening! In such an inn, in such weather, to such a wind have I formerly listened in winter, when intent upon the morning's hunt; but since I have commenced tourist, in what is called summer, I have wished for warm gales from a charming sun, and to be able to take an evening stroll, a modest worshipper of Luna.

20 June   'In the worst inn's worst room.' This is a bad and dismal inn, with the mice running about behind the wainscot and everything rattling with wind; and what is worse I am obliged to stay in it, for all day, yesterday, I felt myself very unwell from all the windings, wettings and starvings of the preceding day; so last night, I applied to Dr James's Pills, which sweated me most handsomely, aided by a great floundering feather bed – luckily for this night, only, but which would have destroyed me in a hot summer. This morning I had the prudence not to rise till a hot shirt was brought to me, and then crawled down to drink bowls of tea. Of all weathers, windy weather is the least endurable in a bad inn; for last night my windows, door and chimneyboard kept an incessant clatter. These miseries are only the lot of gentility, for lower people will never stir a step to stop them, by driving a nail or fastening a peg, but say, 'That they always do so in a wind.' I believe that I left my knife on Monday to the miseries of the moor alehouse, which must be a great prize and curiosity, having a corkscrew and a picker, and if fallen into Scotch hands useless. I am frequently met in this road by Irish vagabonds and sailors going to and from Liverpool, upon whom I bestow charity with the same grace as Gil Blas did to the sturdy mendicant. The day brightened up at ten o'clock when the wind sank; and this tempting me out (my great intention to Malham being given up) I walked over the well-built new bridge crossing the River Ribble, whence is a pleasant view of the vale, closed by the crest of Ingleborough. This led me to the village of Giggleswick, where is a tolerable seat of Mr

Backhouse. I sauntered around the churchyard, and admired a pretty fall of water from the mill; then beneath Giggleswick Scar, where the church shows to much advantage; and so returned by the bridge home. It is from publications and descriptions (and sometimes the puffs of natives) that places and countries are visited; had I not read the poem of Wensleydale, written by (the old codger) Mr Maude (who, by the bye, has much the same kind of glazed face and simper that his patron has; a very suspicious aspect! and was, I find, under His Grace as Surgeon of a Man of War); and had I not studied *The Tour of the Caves* and *A Description of Malham*, etc, I had never come this way. Therefore of infinite advantage to a place and country are such publications. The bread and butter of this country are bad, and I do wish for the fruit and garden stuff of summer; but I must say that in general the port wine has been old and good. I think I understand it, and no man is at more pains to procure it!

That and my writing have been my supports; and a support or supporters are wanted by a man who travels alone, and in untoward weather. Garwood becomes, to my liking, a resemblance to T. Bush by hurrying me along; he is sober, assiduous and careful, and in many respects superior to T. Bush; for he lorded it over me; was talkative in the kitchen, discovering your whole history; made love to the maids; and was very complainant when highly charged; besides, an ugly trick of repairs and of goods broken and out-of-order.

I had an early dinner of beef steaks, lamb chops, pickled salmon and tart; and for supper last night a trout, lamb chops, potted trout and tart; so that under the article eating I have not been over-charged. (Nine pence for each meal!) It was a gloomy, cold forbidding day, and I rode along from Settle without pleasure and without observation (remember I was not well) except at the village of Long Preston, where was another Scotch sale, when I again attended to the different dialects and dress.

I passed through two hamlets and a Leicestershire grazing country till I crossed [the] new canal from Leeds to Liverpool, where they are now building locks for the advantage of increasing trade; but I should honour more the planter or cultivator of 200 acres of moor ground, than the builder of the noblest cotton mill. All the hedges of the country are ruined, as most are by throwing up the ditch bottoms on the bank, instead of throwing upon the fields! The village of Gargrave is by the side of the canal, whence more miles brought me to Skipton – where, after much debate and enquiry, I put up at the Black Horse, the older inn; for there is another, the New Inn, a gawky, dismal, ill-contrived thing built by and resembling the Duke of Devonshire – a thing one would avoid.

At the top of the high street is the church, which street reminded me much of Maidstone. Close to the churchyard stands the porter's lodge of the old castle inhabited by Mr Healer, steward to Lord Thanet. A servant maid showed us the castle, and a most inconvenient, miserable, tattered place it is, with neither beauty of building nor pleasing antiquity; but a melancholy wretchedness of bad old rooms, some miserable tapestry and some (basely) neglected pictures, especially one of the Countess with a child in her hand, are the only relics, for all the furniture has been removed to Appleby Castle. The inner court, with a large yew tree in the centre, reminded me of that of Haddon Hall in Derbyshire. The roof is repaired, that is all; but the ceilings begin to drop down. It is a nasty, miserable place, and only fit to make a ruin. There has been a park at some distance, and around it some walks and trees. I was much disappointed, for I expected more.

I entered the church, the door being open, which is very damp and very dirty! In it are several old tombs of the Cliffords, particularly one of George, Earl of Cumberland.

I had only now to stroll about this nasty, filthily-inhabited town, for I never saw more slatterns, or dirtier houses; my walk was protracted till nine o'clock, when I had a vile supper, for neither the bread nor pastry are eatable. The wind is north-east, and if a man is obliged to stop a window with a towel, either he or the weather are bad travellers.

21 June   I had a tolerable bed and passed a tolerable night; nor did I get up more than once to look at the weather, my first rising is about three o'clock. My drawing room and bedchamber often compose one compartment, but are at present divided.

I walked this morning through the castle yard, and through a wood behind, to a cotton mill which stands in the old pleasure ground, where remain some very lofty fir trees. The castle on this side stands upon a rock edge, and would do well for the ruin it must come to, and will then look much better. Had I not been very unwell yesterday, and weakened by a bad night, I should have taken the excursion from Settle that must employ this day; and thereby gained time and saved much ground.

My ride of this morning (after I had read the London newspaper) was the four miles back to Gargrave; thence to the right where they are working at the new canal. When mounting Bumper, I passed through the villages of Easton and Scrotton, where finding my horse's shoe loose I left him with Garwood at a blacksmith's shop and was not overtaken by them till I had arrived at Kirkby Malham; the vale to the right is very pleasant and pastoral; opposite are lofty scarry hills. A dog fare would be a blessing in this county, where one cur alarms the whole village, and the traveller is barked to deafness by tolling, lame hounds.

Kirkby Malham has a tolerable church, about which and the churchyard, a rural spot, I walked for some time. Three more miles and to Malham village, seated beneath the hill; where I housed at the White House alehouse – a miserable one – and was instantly *tooted* by a guide (*ecce iterum Crispinus*)[1] but not a Jobson; dinner ordered – but no trout to be had. Crispin shoved forward before us, having refused to drink – though he said he was very drunk last night.

A steep and stony ascent carried us to the hilltop – which gave us a view of Malham Water (called Maum Tarn). This produced most wonderful accounts of its fishing from our guide, and of the method of procuring leave for fishing upon this

[1] Behold the Crispin of the road. ('Crispin' often refered to a shoemaker.)

wonderful lake, where trout fishing is certainly to be enjoyed to a greater perfection than at any other place in Great Britain, which is by an application to Colonel Lister, who then sends a card of permission.

His house, built upon the bank for the purposes of shooting and fishing, seems to be well-built and comfortable; and if the plantations that are made around will ever grow (which I must doubt), the house and lake will be much beautified and benefited. There are boathouses at one end of the lake, and we saw one boat full of gentlemen-fishers, who must have had a fine day for their sport.

This lake is not so large as Semer Water, nor of such beautiful boundary; but then it has found a writing to sing its praises, whilst Semer Water deserves description and encomium[1] ten times more. From one corner of the lake issues a stream which quickly buries itself in the ground. After walking for an hour upon the banks of the lake, we returned by a new tract over the moor and descended the hill beneath the cove, under whose summit I took my stand in the fullest admiration of its lofty beauty.

The height is 300 feet, and from its base flows the stream that is lost soon after it has left Malham Tarn. Numbers of hawks inhabit this rock who are destroyed as much as possible, for their destruction of the grouse.

Our guide was ample in descriptions, but now my appetite hurried me back. The stable was external wretchedness and could not produce a halter; the house, and stone floor parlour, so bad as to make me wonder that no public house and stabling were decently fitted up here – where I should suppose many tourists do, or ought to, come. Now I might like a fishing party; several parties come here for grouse shooting (these are the pursuits of the country), but when I intended such a scheme, I should send beforehand to secure rooms and stabling, my servant would see that they were properly fitted up, the windows

[1] Praise.

171

well-glazed, the doors to shut tight, the grate repaired; and when I came, think you that I would lay in their beds and drink their poisons? No, no; my bed and bedding, my hampers of wine, my books, my backgammon table, should be ready to receive me. (When I was a boy and in the active field, and changed quarters every day in Germany, and had entered the boor's house allotted to me, I was comfortable (for I had only German servants) and laughed at the ill-management of my comrades. What the village could produce was mine; my servants cooked and my soup, my boiled mutton and my fowl were quickly produced; though the room was wretched, my bed was good and well-made; and let me recollect a present from our Lieutenant-Colonel J— of a sort of a large tea-chest, with a lock, lined with iron, and with a lower drawer for a heater. Beginning a march, I filled the upper space with a fowl, chops, portable soup, greens, etc, and to the brim with water, marched some hours, unlocked the chest – and behold – presto – a delicious, hot, smoking repast.)

After attempting to eat and throwing it to Ranger, I again commenced my touring drudgery; for as Butler says that 'Folk in merriment do drudge and labour', so does the tourist. He sweats, he toils, more than any drover, or like a dancer, tired to death, who wipes his brow and extols the pleasure. Now for a walk with Mr Crispin, to Gordale, for the way is not long and the horse road from stones and steepness almost impassable; however we met a damsel on horseback of youth, and well-dressed, whom Crispin described as a great huntress, and who would gallop down this road. 'Think you,' said I to Garwood, 'that your mistress could be prevailed upon to walk a horse down here?' 'No, I should hope not Sir.' We crossed over difficult wall stiles to near Gordale, above whose brow browsed some goats, a Welsh and novel scenery here. Gordale is of easy and safe approach, and is likewise of formation and curiosity, totally unlike the other forces I have viewed; and perhaps as the last, I esteem it the most, as most dwelling upon my memory. I think I may now say that I have seen the principal waterfalls of the North; not that any inspection can exceed the three beautiful waterfalls that are near together and at a short distance from Dolgellau, in North Wales, which are buried in deep woods, and in this respect differ from the northern cataracts. A view of these occupied one of the most luxurious days of my tourings.

Gordale, though undescribed in prints, could not be so well explained by any pen. (I wonder never to have seen paintings of it; but I believe that the curiosities of Malham are not much visited.) Beneath these cliffs, these lines were explained to me –

> A vaporous drop profound
> I'll catch it e'er it come to ground

– by watching, and catching, the big drops that fell from the summit.

Our guide, a great hunter, told us that the hunted hare often skipped about the rocks, when the clangour of the hounds was very delightful. He added many curious accounts of his fisheries at the foot of this cataract, and of the many trout he caught in this stream. This Crispin was a very communicative good guide, though not of the wit, figure and address of my first Crispin. He next led us to where the stream pours a very pretty cascade, and on one side of it a little, snug, dry cave which he said 'was once inhabited by fairies – but that now they were quite out of fashion'.

All this survey employed one hour and a half, and fully employed, though with much fatigue. In our way of return he showed me what lands had belonged to Mr H— (the schoolmaster, and writer of *Malham and its Environs*) who he said 'had *swallowed up* all his substance, and was now as *crippled* as he was'; and at my desire, he showed me Mr H.'s cottage, which *here* and to me was a curiosity.

I was heartily glad to set myself down upon a wooden chair in the stone parlour, being heartily tired; and though I had enjoyed what I had seen, yet, being alone, the thought of selfishness and want of participation drew tears to my eyes. No mutual remarks and observances; no joke about tumbling over stiles and stones; no incitement but 'I will'; and then two of us had dragged from Crispin all the ridiculous scandal of the village. Before Garwood I dare not speak.

The evening became gloomy after a very fine day; but having finished this grand survey (a great object of desire) I did not much mind the twelve miles of return which I rode, upon Bumper, in two hours. That I call hard riding, and these stony lanes are hard riding. I had for supper a roasted fowl and a tart. No sooner had we returned than the rain began, and continued slightly when I went to bed.

22 June   Are the days now to shorten before summer has made many, and those but faint efforts! This was a warmish morning, in comparison of those we have had. As I had often called at the post office to enquire for letters, the postmaster this morning called upon me, to state 'that several letters had arrived; but that fearful of losing the postage he had sent them back except one, franked, which he had delivered to Mr John Baine of this town, as the nearest sounding name.'

My astonishment was great (anger would not serve me)! I said, 'It seemed to be, in his part, a most wonderful procedure, not to wait some few days; that my letters had always been kept for me at other places; and that Mr John Baine must be an extraordinary gentleman, to read and destroy letters not directed to him; and that if this became a custom, the Post Office must shut up, as no person could trust to the post his secrets or his bank notes!'

Waiting for the post, writing and this eventful history detained me till eleven o'clock when, mounting our horses, I continued the vale for some distance, when I ascended a *steepish* hill (so I believe it would be thought in the South) leading to the moors; where a scud of rain, and more seemingly in advance, hastened me into the vale, having Bardon Tower in view. Here I thought myself lucky in finding the shelter of a cow-house during a heavy rain for half an hour, during which time I employed myself in a sketch of the back of Bardon Tower.

When it cleared up we got out from our calvish society. The farmer appeared, who dwells in an adjacent house attached to an old chapel. He took me round the ruins, but when I heard that this castle was only demolished about twenty years ago for the sake of the lead, slates and timber, by the Duke of Devonshire's order, I could not but exclaim on the folly, waste and stupidity of the possessor. 'Why, wantonly, destroy what Pembroke's Countess so honourably repaired? Why not preserve such a venerable mansion as a home for your steward, or for the farmer? Or (but I am preaching to the wind) lend it with some land, and tax free, to a worthy companion or friend, who will find methods of return in gratitude and assistance, and by his society when you come into this country. But lay not waste the land, nor triumph in destroying useful antiquity. For this house is still very stout and easily repairable.' In the old adjacent chapel, clean and new-glazed, there is divine service performed once a month.

The vale is beautifully wooded, and watered by the River Wharfe (my now old acquaintance), above which I rode till I arrived at Bolton Abbey, when I dismounted to survey the Abbey ruins, which are very magnificent.

The foolish possessor, by some advice (the mason's I suppose), has ordered that they should be repaired, which is now doing – not with proper rough stone but with white quarry stone, without any intention, and disfiguring the building. The eastern end and cross aisle form a fine ruin; the west end is preserved as a church, if a place can be called preserved which is unpaved and in filthy neglect! The steeple is fine; the west end is noble, where some stone figures are left, as two baboons.

Close to this desolation of place and shame of church, the Duke of Devonshire sometimes resides in the Old Gateway, preserved by Lord Burlington who built up the inside, for the pleasure of grouse hunting; but within, there are neither comforts nor cleanliness. An old woman showed me up to the leads, whence is a fine view of the park and of the old Abbey ruins. Another mile and to a snug public house, the Burlington Arms, a house of much better entertainment than Bolton Priory Gateway, for here was good stabling and rational treatment, and a good parlour, wherein were quickly served mutton chops, salad and cold veal pie.

Comfort, but in society; Garwood seems languid for want of society.

After dinner, I took a long strolling walk over Bolton bridge, and sauntered, for some time, in a meadow that sweeps from the inn to the bridge and is famous for the fattening of cattle. At my return, I ordered tea and delayed as long as possible, before I crawled back the six miles of return, when I walked (no rain fallen here) into the wood behind the castle, where I discoursed with a man about their wages in the cotton mills, who said that they could earn 2 shillings per diem, women 1 shilling and children 6d.

Here, and in most places where water must be pent up, they work in the cotton mills only during the day. I wandered about this wood for an hour, till I had heartily tired myself, when I returned to my supper – a trout, etc. – hoping for better and drier weather, though these high hills must for ever produce rain.

Biggleswade, after all, for my money, with its young rabbits and silver eels, and a sandy flat soil to ride upon. I saw a one-horsed hearse with two wheels pass by, which I understand to be the fashionable vehicle of death.

23 June I was glad to leave this dismal town and dismal inn of Skipton, where I had been very hoarse and unwell. That horrid ride from Askrigg half killed me.

My eating here is charged cheaply; wine and horse meat are in the North as dear as elsewhere. I walked forward a mile in a tolerably warm morning; soon crossed Ingay Bridge, and then through Broughton village by Mr Tempest's seat, Broughton Hall, a shaded situation, with a stream in front which turns a mile below it, beautifully hid in wood, and there is a very lofty bridge over this stream. The country beyond Broughton consists of large, wild pasture grounds, twenty fields laid into one; for the cotton trade, with its high pay, has put an end to all thoughts of husbandry, canals and cotton mills are the only thought. Throughout this once well-wooded country (and, indeed, in all others) the farmers have dared, for a greedy ill-judged acquisition of ground, to stock up all the thick hedgerows (forgetting the warmth afforded to cattle, and the expense incurred by hurdles), by which practice all beauty of the country is destroyed and the game is annihilated; and, what is worse, the grand nursery of timber destroyed. For no sooner is any tree felled than to work they go to root up the brushwood beneath, which (like the Goose with the Golden Eggs) has afforded an everlasting advantage to the landlord, and has furnished Britain with her wooded walls. Nor does the landlord ever look to this, and his steward is *easily overruled.*

Some trees of beauty and utility, that abounded, are now almost lost, as the sweet chestnut and the sycamore, which heretofore abounded in our woods and hedgerows. Of the former I know where some quondam[1] hedgerow tenants remain; and of the latter the ascent to Highgate Hill yet furnishes, and a wanderer may be seen in other places. The scrubby favourite of the day (like other favourites from their forwardness) is the Lombardy poplar, who does well enough to form a screen or drain a swamp, but must not be compared to the two old Englishmen.

Below the village of Marton they are [-][2] and a new canal to Leeds; at the village of Little Marton, placed in a pleasant dip, I housed myself for half an hour under a tree, to avoid a pelting shower. From Little Marton the road becomes very stony and disagreable, passing by Denston House, a new-built, staring, high house upon a high hill; 'Pillicock sat upon Pillicock Hill'.

[1] Former.
[2] Portion missing from manuscript.

Another severe storm of rain drove us for shelter to a farm; thence, upon rather better roads, to Gisburn, a small market town adjoining to which are the seat and grounds of Mr Lister (mentioned at Malham Tarn). From a hill there are fine views of Sawley dale and village, where I dismounted to survey what ruins remained of Sawley.

To the village of Charndon the road is very bad, very broken up by the coal carts, and here I contrived as usual to miss my road, from not deigning to ask the way; so went two miles about to Clitheroe, whose old castle remains and high-standing church make it appear to advantage, whereas it is one of the meanest borough towns. Pendle Hill rears its noble summit above this town, and at a distance, to close the vale, appears the mountain Ingleborough. The Swan Inn, a poor alehouse, received us, when Garwood (like T. Bush) was much out of humour with the stable and said, 'Let us go on, Sir.' 'To where, man, would you go? For I know not. Let us stay and get our horses shod.' 'Here I am sure they cannot be.' 'Better here, Garwood, than in a better place; let us not shoe them in a manufacturing town.' Broiled and buttered mutton chops; but luckily there was a cold round of beef and a good fire, for it is very cold. After dinner, when the nags went to the tremendous operation of shoeing (when Garwood was to stand to prevent buttressing, and act according to my orders about small nails, wide heels, etc.), I walked to the castle hill, by a foolishly-fancied Gothic house of Mr Richardson's. The view from the keep is very extensive; and this tower is of great solidity, surrounded for the most part by a rampart wall. Within the precincts is [an] ugly house of Mr Richardson's, built in what is called the Gothic style.

Then to the church, a mean place, and round the church-yard, but without any sport. Nor did I omit, you may guess, twenty calls at the blacksmith's shop whilst the horses were shoeing.

In my second walk I passed under the castle hill and took a sketch. I am very hoarse and weak, with lungs much oppressed, and have deferred, idly perhaps, the putting a blister upon my chest. There was a young moon that tempted me to try a walk after supper, but the cold soon drove me back, and to these reflections over my newspaper the *Morning Chronicle*.

24 June   This finishes my month: not a month of cake and candle, but a month of much pleasant observation and of discourse for hereafter, and much chewings of the cud turned over in my mind and reproduced from my short notes.

I say that this is the last long tour I will ever take alone; and, indeed, it is the only one I ever took to be alone for any time. But I have seen what I wished to see and what I *longer'd a'ter*.

My bedchamber was very wretched, with an old broken deal door which I fortified with chairs, and through which every passenger in this house might see me in bed!

After seeking Ranger for half an hour – an old Mark Anthony, whom I repented having brought with me, for his dullness and want of activity – I left Clitheroe; and upon an ugly stony road for four miles till I arrived above the Vale of the Ribble, which opens beautifully. Whalley is a pretty village with two good-looking inns, the Swan particularly so; but no person will give you this information, nor can you get any hint after you have left London. Of Whalley Priory there is left a profusion of superb ruins, though Mr Cannon, building upon the foundation of the old dwelling, has pulled much down and neglected the rest; there is, in the first place, a whole gateway of approach, leading to the tasteless house of Mr Cannon, attached to the remains of the old house whose ruins, overspread by ivy, stretch themselves along the river's bank.

At the end of these ruins stand the noble relics of the church, behind which and all about is antiquity sufficient to amuse the tourist or supply employ for the painter. Strange that no drawings have been made of a place so curious! (Perhaps its obscure situation has prevented it being known.) But more strange, and to be grieved at, that Mr Cannon should permit dilapidation, and not secure and plant about these beauteous ruins, where he might form for a trifling expense a garden of wonderful charms and curiosity. I took the whole survey at my leisure, gratis, for no one came near me. There is a long large building which I entered, now a barn, which I take to have been the dormitory. At the further angle of the close stands this fine old gateway, under which now passes the common highway to the village. Leaving this charming survey (of which I have said so little, and of which I believe nothing has been written), I rode to the bridge, upon the Blackburn road, whence is the best view of the abbey ruins, of the river, and of much rich and wooded scenery. (May I be able to find a good description of this place.)

A new and well-made road carried me from Whalley near Mr Waller's house and grounds, who has, with miserable intention, built some strange ruins upon a hilltop – being probably ignorant of the splendid ruins at the hill bottom! Such a man will furnish his house with base copies of Correggio. Upon this new road I could trot along, followed by Bumper in a new thick snaffle, the last having much galled his mouth.

Arrived at [Padiham] Bridge upon the River Calder around which are numberless coalpits, for the whole country seems to be a bed of coal; crossing a common, we passed by the village of Accrington where they are building rows of houses, as every vale swarms with cotton mills – some not bigger than cottages, for any little stream, by the means of a reservoir, will supply them. Cotton mills have chosen the old abbey situations; in the abbeys there was religion and decency, in the cotton mills, blasphemy and immorality. Religion might have overstretched her power and intention, and was blown up. I hope the cotton trade will flourish; but it may crack! And then they must be converted into workhouses? No corn is raised where cotton mills abound, for no hands could be found for agriculture; so all the flour is brought from a distance; and wonderful is the import of wheat to Liverpool, from America etc.!

Haslington church stands high in a bleak country, which however, from the population, does not appear melancholy. Being very hungry, I hastened to an inn – the worst of the place it must be, for it is the worst in the world! Mutton chops, not eatable, upon a dirty cloth (I should fancy that my landlord came from some dirty country[1]; and dropped the Mac by the way); as for the port wine – the pint, that I poured upon the ashes. Here I stayed not an hour, being eager to find better accommodation.

In two miles I sent Garwood forward, but learning at the turnpike that Rochdale was a much better town to stop at than at Bury, and only some few miles' difference, I trotted after and overtook him; and then quitting a very good road, we crawled up a stony lane of two miles to reach the Rochdale road, which was very bad, and over a wild moor till the hill which descends into Rochdale! The rain now came on, but I was consoled by the thoughts of a good inn. All round Rochdale they are building away – and have swelled it from a small market town into a great city. Crossing the stones, and a bridge, I arrived at the Roebuck Inn. Oh! What a Wapping alehouse, and what a Wapping landlady! Discoursing with me, with her great back against the table. Nothing clean should enter this mansion, for nothing clean can go out of it. She said that the Players are here and will act tomorrow night. I wished for Players, I have found them; and now won't stay to see them! Why, can I stay in an inn where my parlour is adorned by escutcheons, with a door that don't shut, and there is no straw in the dungeon stable?

This may be the grand tavern of Rochdale, but people who are acquiring riches are ignorant of enjoyments and comforts; those are left to the succeeding generation. I was hasty in wishing my horses to be littered down with cotton; for [so] had I heard. (If you dine in the City of London, you will find (even there) a strange dinner: expense without comforts; two-pronged forks; Birmingham broad-ended knives; and, at every turn, some wonderful want amidst wonderful expense!) In what a lawless state of indecorum must these great manufacturing towns exist, when, from a want of hands, character and good behaviour are unnecessary, masters wanting servants, not servants wanting

[1] i.e. Scotland.

masters, so the workman demands excessive wages, is insolent, abandoned, and drunk half the week!

In the evening I walked about the churchyard, and in several walks thronged by Sunday company, naked-legged boys and impudent wenches, before I returned to my supper of a black fowl with bad bread, and one candle; however, at last I did get another.

I have read with astonishment a new newspaper, called *The Manchester Herald*, fraught with sedition and every species of rebellion; to your tents, O Israel! Tom Paine, the hero, with extracts from his damnable publication. I say prosecute them boldly, and let the nation, in general, be the judge.

25 June   Midsummer Day. No characters of workmen are required here, so drunkenness and impudence are in full revelry, and all other counties are to be drained for their supply. Instead of clean, jolly husbandmen strutting about, the '*lean unwashed artificer*' here rules alone, to the dismay of modesty.

Upon my offer of a £10 note for change they refused acceptance, unless I would give 1s. 6d! Is this to be justified, or is it part of their treason to decry the lawful money of the Bank of England, to serve their own notes?

(If Garrick had acted I would not have stayed in this Inn.)

In Bury I could not have fared worse than I have done here, besides the having to consider the detour and the bad road I endured. Leaving Rochdale, I found the surrounding country rich, well-studded with houses, and the roads crowded by idle fellows to enjoy the holiday of Saint Monday, or of Midsummer Day.

Middleton, which was a little village (where Lord Suffield has a bad old seat), is now becoming a large market town, where they are building streets and a Grecian Market House. To the right is the ugly, vulgar house and grounds of Lord Grey. I now come upon a pave[d road] within sight of Manchester, passing through the village of Chetham and, by the public house, the assemblage of the Manchester Archers, who have ever maintained their precedence over every other archery association.

I felt very hungry, having had nothing eatable before me for some days! I want not dainties, some good cold meat or a tolerable mutton chop are all I seek for; but, lately, I have neither found tolerable bread and cheese. But, now, at Manchester I will gratify myself. By advice, to avoid a noisy tavern, I put up at the Bull's Head in the Market Place. Oh what a dog hole is Manchester! For the old town is like Wapping, and the upper, the new town, like Spitalfields, in the same gloom and dirt.

I hurried to the Post Office, there found letters, my best and only treat; then wandered about the town till dinner time, without seeing anything that I should ever wish to see again. Now for an indulgence of appetite, after a long disgust. My dinner (ordered magnificently) was a salmon, veal, lamb chops and peas. Look to the product: peas were not to be had; the salmon served to me was too stale to be eaten; and the thick, raw, fried chops swam in butter! 'God sends meat; but the devil sends cooks.' I could not eat; I tried to drink of the port wine, but could not; the bread was intolerable and the cheese was in remnants. I said, 'Take away, I cannot eat.'

In places where wealth is procured, it is ignorantly spent, for the upstart man of riches knows no better. The inns therefore are bad, dear and presumptuous; but on roads where gentlemen travel, and scold, there will be a reform. To increase my spleen, it began to rain. They would not change a £10 note, and they refused to take a guinea I had taken this morning, 'because it was a light one'. One cannot travel about, like Shylock, with a pair of scales.

As the rain fell fast I turned back for an hour, to write a letter to Mr O. I pity the officers of the Scotch Greys, quartered here (although they have made the Bull their headquarters). For such living must poison them.

I gave the waiter a shilling for his non-attendance, and for taking a letter to the Post Office, which, when received, he said,

'I hope you will give me something for my trouble of taking it to the Post Office?' I snatched my letter out of his hand, damned him and the inn, and walked out immediately.

At the end of Manchester (to which, soon, there will be no end), I overtook my horses. Under a misty rain I traversed the bad stony road of seven miles to Stockport in Cheshire, where all seemed holiday and drunkenness with a grand procession, with music, of idiotical Freemasons! Here, drunken weavers leading home by their soberer comrades; there, men and children, killed by gin, carrying to their graves! ('There the black gibbet glooms beside the way.') For near to Stockport hangs a weaver in chains, for the murder of his wife, and my wonder is that murder does not happen every hour from eternal drunkenness! I quitted the park incessantly to avoid staggering insolence.

Oh! That the wastes of this land were cultivated, and that the property of the land was properly subdivided for the support and encouragement of the honest kind, and that it were not thought useful (nor necessary) that vicious unwholesome trades should be encouraged to the immense gain of a few by the loss of the lives of thousands. Amidst all the crew of artisans, you may search in vain for healthy looks, for, alas! they are all squalid from unwholesome toil and relaxing debauchery. At Liverpool the importation of wheat from America is very great, for this great cotton trade cannot support itself; consequently as their husbandry keeps pace with our manufactories, who, think ye, will last longest, the ground work or the cotton work? The one fixed as the globe, the other as precarious as the wind. The one rearing hardy honesty, the other supporting enervating debauchery. Now were five hundred of either side of such men to come to combat, what could the sons of the shuttle perform against the followers of the plough? Why – they would fall before the latter.

After my late bad stops and bad sceneries, think of the pleasure of finding myself in the snug Dishley Inn, in a parsonage kind of parlour, and my horses in a dry good stable, eating sweet hay.

I walked about the little garden in peace and ordered my old bedroom (for I have been here before). But that made me sigh, for the weather was gloomy; then it was very fine, T. Bush and poor little Poney were with me. Foolish thoughts. I supped upon mock turtle and mutton chops, with good bread and cheese, but no peas. At Manchester, I was directed to a great fruit shop, in that great rich town, to get some strawberries, my favourite fruit, and some were handed to me such things as boys pick up in Covent Garden Market; I bought six pennyworth and, having swallowed two, threw the rest into the street. At eleven o'clock, I felt sleepy and retired to bed.

26 June   Where I did not wake till nine o'clock this morning; long after Garwood had gone, by my advice and permission, to spend the day at Buxton ten miles distant.

A long toilette was as necessary as refreshing, having been for some days hurrying about from bad inn to bad inn, and like Noah's dove without a resting place, buffeted about by incessant rain.

After breakfast, at the late hour of eleven, I sauntered on foot to the blacksmith's shop, in that sweet spot at the entrance into Lyme Park, which is all in waste and ill-keeping. I stood before the house when my lady housekeeper came out, in civility, as I thought. So I said, 'Is there any family here?' 'Yes, to be sure.' 'Mr Legh?' 'No.' 'Then I can see the house?' 'Indeed you can't, I should have enough to do then.' 'Pleasing business, surely, for a housekeeper?' 'We never show it but to those we know.' 'Then I am happy not to be able to see it.'

Thus we parted in mutual contempt, though it seems to be so miserable a house that she would not be over-fatigued.

One side of the park is covered by rabbits, and the other is a dreary swamp, with withered hollies and some very large old alders which they are now felling; and why? Unless a large piece of water were intended, which might be formed. I wandered over the holly side and only met some tremendous red deer. Who were most alarmed I cannot say; though I walked on and

185

they moved not, so it would be given against me, as quitting the ground. The day was soft and gloomy, a fine fishing day; and as I get southwards, I hope the sun will get warmer.

I returned back by the park gate and then to the left, up the hill, by the pillars, into the high road – a charming walk. Garwood returned at the same time, two o'clock, from Buxton! So, he was soon tired of a gayer world.

I dined upon the mock turtle, and then for an hour worked at the drawings I had sketched, though in that way I have been idle. But then the weather has been too cool to stop in; nor can I think that I make any improvement.

At six o'clock, preparing for a walking ride, the weather set in for rain – a settled rain; but it came at a good hour and found me at a good place. Let me reflect upon my happy or ill luck since I left London. The weather has been cold, with some rain; but not enough to confine me long or to baulk my intentions. In spring and autumn now, we have often warm weather, while the midsummers are cold. Of the mock turtle I tire not, so had some more for supper, after a long stable inspection.

27 June   For some reason, but not probably from the devilish mock turtle, my head ached terribly through the night; so as the best cure I drank cold water, wrapped myself up close and perspired beyond all reckoning. At eight o'clock when Garwood came to call me, I begged a respite for an hour; and then crawled down, much exhausted, and hung for two hours over my brandied tea whilst my night cap was drying at the fire. At eleven o'clock, a dark morning, finding myself better, I beat to horse, then crept along through Lyme Park, there enquiring my road to Edlington.

From these hilly, wild divided parks, there is a noble view over part of Cheshire into Lancashire.

Descending this hill and through a wood came to Edlington, and then into the turnpike road, fronting which is an ugly, staring red brick house of Mr Legh's around which is much timber (though shroved!)[1] with nasty Scotch firs in the hedgerows.

The weather became now hot all at once, so much to my delight that I inwardly muttered, 'Ha, Ha, Mr Summer are you coming? Well, I can bear you.'

My mock turtle headache vexed me, however, so much as to take off from the pleasure of the view of the vale to the left, and of the rising hills above it. At Macclesfield they seem in prosperity from their trade, and are building away. I put up at the best, though a bad, inn (where I have been before), the Angel, where the house was so crowded by a grand dinner that I betook myself into a small room behind the bar, desiring to be served from the remains of the grand dinner. 'And pray, of whom is the Club formed?' 'Why, Sir, of old women of this town, who having established a fund for the benefit of their helpless, their sick, etc., and for funerals, meet at this inn to settle their accounts and to enjoy themselves over a good dinner'; from part of which, particularly a good ham, I dined. (These subscriptions – not missed at the payment – are a most excellent invention, strengthening the bands of fellowship, destroying the chains of poverty, and rendering overseers of the poor needless.)

The streets here are newly-paved, a large addition made to their old church, and the silk and copper trades in a most flourishing state; were the Pretender to rise from the dead and review Macclesfield, he would be surprised, and expect a great augmentation to his army from such a town. The people here, I suppose, are kept in high health from the number of their *water-carters*.

In my way to the copper works, I entered and observed a silk mill in the lower town, but when I came to Mr Roe's great copper works we were refused admittance, from the want of a ticket which we should have applied for. Now this was very provoking! And to have to trudge a mile back to Mr Roe's

[1] Pollarded.

187

banking house. So I was properly peevish at the inn, where they knew my intentions, but the weird women had bewitched them.

Horses in hand, we returned to the copper works, where I took an accurate and gratifying survey of their mixing, melting and flattening the copper, a most unwholesome employ for which the workmen, I think, are meanly-paid, as the best earn but 14s. per week. The road from Macclesfield is exceedingly pleasant, passing under the hills, with beautiful views into Staffordshire. The evening was fine, the country of a wild irregularity, and the road of a reddish sandstone. To Bosley Marsh, and passing near The Cloud, a steep and lofty hill, soon passed [Dane] Bridge which divides the counties of Chester and Stafford, whence four more miles brought me to the town of Leek. (Not a Welsh town, as some ignorants might imagine.) Putting up at the George, securing a good parlour and bedroom, I hurried to the Post Office (very successfully) for letters; and in the market place purchased a long riding whip, to prevent my waste and trouble in cutting down the farmers' hedges for switches, a dozen of which I destroyed this evening. Eating a good supper, deciphering and answering Mrs Byng's and her sons' letters, fully employed my hours till bed time. My landlord was the most ignorant of the ignorant! This was the finest day I have met with, and the moon shone brightly in the evening.

28 June   As my expression concerning switches might lead my readers into a belief of my whipping my horses to death, I wish to have them informed that I only strike them, and that tenderly, over their hinder quarters (not cutting eyes, ears, shoulders or flanks), by which usage, aided by a running snaffle and a pistol bit, my horses, instead of pecking against every stone with a straight leg, afford me the satisfaction of seeing their knees at every step they take. Now this my weak and unfashionable notion, as it is, sounds ludicrously in the ears of modern horsemanship; for modern management doth ordain that a martingale should so confine the horse's steps that he cannot walk two miles an hour, or miss striking the smallest pebble.

Now by way of conversation, not vaunting, I will suppose myself on the descent of an hill, in company with a long-spurred jockey upon this martingaled nag. We would trot it down; now you perceive the modern equestrian pulling with all his violence and spurring his shoulder-rolling steed, whilst I (now don't laugh) lifting up my arms, calling out Ha! Ha! Ha! and applying my switch to the rump of my nag, am carried down the hill safely and straitly, with neither mine nor my horse's shoulders being ground to shivers, from his quarters being properly and easily collected under him.

This I state, as an answer to such wits who, not choosing to depart from fashion or to understand horsemanship, indulge themselves at my expense on the quantity of my reins and the length of my whip. 'Well, I would not be so encumbered with so many reins, for the world! Pray, Sir, are you going to angle? That is a very fine fishing rod in your hand! etc.! etc.! etc.!'

Now to such ribaldry (for an attacker has great advantages), what is to be answered but by way of retort? And that produces spleen and passion. Were I to say, 'Pray, of what use is that short thick stick of yours? Is it to knock your horse down? Why are the necks of your spurs four inches long? Why do your breeches reach to your ankles? And why should not your boots cover the calves of your legs?', my assailant would become peevish and moodily retire behind the weak shield of fashion.

I shall conclude my episode, in the indulgence of a little harmless vanity, by saying that I knew Sir Sidney Meadows, the first master of horsemanship, that he honoured me by a permission to enter his *manège* on horseback, that he often flattered me by saying, 'That is right, Sir, you work your horse properly.' Under the impression of this memory, I can endure a volley of smallshot wit, which offends but wounds not.

I took an early walk around the churchyard, whence is a very pleasant view. The church is well built. In the churchyard is a very old engraved pillar of the mouldering red sandstone. This inn is a goodish shop, and I had good hot rolls and coffee for breakfast.

189

From Leek, an up-hill and down-country to Cheddleton, where the view of the bridge, navigation and church compose a most happy scenery. Having enquired in vain of my landlord at Leek about some rocks of curiosity, I here popped upon them by the roadside. They are called Wetley Rocks and are a romantic cluster of craggy cliffs; upon these I climbed, and rested for some time in a very happy feel of mind, for the day was fine and I felt hearty.

Thence a high, pleasant road brought me to Weston Coyney where, upon enquiry, I took down a lane to the left which soon brought me to the village of Caverswall and to the object of my research, Caverswall Castle.

At the gate I was received with much civility by two young farmers, brothers, one of whom remained with the horses whilst the other attended us into the house.

This house, belonging to Mr Grey, I expected to have found a deserted ruin, whereas it is in perfect repair, usefully furnished and perfectly habitable. All the corner bulwarks remain, and the moat well-stocked with fish must be productive of fine sport to the angler. I ascended to the leads, whence is a wide and tolerable prospect.

I was now quite undetermined to my purpose, whether to Stafford, to Stone, or to the left to Bromley. The fall of my stick had determined me; but learning here that the pottery country began in two or three miles, which is highly flourishing and wherein is much to observe, I was resolved to pass through it, though it threw me considerably out of my first intention. One of the young farmers attended me through the grounds till I entered the public road. At Lane End the population of the pottery commences (where the roads are repaired by the fragments, 'broken in pieces like a potter's vessel'), and continues a street of many miles. The men, whitened with the powder, are supplied with coals to keep alive the everlasting ovens, from every adjacent field; hundreds of horses, and asses with panniers, are incessantly taking in their lading. Through there I passed along, slowly, in pleasant rumination, but wondered much at no market being established for such a multitude.

I now descended to the village of Stoke-upon-Trent, around which are numberless new buildings and many pleasant villas for the principal merchants, and there is likewise a good inn building in this place. Here I crossed the Trent, and soon, many branches of navigation. These intersecting canals, with their passing boats, their bridges, the population, the pottery ovens and the bustle of business, remind me of a Chinese picture, where the angler is momentarily interrupted by a boat.

The late village of Hanley, now a great town upon the hill above, cuts a flaming figure from its new church and newly-built houses. The village of Skelton, likewise, is swelled into great bulk.

Now I enquired for Etruria, the grand pottery established by Mr Wedgwood; and putting up my horses at the adjacent inn, sent up my name and compliments to Mr Wedgwood, with a desire to view his manufactory. In the meantime, as the workmen were at dinner and would be for about an hour, I sauntered about Mr Wedgwood's grounds, which are green and pleasant, with some pretty plantations, views of navigation, etc., etc. The house seems to be good, and is built of staring red brick, as are many in the vicinage, belonging to the principal traders. I was now shown about the several workshops of this great pottery, wherein are employed 300 men; but this is a dull observation for any person who has seen china manufactories. The painting business, performed by females, is a hot, unwholesome employ; the work to be painted is always lifted up in the left hand. Except some Irishmen, who were put in purposely, for the intent of desertion, I did not find that any persons had attempted to carry off any secrets of the art.

My horses remained at Mr Wedgwood's inn, where was no corn to be had! (Ah, we are rich, but we don't understand these things.)

After an hour's inspection, hunger hastened me away, and I thought the mile to the town of Newcastle-under-Lyme grievously long, but as this was a large town, upon a very high road, I knew I should fare well.

The Roebuck, the largest inn, is one of the most savage, dirty alehouses I ever entered. (Traveller, beware the Roebuck in Newcastle.)

The cold meat was not to be touched, the bread was oniony and buttery! I could not stay, and was loath to go; despair forced me to order out my horses. (A hungry, tired man does not do this without sad provocation?) Then came some mutton chops, but not eatable.

I then walked away, and was soon overtaken by the horses, and too soon by the rain which hurried me along to Trentham, where into a smart-looking inn I entered; but the house being full I was shown into a bedroom and ordered tea. 'Up with my tent' – I go no further; no one would warn me against the Newcastle Roebuck, or tell me of this inn. After tea-drinking in this good bedroom (I should not dislike, in winter, the French custom of supping in a bedroom and slipping, full and warm, into bed without changing ground), I walked into Trentham Park. Trentham House has been wonderfully altered, from the grand to the modern. In the park, my old friend Lancelot Brown is to be traced at every turn; he certainly was a grand planner and leveller of ground, and a judicious former of water (the lake here is very fine, but above the house), but he was too severe upon avenues. Now, narrow avenues are charming, shady walks, and if wide, grand things.

But the glory of Trentham is the fronting wood, of age and magnificence. Such a bosom is not to be met with! 'For which your sister Gertrude was so famous.' Through this wood did Jacques (for I have heard of his character) wander in happy meditation, wanting, only, warmth and summer thoughts. Nor did I return till nine o'clock, when over a fire, sitting in my greatcoat, I ate the first peas I have seen this season. Oh! November, you will be quickly upon us with your threats! Why will not an end of June cheer us?

I would have enquired many things of my landlord, but he

knew little further than his own bar, and enquiry becomes fatigue and desperation. Turn the landlords round by three questions, and they are undone!

A good inn near your park gates is an excellent plan, but the landlord should know that the stabling were good, with wide stalls, for ground is cheap enough in the country. Yet under what disadvantages do people hazard an invitation. 'Oh, come to us.' 'You will find our rooms warm and your bed comfortable, and the stabling at the inn is excellent.' Are you sure of that, Sir?

29 June   A dark doubtful morning, much rain had fallen in the night, and the roads are as dirty as at Christmas. This inn is well placed, in good country, and with a good kitchen garden; but, as usual, there are no feathers in the bolster and pillow. (In gentlemanly houses it is often [not] better and down falls your head till it reaches the wood, the cord or the ticking!) After breakfast, and a complete suit of clean linen, I walked to Trentham Hall; horses to follow. The church and churchyard are attached to the house; surely when Lord Gower took down the steeple, he might have removed the church?

A grand housekeeper transferred me, for my survey, to a servant maid. (The old front was magnificent; but the present ones are quite ugly and mean.) The inside contains no vestige of antiquity or of old furniture; and what is very extraordinary, there is not one old family portrait in the house!

'Were there never any, Betty?' 'I believe there might be when the house was altered, but they were old shabby things, and were thrown aside.'

There are several portraits of the present Marquis, and one of Lord Gower in an old English habit with dressed and powdered hair!

The apartments are well-sized and well-doored, but the dining room is neither chaired nor carpeted, and the drawing room is too French and fine for me. The library is dark! This is to make people attend to their studies? (When I build a library in the country it shall open into a flower garden, so that it will be perfumed by the flowers in the summer, and in winter the surrounding evergreens will afford a warm and studious walk. How like you that? Another taste I have, out of taste, of choosing a fountain in the midst of my flower garden, and orange trees. How like you that?)

I would not view the bedrooms; and the kitchen, the maid said, was a bad one! That's odd *methinks, I,* for I *thoughts as how* that his Lordship understood the *right thing.*

I now mounted and crossed the park into the wood, which is ill-managed being too thick of trees, and the drives are not verged by pleasant shrubs. However, this is a noble building. Passing the lodges, I proceeded into the village of Tittensor and the high road, when the rain came on and forced us into (another) saw pit shed for shelter. Hard this upon the poor tourist? And grievous for the country that wants sun.

Quitting the hotel, I soon came to Mayford village, a beauty of situation as to river, wood, bridge, etc. The situation of Mr M.'s house is spoiled by a kitchen garden, which detaches the beauties; a kitchen garden should be in a concealed bottom, screened from the north.

As the rain now returned with violence, I trotted briskly along by the side of the navigation to the end of the town of Stone, where I re-hoveled for an hour, when finding no cessation of rain I ventured out to take a peep at the inn, and to this, liking the appearance, I removed my quarters. The Crown appeared to be a good house, with symptoms of civility, where, taking possession of a good parlour (with a good fire, June 29th!) I ordered dinner, and then read the London newspapers with great avidity after my long ride. I was much entertained from my window with the sight of four lusty Irish gentlemen coming forth from a hackney post-chaise with four horses; and afterwards being repacked in another, instead of going in two chaises drawn by 2 horses each, which I should have thought a pleasanter way of travelling.

These rains make me sluggish, I want the spurs of sun and

summer. My touring of today has been from Mile End to Hackney, but when I times speak with affected humility, I seek applause for what I have done (alone). At three o'clock I ventured out to survey the church and the churchyard, wherein are some recumbent figures upon monuments, and two very old carved figures upon the earth which I should suppose were removed from the old church, for there is a new, miserable Gothic-like church erected. In the churchyard is much rhyming and much lament. One epitaph of excellent metre I took down:

> Consigned to death are all mankind
> Behold four sweet infants here entombed.

The rain hurried me back. This weather I could endure in London, muzzing at home or crawling to the Haymarket Theatre; but not to have seen one rose yet! And here is winter coming, and my flannel under-waistcoat not yet changed for a calico one!

It looks now like a November evening, and I feel as if in one of the streets at the back of the Exchange. I would that the Rochdale actors were here; with pleasure would I give a crown to see them, or I would with pleasure lose double that sum at whist, to three quiet, steady players. This is by much the longest and most desponding day that I have passed; and I have passed it like a solitary officer of Dragoons, without having a quarter-master at his command to order about. I read in the papers of several robberies and abuses of travellers, upon Hounslow Heath at ten o'clock, and upon Finchley Common at 11 o'clock at night; and here are passengers at nine o'clock at night, stopping only till another chaise is got ready. Now, such travellers are the encouragers of highwaymen and ought to be punished accordingly. Why, twelve miles further is a worse inn and a bad bed? By being early I receive the best stalls and the best bed, and then laugh at the fashionably benighted traveller. Lamb chops and peas for supper. This has been a day of delay and of depression, for the rain continued almost incessantly, though I should hope without yet driving the rivers over their banks.

30 June   June is going without sun! Now advance, Mr July, enliven us, and toast us a little. I slept in a wide, good bed, and came down in a rainyish morning to some excellent hot rolls. Walking forward on foot, as usual, I had got three miles and no Garwood appeared! 'How comes this? He must have taken another road.' And so he had, and when at last he came up with me, his horses were covered with sweat and mud.

He had been directed (mischievously) the wrong way and appeared so flustered that in attempting to remount his horse he fell over him. Now this did not happen from delay, for a horseman that overtook me informed me of his wrong guidance.

I now came to Sandon village, beyond which is Sandon Hall, the seat of Lord Harrowby. This is a new-made place, with young healthy plantations; the house, to which I rode, seems good and is placed, *à la mode*, on the hilltop. Now, quitting the road, I crossed the river, and at a short distance entered Ingestre Park, through which I rode with a civil groom of Lord Talbot's. We held much discourse about hunting, and in the midst of it I was lucky enough to meet Lord Talbot's fox hounds, trotting out for exercise. They appear to be a sizeable, well-bred and fleet pack; for who would lose their time in chasing a fox for 2 hours, when you can burst him in 20 minutes!!

We next saw the gamekeeper catching fawns with a grey-hound, to mark them. Is this barbarity necessary? Or is every creature, that would be domestic, to be worried and hunted about by brutes and park keepers?

The sheep of England are hooted and chased about, that they are never at peace, and all beasts are beaten and baited without any cause; aye, and under their master's eye too!

Blackguards and boys should be deprived of all hostile and barbarous weapons as guns, whips, goads, spurs, etc, etc. And people who are to have the care and guidance of animals should be chosen for their sobriety and mild disposition.

Garwood rides without spurs; and most luckily today, else he had been thrown by the violence of his beast – who was quite wild at the sight of the hounds and the coursing.

The grounds about and views from Ingestre are beautiful; and this country seems to have been formerly studded with spacious parks and noble mansions, at the time when the nobility resided with magnificence and hospitality in their several counties, before operas were known, or that it became necessary to huddle all together in miserable, mean lodging houses in London, there to pay extravagantly for what is brought, or stolen, from their own lands! But the ladies command, and here has been this old magnificence of old Ingestre Hall ruined by late modern alteration, and the grand drawing room is so frittered out with French festooning (contraband probably) as to make me sick; the old hall is turned into a comfortless dining room, the windows modernly sashed, and everything altered without being improved.

The church adjoining and the road close in front are miseries; sometimes very difficult of removal, these were the bad taste of our ancestors, but then we must consider that the whole family, or part of it, went to church as least four times in the week. The views around are fine, to Chartley Park etc; but why mention I these left behind, and for (I hope) another tour. Tixall Park is only divided from Ingestre park by the road; here has been till lately a finely wooded place, but all the timber is cut or cutting down, for every remaining tree is marked. (Just such a destruction as I formerly observed in Hampton Court Park in Herefordshire.)

Here are great pools of water, now in full exposure, and the park, speedily to become a wild heath, is cut to pieces by the timber wains; and all this is done too, in sight of the house, by the owner Lord Chetwynd, who seems to possess the most cruel taste that ever man possessed!

He is now demolishing the remains of the grand old mansion to erect offices upon, adjoining to his new mansion house. Now the old gate of approach (wonderfully left) being in strength and soundness, would have made an excellent dwelling.

This gatehouse (upon which is written *William Yates maide this House MDLV*) is of that Grecian architecture which succeeded the Gothic, and was as inferior to that as our modern taste is to this. The inside is entirely scooped out, in filth and dirt, and only a receptacle for cats or the resort of pigeons! Surely a small expense, with some little taste, might form something very grand or pleasant within these old walls. Suppose a *manège*[1] – or a playhouse – or a fives court – or, in short, anything but dirt and ruination. I saw not, I wished not to see, the destroyer, whose modern house and pretty, petty approach (after beauty and grandeur are gone) would not be an ornament to Hackney.

Passing through Tixall village, and on a good road by park pales, I enquired what stood here? And was answered Sir Thomas's, an old house pulled down by the late Lord Spencer; and the timber cut down of course – that both lord and tenant desire to be done speedily!

I now arrived at Stafford, around which town the waters are much out; it is very mean, though the county town, but then it is *honourably* represented by two members – one of whom cannot utter, and the other can utter nothing but treason, and so I feel warmly towards the constituents.

All the inns here (the Swan, perhaps, the best) are merely alehouses and fit for the market folks only. Not choosing to dine with the ordinary, I got what I thought a private room, and some leavings from the ordinary, when a company was put in upon me – good kind of farmering people. But these are always whining and complainant, as, 'Weel I never heard on't – that's strange – but, I hear, God be praised, that wheat is rising? Well – all the better – but oats keep deadly low – though mayhap this weather may meak a change for the *better*.' 'You've grown woundy fat!' 'Aye so are you methinks!' 'How does your sister,

[1] Riding school.

Peggy?' 'Whay – sister Peggy – whay – sister Peggy has been dead this twelve months.' 'Aye has she so?' When gentlemen meet, there is a warm and rapid address; but farm men and lower people, like children, never know what to say.

Glad to quit this society, I walked out to the market place; and it being market day I bought under the market house a pint of clean small strawberries as a curiosity! Then walked around the grand church, whose windows are shamefully broken (by some *Tories*, I suppose, or *Lords of the Bedchamber*) and there are stopped-up cloisters, within which is a school house. In this town there is another, smaller church where *service is done onc't* a month. Returning after my detour of the town and market place, and a purchase of pound of powder (without a stamp, which the old woman said was quite unnecessary) to my parlour friends, I hastened from Stafford as soon as possible, with good directions of my road, and to a most excellent night inn. The country I passed through was very pleasant (with a view to my right of the hill upon which stood Stafford Castle), though the air was very chilling, with frequent storms of rain. I first came to the village of Dunston, and at a short distance to the small, ill-paved, little market town of Penkridge, whose church, well-built and formerly collegiate, I ought to have inspected. Thence, soon turning to the right and keeping the old Roman road, I came in a few miles to the inn I was directed to, at Ivesey Bank. But such a horror of a place, with shattered casements, was only fit to receive Irish trampers!!

Luckily the day was long, and I have always time to spare, so I resolved upon pushing on to Shifnal in Shropshire, to which place I had ordered my letters, and where, no doubt, as being upon the high road to Shrewsbury and to Ireland, good inns are plenty. Weston village is a pleasant situation, and here are the house and domains of Sir Henry Bridgeman. Thence through new enclosures, over a hill which afforded a fine view towards the Wrekin Hill, I arrived at the town of Shifnal having enlarged my ride six miles longer than I intended, and having performed a day of good observation.

The Talbot, the best inn, by no means answered my hopes, being a miserable inn; but here, my standard being fixed and my horses ill-lodged, I walked to the Post Office for letters and to the churchyard as usual, there for my living, and dead, information.

I was comforted on my return (stable business ended), by reading my letters, over a good fire, and making a hearty supper upon cold meats and hot peas.

1 July

> For solitude sometimes is best society,
> and short retirement urges sweet return.
> *Paradise Lost*

Had the inn and town suited me, I might have been tempted to make a day's halt and to have attended divine service. Here are an old drunken ostler and a mincing fine landlady, who will never come near you, nor your horses. After my coffee and hot roll, and enquiries of road, I took my departure and was not long in reaching the village of Tong, before whose church porch began to assemble the villagers for divine service. This church is of beautiful construction, and of beautiful situation, as commanding a view of Tong Park to the castle, and becoming a charming object from them. Below the church are the ruins of extensive buildings, and a remaining wall, with several arches of windows etc.

With the clerk and a civil farmer I entered the church, which is rich in monuments of antiquity, of the Stanleys and of the Vernons, as also stalls and much stained glass in the chancel. These the Saints missed, though they spoke here of Cromwell, of his cannon balls and of his attacks upon the castle.

There is a small chapel of beautiful carving, that is now elegantly fitted up as a pew. There are six tuneable bells – with six fine handsome fellows belonging to them. I ascended a circular staircase in a pillar, with the farmer, to the great bell, which weighs fifty hundredweight and requires three men to pull it. The bells were now chiming for church, and [I] ought to, and might have, stayed had I not learned that this was the best time of seeing the castle, as the family would be to church.

In my way to the castle to which I had sent forward, and which is hired by Mr Plowden, I met Mrs Plowden, her daughter and family. This place, purchased by Mr D—, has been rebuilt in a most overgrown taste and would require a very large fortune to keep up. How people can build these pompous edifices without a sufficiency of surrounding estate is wonderful! And yet how commonly it is done. Vanity easily triumphs over reason. It impoverishes the first and now ruins the succeeding generations. And how a tenant can be found is surprising, to ramble about such an edifice instead of the quiet cheapness of a smaller house!

It is a grand and beautiful place. Attended by the housekeeper I surveyed the house; the staircase is very fine, the rooms well-sized and well furnished, the bedchambers excellent, there is on the first floor a vast music room; but no library! Your hasty wealth thinks not of that. Every part of this magnificent house is covered by pictures – from Christie's and other auctions, of dying saints, naked Venuses and drunken bacchanals.

Now why all this offensive show, disgusting to every English eye that has not been hardened in Italy? Surely the intention of paintings was to cheer the mind and restore your pleasures, to survey your ancestry with conscious esteem, to view the beauties of Nature, to restore the memory of famous horses and of faithful dogs; but why produce savage and indecent exhibitions before your children's eyes? Why is Ovid's *Metamorphosis* to be produced in full display?

Why are the glorious feats of Jupiter to be held before our eyes, and why are we to be encouraged by Satyrs to peep at naked, sleeping beauty? Now with all this show, the first of comforts was wanting, some good fires. I came from a large one at Shifnal and shall, I hope, set over another at night. With an encircling estate of 10,000 per annum, this would be a grand place; as it is, some West Indians may hire it for a few years, but, if once deserted, these great houses soon tumble to pieces. The pleasure ground behind the house is pretty, and the trees and shrubs grow well. The water that twines through the park is beautiful, but might be much improved. Neither its banks or the park are half planted, but this is the case everywhere – views and wind form the present taste.

Returning by the church, I enquired my road, which continued for some time very good, when turning to the left, I entered into deep lanes in a country very enclosed and till very lately shaded by timber. I now felt very eager in the hopes of near approach to a long object of my wishes, and suitable to my *tory* sentiments and my love of curious historical anecdote: Boscobel House and Wood, where King Charles II found safety and concealment after his defeat at Worcester.

Instead of finding what I expected, a low retreat in the midst of a great wood, behold, a house upon a hill exposed to every view; nor could I have supposed it the place had I not seen a tree in a ploughed field, surrounded by a brick wall!

I had passed by 'White Ladies' in the bottom, without knowing or enquiring for it. Now that I did not visit it has much vexed me since, as I have been told (in London) that these ruins are highly worthy of observation.*

Approaching Boscobel House I was accosted by the owner, a yeoman of genteel appearance, with whom the following conversation passed:

(B) 'I am surprised at the appearance of this place, expecting to have found it in the midst of a wood.'

(Y) 'Aye, so it was till lately, till within these two or three years; it was sadly encumbered with trees; you could not see the stable for them, nor the prospect – there, Sir, the Clee Hills, there the long mountains in Wales. All the wood to the left, and about the oak, was felled and grubbed up by me last year. It

---

* At Shifnal I had enquired about the Pendrills, and learned that the family still lived in this county and that a descendant enjoyed the pension bestowed upon *Honest Dick Pendrell* and his heirs.

was quite like a forest, and so again behind the house. But I left the tree – will you walk to it?'

(B, sighing) 'It seems to be withering, and has but few leaves, which I should fear came from being thus left alone, and that it will soon perish!'

(Y) 'Why, Sir, the king might have been in it, or not? For my part, I don't believe much of the story.'

(B) 'Surely, Sir, never was story better authenticated or by honester historian?'

(Y) 'Well, Sir, if it pleases you.'

(B) 'It certainly does, Sir, for I am a royalist; the royalty is going out of fashion, and kings now seem to be liable to more insults and dangers than any of their subjects! Ah, there's the mount upon which the summer house stood, and to which the king retired.'

(Y) 'When the king was in such a taking, was it likely for him to go and sit in a summer house!'

(B) 'Why not, Sir, it was a quiet retired spot; and I cannot think that improbable either. But I am much obliged to you, Sir, for your trouble and civility.'

(Y) 'Will you enter the house?'

(B) 'This is a curious old parlour. There is a picture of Charles II.'

(Y) 'On this side were the folding doors, behind which, they say, the king slept. But I have stopped them up.'

(B) 'I am not yet satisfied. Might I not see the place upstairs where they say he was concealed?'

(Y) 'Aye, certainly. Here, Sir, is the place by the side of this bed. I will lift up the trap door to show you, and below it are stairs that lead to a door going into the garden, etc, etc.'

We then walked about the garden and I stood for some time upon the mount, then took leave of the yeoman, who must wonder at those silly fellows who come from far to see a tree and an old parlour. He advised me at parting not to quit the neighbourhood without seeing the beautiful seat of Mr Giffard at Chillington.

Though I had passed by White Ladies, yet I was resolved to

make Black Ladies in my way, which lies at a short distance from the road to Brewood. This is a very old house, and wherein the Catholic service being then performing (for many Catholics dwell in this neighbourhood) I abstained from entering, though I have since learned that I should have seen therein the original portrait of Trusty Dick Pendrell.

Returning into the high road, I began to feel myself quite peevish for dinner and hurried along to Brewood, whose tall spire was in sight.

In this mean market town the Red Lion alehouse received me; and being put into a whitewashed room, got a miserable neither-hot-nor-cold dinner, and then took my usual walk about the churchyard. These the best epitaphs:

> JOHN ELLIDGE
> Near to this place I do lie
> It was the Stone caused me to die.

> JAMES TAYLOR, aged 3 years.
> Near to this Stone, beneath this earth
> Here lies the mildest babe that ever drew breath.

Having a sufficiency of day, I resolved to take Chillington in my evening ride, to which I approached by one of the finest avenues, 100 yards broad and edged by a belt of plantation. The house, now under repair, is an ugly staring thing, unquestioned and unmolested. I took into a drive betwixt a forced-up canal and the old stream, where all is misunderstood and larches and beeches are planted in a bog. Crossing a little, ugly bridge I came to the great lake which is really a grand sight, but it looks like art; besides, by this uplandish water, the park becomes swampy and everything appears in neglect and confusion. If I was sulky here, how much must I be shocked when I saw, on my return, that from the house to the top of the avenue every tree was marked for felling, to the number of 2000, which will deprive this place and neighbourhood of a capital beauty. Surely Mr G— must be in great lack of money, or taste.

I can guess the appearance of this county of Staffordshire fifty years ago; and I can suppose its appearance fifty years hence. It must have [been] gloriously wooded (read Plot's account of wonderful timber), and will be an openish county – like most others. For the kingdom being now intersected by canals, timber is easily conveyed away. If a gentleman alters or repairs a house, here are the means; and then he thinks, most ridiculously, he makes reparation by sticking up some larches and Scotch firs. Besides, the now general practice of stocking up thick hedgerows, and mixing the earth with lime for manure, actually destroys the nursery of timber; and what few oaks may be left in the trim hedge are shroved, so they will never be worth twenty shillings!

This place is so grand in parts, with water so capable, so much wood and (yet) such an avenue, that did taste and cleanliness prevail it would be of the foremost inspection. (Agreeable to my ideas on Modern Taste, I was not surprised at the comments and remarks of a young couple who have lately succeeded to a high title, a great estate and a noble old park. Glorying in its timber, the lady, a shallow ignorant of pert ill-bred manners, told me that the park they were hastening to improve 'was a foresty wild, so dark and so gloomy that it seemed like a harbour for wild beasts; and wanted much clearing away of timber to make it look cheerful.'

> A park is purchased; but again he sees
> The fair in tears – oh odious, odious trees.
>
> Pope

How I tremble when I hear women talk upon subjects foreign to their capacities.)

Now, almost all parks are so sprucified, and levelled, and opened, that romantic, wild scenery is destroyed; nor does there remain the least encouragement for imagination, for ideas of retirement, or a thought of feys, hermits, etc. The haste of opening lawns, of discovering new prospects, and the temptation of a sale of timber, hurry on every practised vile destruction.

But to proceed. As the lady was so shocked at the rudeness of the park, so was the lord as eager to lay waste, to modernize, to improve. And when I dined at his table (for the only time) and heard his answer to the enquiries of an old gentleman who enquired after a mighty oak in the park, known by the title of the King of the Woods, and was answered, easily, by his Lordship: 'Oh, Sir, he is down,' I sighed and knew what was going forward, and if the king was overthrown his subjects of the park would be quickly dispersed.

I returned up the avenue, at the top of which is a wooden cross! The first I ever saw, or heard of, in this country. From this avenue another, of clumped firs, leads into the vale, which is likewise destroying in another way, by shroving! Whoever heard of shroving firs? For Scotch firs shrove themselves, and spruce firs should be feathered to the ground. In this avenue I listened to the anthem singing of some pious men and women, who performed with solemnity and judgement; such melody was to me highly gratifying.

Passing by the forge houses I was directed into a road, by no means good but passable, till I came to the Anchor public house and the navigation. Here I received another direction, for my road was now through deep, boggy, stony lanes, often danger-ous, where no carriage passes. Garwood in bad roads piously remarks, 'These are our Sunday roads, Sir.' Probably, he may think it better to lay still, at least for the spinning out of the time. In this uncertainty we plunged on till at last, bemired and fatigued, we came to Moseley village; where the manor house, an old Catholic one, was one of the hiding places of King Charles II. This was my object. Around it has been lately a destruction of wood; even the old pleasure ground and the walk, called the King's Walk (in which the king delighted to walk), at the end of which is a yew tree, is cut down. The farmers are very civil and I saw a sneaking priest glide by me; of what should they fear now? This is an old striped timber house, as old as any remaining. And I again here saw the recusants'[1] hiding place,

[1] Roman Catholics, who were still subject to civil disabilities.

and some very ancient rooms. When I came downstairs I said, 'But where is your chapel?' So the young farmer took me up to it in the garrets; and here I saw their adorned altar etc. etc.

Religion and royalty are on the wane; and must be soon found in scenery, or read of in history, not to be boasted of in this land. Anarchy and irreligion are striving to reign.

Some long stony lanes from Moseley and then into a turnpike road, which soon brought me to Wolverhampton, a large black, ill-paved town, swelling by commerce. At the Swan Inn, I was received civilly and put into a tolerable parlour.

Having some daylight to spare, and some little inclination left, I strolled about the market place, into the best streets and about the old churchyard, etc. At supper, a large duck (a bigger never waddled out of any alley) with peas, and cold meat; then a regale of newspapers; and then I begin, somehow, to slumber, and sometimes I fancy that I have had a little nap. Garwood had chosen for me a double bedded room, and mine a tent bed, a vile thing, because the curtains never draw and you look all round; but it can't be helped now.

2 *July*   At four o'clock I always wake, look at the weather and extinguish Mr Rushlight, else he stinks me to death.

In the market place (a very good one) I bought all the strawberries that were brought, which were small but clean.

My road of departure was to Willenhall, a village once but now a long, large ill-paved town, occupied by lock- and gun-smiths. I have enquired and soon found my way to Bentley Hall, which is now fast going to demolition.

The front wall, the summer house and the stables remain; but instead of gentlefolks (in cravats and farthingales) only an old farming woman and a maid-servant were to be seen. The latter attended me, at my desire, to show me the old parlours and the king's place of concealment.

This farm belongs to Mr Anson. At my descent I was questioned by the old woman as to my curiosity and 'if I was a foreigner?' 'Why should you think me a foreigner?' 'Because there was once a foreigner here – as I thought him, as eager of enquiry as you are. I will tell you the story. I have been here forty years, and in a year or two after my being here a gentleman called to see this house, and the hiding hole, whom I took to be a foreigner – his servant, I am sure was one. Well, he behaved very civilly to me, and after he was gone a thought struck me. That it was Prince Charles himself!' 'Well, good woman, and so it might be; for I understood that he was in England in the year 1754, and might like to take this ride of curiosity.'

I returned across the Walsall road, and then by a lane came to Wednesbury, another overgrown village, blackened with its trees and hedges by the forge fires; nay, even the sun itself is obscured by them!

Every field is scooped by collieries and canals; and the ironstone (happy distribution) lays under the coal. Iron foundries around are numberless, and the roads are made of the iron dross.

Dudley Castle ruins, to which I now approached, appeared in grand situation, and I thought it as well to send my horses into the town, that I might view it quietly on foot.

Nothing can be in greater disorder and neglect than this ruin, and so is all the hill around, whose greatest beauty is the remaining ash trees. If this hill were properly leased, and properly hired, to what advantage of beauty and profit might the ground be laid out?

Some easily-formed walks and plantations would tempt visitors, and the area of the building a bowling green might be made. But the possessors of such noble ruins (and here, too, the possessor Lord Dudley lives at hand) disdain to preserve, or think of such possessions. Devoid of proper pride, or of taste, they abandon them to dilapidation and plunder.

Ranging within the buildings, I could clearly trace the hall, the kitchen, the chapel and all the good apartments, the brick chimneys of which, of a latter date, give a bad look to the old buildings.

Having made this melancholy, lone survey, and sketched a

view of the gateway (which I was pleased to observe did not ill correspond with the prints), I walked around the outside wall, where in the vale beneath I descried[1] the ruins of Dudley Priory; and to them I scrambled down, crossing two fields beyond the road. Much yet remains, as several arches and the body of the church, but adjoining the tower and against those walls is built a very disfiguring house.

After a long and fatiguing walk of an hour, I was glad to enter the Dudley Arms Inn in the town of Dudley, at the look and building of which I was much surprised. At Shifnal and at Wolverhampton, upon the high road, I found two very indifferent inns, and here, upon no road, I found a grand and comfortable hotel with good wine, good cookery and good stables!

My dinner at Dudley was well-served and I was well waited upon, and I believe might have stayed the night had not the newspapers informed me of Mrs Siddons playing at Birmingham. This temptation was too strong to be resisted.

I chose the shorter road, as they said it was very tolerable; and so I found it, and very green and wooded. The avenues to Birmingham are marked by citizens' houses all for a stare and to be stared at. Before we entered this hourly-increasing town, I told Garwood of Mrs Siddons playing tonight, and that I should treat him; at which he seemed highly pleased, having never seen her. In the High Street there was an amazing crowd before the playhouse door, striving for entrance, and near them, in pleasing contemplation, stood Mr Siddons (for it was Mrs Siddons' benefit), whom I addressed, and he begged me to come to the stage door where I would gain admittance.

At the Swan Inn, no room could I obtain for myself and horses; so I walked with a boy to many other inns, the Hen and Chickens, the Castle, etc., etc., and was refused at them all, though not without examination, as should I want a post-chaise?

[1] Spotted.

Was I for a stage coach? and many such impertinent mercantile questions.

So I began to think I must depart, or lay in the streets. However, at last I found reception at the Dog Inn, a stage-coach house, and had a bed allotted to me from the gallery, wherein I powdered my hair e'er I went to the playhouse.

Behind the scenes I conversed with old Mr Yates the manager, and passed most of the time with Mrs Siddons in her dressing room when she quitted the stage. Mrs Siddons is a woman of such retired notions as to drive off my conversation. Speaking of her friend Mrs B—, who lives in the north, she said that 'she had written her intention of a visit', but that Mrs B— declined it, being apprehensive of a miscarriage!

(B) 'Why, Madam, you might better have declined your visit from fear of an overturn.'

(S) 'Indeed it might be dangerous for her to have a child from the deformity of her make.'

(B) 'That she should have considered before matrimony.'

(S) 'Do you know her sister, Miss A—?'

(B) 'Yes, by sight, and dread her. She will never be married.'

(S) 'Why, I think she will not like to say the word obey. But I love characters.'

(B) 'Characters, Madam, can never be formed from conceit and pride.'

I never saw a coarser company than this of Mr Yates's, but he gets them very cheap I suppose. The play finished, I left the theatre; and returning to my alehouse, procured some cold meat in a back room and then crawled up to my gallery chamber.

3 July   How luckily does one wear oneself out in touring; else the beds were not [to] be endured. No strawberries here, eatable! No booksellers! I breakfasted in a public room with the bag men, and then took a town walk, and to Clay's manufactory, but the workmen were absent; and thence to Mr Siddons's lodgings in Charles Street where he, though very unwell, showed me the working shops, stampings etc, etc of the merchant where he resides, and Mr Siddons ingenuously said that when here in 1777, Yates only gave Mrs Siddons £1. 1s. per week, when Mrs Yates could fill houses and was deemed a grand actress. (This marks life, where the fashion or whim of the day is to guide, in spite of reason or truth.)

How eager was I to get from the insolence of Birmingham, a town wherein I should be crippled in a week from a want of flagstones. Tell this to a bucklemaker and he would stare, and say, 'That he never remarked it'. Even Manchester has a flat stone footpath.

The road from Birmingham is as sharp as their streets, being mended by great pebbles; the country is flat and enclosed, nor is there any rise till beyond Shirley village, where I shaved at a barber's shop, a penny barber who never makes wigs nor has a shaving-brush in the house, 'Because my customers complain that it tickles them; but you, Sir, handle a razor well.'

All this country was the Forest of Arden; and today the gentlemen archers, the woodmen of Arden, shoot their match with the Manchester archers at Wellesley Bridge in Staffordshire.

To the right is Lord Archer's seat at [Umberslade Park], to the left the church of Tanworth. From Leveret Hill is a gay view, and over the town of Henley. Since I was last along this road, it has been much widened and straightened; but give me the old curves to beguile the way, I love not straight Roman roads.

I put up at Henley at the Swan. Think of the inns being casemented at the first stage from Birmingham! Here was a tolerable stable, a thing not to be found in Birmingham, where my old corps the Blues are quartered to maintain the peace. I saw them parade in the High Street, and think I never saw a regiment in worse order or looking less like soldiers, dirty, slovenly, ill-dressed, with neither fashion nor pride about them; and their horses were as dirty and ill-dressed as their riders! Such a corps should be instantly re-formed or reduced.

At Henley I dined upon some good (uncut) cold lamb, with

good cheese, after a walk over the brook to another church, Beaudesert, where is a fine Saxon arch.

Henley is only a chapel of ease to Wootton [Wawen], through which I passed in the evening, and would have stopped at the church (near to which is an ugly house of Sir E. Smith's) but that it began to rain.

Here were a crowd assembled, the remains of yesterday's wake, and two fellows upon stools, grinning for a wager (a sport I thought disused) so happily described in *The Spectator* – 'The frightfullest grinner to be the winner!'

The road now mended, as the inns will do; for I told Garwood that we were now coming to charming inns. 'I am sure I am glad of it, Sir.' At six o'clock we entered the town of Stratford-upon-Avon, rendered famous by Shakespeare and the jubilee; but at the noted White Lion, I met with nothing but incivility, and I was put into a servant's room though the house was empty. The stables are very bad. When I toured with Colonel Bertie, and never more will I take a great tour alone, his figure and discontents were often of great service, and here they were much wanted. As for poor, foolish Ranger, I could have spared his company, having afforded us no diversion and drawn the dogs of every village upon us.

The evening was cold and gloomy. I walked about the town in a Shakespearean reverie. At the house of his birth they would have tempted me in, but I said, 'Where is his old chair, that you have sold? I, now, enter not.' My words seemed to shock them; and they have discovered that they have sold the goose that laid the golden eggs!! Had they been makers of Italian policy, they had all always kept an old chair ready to succeed the one sold; or rather, kept the old one and parted with the substitute.

I looked into the mulberry shop where the goods are most wretchedly executed; and then to the old bookseller's, who have the best library I have seen in my travels, and had I time and spirit I would hunt his garret (though well sifted) for he formerly bought the library from the house wherein Shakespeare resided.

On the opposite side of the bridge was a mountebank with his

Merry Andrew, but I went not to hear him as I would have done on a fine, warm evening. At my return to my dog-hole room (in this fine inn), I was obliged to order supper, for here they keep a man-cook and profess elegance. I saw him, and longed to kick him for the veal cutlets, that Ranger would scarcely eat. There was not a fire in my room in this inn; for all blackguard inns (and indeed, most houses called genteel that I know) put out fires at a regular time, and freeze because it is July. A good inn is known by the fires and well-littered stables. I thought it behoved me to lay out some money at the booksellers, so I most *generously* gave sixpence for *Heroick's Portraits*, 1660; and well supposed it was, as it served for my evening reading, and in it there is 'The Picture of an English Inn'. At eleven o'clock I went to bed, a bed like everything else in the house; but no chambermaid knows how to make a bed (that sounds like bold assertion) nor will ever roll the undersheet round the bolster!

4 July   I seldom want calling. I was up when Garwood came, who is proverbial to a moment. I breakfasted ill. I saw where I was and hastened to get away, though in dread of rain from the gloom of the morning. The stables are all in common and everything is left-handed; in my bill the beef was overcharged, so from peevishness and prudence, I cut out sixpence. I am always penny-wise.

I went, to oblige Garwood I think, more than myself, to visit Shakespeare's tomb (having often viewed it). The church, which was collegiate, is a handsome pile, and an old mansion near is called the College.

Churches and chancels should be repaired and whitewashed, but the minister should direct the churchwardens and not permit any havoc of stained glass, or any ransacking or disfiguring of the right as is done in the lately brushed-up chancel. Had they restored Shakespeare's monument to the natural colour of the stone, there they had been right; but what could inspire them to daub over, with yellow paint, the fine old oak stalls? I declare, if

213

I lived near or could afford it a distance, I would desire to be permitted to restore them to the shining brown natural ebony. Upon the under part of the seats are carved, as usual, odd devices, whippings etc., of the strangest tendency. Of the Cloptons and John-a-Combe there are fine momuments, but the best are those of the Earl and Countess of Totnes.

These stony roads make me nervous; and their shroving the trees (here particularly maypoled) render me irascible and full of wonder at landlords! Mrs West's park, on the right, is a cool-looking green flat with some deer.

At Alderminster, the church stands in such a sequestered, pleasant spot as to tempt me to walk to it and there try the exertions of my pencil; but the cottages are mud without, and wretchedness within, because their portion of lands and of commonage is taken from them.

(Upon my estate, there shall be no mud cottages; and my comfortable cottagers shall be obliged to have land and to be happy. Let me feed a child with potatoes and buttermilk, and I will show him, at any age, against the one fed with hot, black tea.)

At Burmington the church, which stands exposed, is close to the Hall; the Parsonage House might be rendered pretty. Passed near Hollingdon, Mr Townsend's, a good-looking house (though a red one) with water and some shade. I could live in this very comfortably.

To Shipston, a small market town, with a tolerable-looking inn where I must have fared better than at Stratford. No legible milestones upon this road; which are an amusing study upon travel.

The roads now began to mend, because the pebbles are gone and the limestone begins, which pulverises into a tolerable track. The old seat of the Sheldons, Weston House, now abandoned by that family, is let to Lord — for a hunting seat.

Some steepish hills, one into Long Compton, a mean dirty village. At the top of the opposite hill I detached Garwood (to make him an antiquary) to survey Rollright Stones which are at a short distance; the larger one, which guides the way, may be seen from the high road.

The day was close, and many sultry showers fell around (my mare sweated for the first time). To avoid these, and to indulge my appetite, I hastened to that capital inn, Chapel House; and was there received and slighted in the same manner as at Stratford-upon-Avon, with nothing that I could touch, though faint and hungry, as at Stratford-upon-Avon. Port not drinkable, a cold, fat, raw ham, some stinking cold lamb, with a black doughy tart and cheese that never changes its dish, composed my repast! It rained whilst I was here, but had it rained ever so hard I had gone on; and the road is now rideable.

Not to delay myself or my journal, behold me at seven o'clock on Wednesday evening, July 4th, at the Bear Inn at Woodstock in Oxfordshire. And here, I think properly, my touring ends. (Like a voyage of discovery when the ship quits Batavia, you hear only slightly of the Cape of Good Hope, the Madeira Islands and of their safe arrival at Spithead.)

I was received with civility. The stables are excellent; and after my past, my repasts and various treatments, all things seemed good. I supped at nine o'clock, and talked to Cross, whenever I could make him stand still for a minute. I unpacked, I bought gloves; I sent my unfortunate old black coat to the tailor's for reparation and my shirts to be washed and collared. We seem all tattered, except my mare, who looks so fat and so sleek! You may say that I have not ridden fast nor far in a day, but then I have been at it constantly, over much bad road, and have hung the whole day upon her back.

A cold supper, and some elegancies as jellies and blancmange. In the great houses I have seen (and those of estimation) I have observed a want of comfort, of habitation, of warmth, of proper furniture (according to my plans and likings). At Raby Castle, a great seat in the North, there is a contrivance of the smallest utility and of the most devilish effect, viz. the coach passage through the hall and the house. A fine hall, finely warmed (every day almost in the year) with mountains of coals, upon forest-grates, is the first comfort of an house; but to make it a thoroughfare street is wretchedness indeed! In the drawing room, instead of large chairs rolling upon castors there is nothing to be seen but little, light French chairs; and thick, welt-lined damask or velvet curtains have given way to French linen festoonings. I love large, firmly fixed writing tables in my library, and to have my breakfast and dining tables substantial and immovable. And when I say immovable, it is because my rooms, and every part of them, should be of an equal warmth, and there should be no need, as I see at present, of little scuttling tables being brought before a hearth. In my house, I repeat it egoistically again (and upon paper this may be allowed), I should desire that no one would come within six feet of the fireplace; nor would anyone wish it, because the grates would be ample and the fireplace high and extended, not a little, low, dug hole, as at present, surrounded by a slip of marble for people (genteel) to clap their elbows upon whilst they, by turns, toasted their shins.

At Trentham House there are no comforts (here I did expect them), nor is the library fitted up as it should be! A library is the first of rooms. What stores of paper, pens, wax, ink standishes, albums, grand writing tables, should furnish a library? People spend fortunes, and waste great estates, without ever having passed one hour in a comfortable room, or in a good bed. A good bed is a great rarity.

When I enter a great dining room in the country, I am generally told, 'That this is not used in common, but that the family dine in a smaller room, unless there is company.' What nonsense is this, arising from mean ignorance? Because they know not how to warm their rooms; and what room is too great for even two people? I love to rest, and walk, and return again to my book or my pen. At Tong Castle, every room opens into another! It is all a passage! And covered by filthy, naked or dying pictures! Comforts should be first studied, then pictures, if you will, and those of beautiful women, men of the sword, or views of the finest scenes of nature, as groves, waterfalls etc. In my great hall (for I love a great hall) would be pictures of magnificent horses by Wooton; in my dining room, full length van Dycks as Dukes of Richmond, Hamilton etc; in my library, some rare Holbeins; and in my drawing room the most finished pictures of Hobbema, Ruisdael and Berghem.

In London and in the country (strange to see, and to relate!) gentlemen of great fortune burn small coals, when in London, even for a small advance, large coals or billeting are to be bought. The Duke of Marlborough here in Blenheim in July is killing and eating stalled-fed deer, flesh as bad as that of swine fatted in Southwark. No, no, I like to eat the flesh of bucks, seven year old, who have fatted themselves.

To bed, to bed, to bed, says Lady Macbeth.

5 July   Here is always a racket of company in this house, and everything unlike the quiet management of Mrs Knight at Biggleswade, which upon the whole I can prove to be (one of) the best inns in England.

When travelling, I sometimes think myself a judgment upon that family from the time of one of the Tracies, with the wind always in their faces, their ancestors slaying Thomas Becket. Amongst the other hard obligations upon a tourist are the being obliged to travel after a bad meal, hungry and discontented, and the being obliged to travel after a good meal, when full and happy. I have toiled like a post-boy; I have set my mind to it, and I have performed my task of pleasure. But never again (I now trust) will I go alone, but upon a short trip; if further, it must be in society, urged on by their support. It becomes, single-handed, too arduous a task. There is a gloom, a despair, a want of assistance in misery, a want of participation in joy. If a man alone views a waterfall, he turns round to find who is with him; he soon is obliged to converse with his servant, to ask his horse if such a thing be not fine. He presses forward to get rid of the good, or of the bad, he dreads illness in himself or in his horses, for the smallest pin lost unhinges his scheme.

217

Why then, I have been lucky? Neither malady nor accident to myself, and my horses have proved safe and sound.

I dined well today, beans (for the first time) and bacon, with a roasted fillet of veal etc. Now I sally out (for I have been stilling all the morning) and walked to Blenheim kitchen garden to enquire for Mr Shipley, the head gardener, with a letter from Mr Cross in my pocket. Blenheim kitchen garden is a grand space not sufficiently divided by walls, and they wants the eye of an intelligent master.

What shocked me much was to hear the firing of guns, and to see a set of Jacobins armed against the national guards, the birds. Oh fie! What, for a few cherries, destroy all the songsters? And here will they come to perish. 'Stretch forth, Marlborough, thy hand of mercy, and of pity; and let not infamous slaughter prevail.'

The old elms, the newly-planted beeches and the (*supposedly decaying*) limbs of oaks are all shroven, and I found that the flues of the hothouses were supplied by wood! In this garden there is not a sufficiency of hothouses and pineries, by one fourth. Mr Shipley being absent, I dared not to pluck a strawberry, but strolled along the drive carried imperceptibly forward from beauty to beauty, from view to view, fancying myself another Jaques (for I have all his spleen and hatred of the world) and lolling against or under trees, and sneered at the visitors whom I saw driving furiously along, in fancied observation like a hustle to a horse race (as Mr Cross furnishes phaetons, single-horse chaises), idly and ignorantly hurrying to and from pleasure. This part of the day was very hot; rainy morning it had been; and the evening, as in general, became very cold. At my return, rather jaded (for the walk was too long, having wandered to the High Lodge) and not satisfied, I mounted Bumper (the only bumper I must mount, as Cross's wine is not for me) and then rode up the avenue, wondered at the obelisk, observed the hares at feed and came in at nine o'clock to a cold supper and a cherry pie.

At eleven o'clock (my fixed hour) I retired to my bedroom.

6 July   As the maids would wash round my parlour this July morning, I was obliged to breakfast in another room. Then Garwood equipped *en femme*[1] tried the disposition of my mare, whom I knew would be entirely gentle and free from flutter.

When in London, to make my way sure (as is my custom) of an intention of fishing in Blenheim Lake, I had waited upon a brother of Dr King, the rector of this place, who answered me that, 'I had only to send to his brother at Woodstock, who would then give me permission.'

So being certain of my ground (or rather of my water), I rounded my tour to this place (here to sit me down in quietness upon a bank after all my hurryings and uneasiness) and had even invited Mr King, of the Stamp Office, to escort Mrs Byng here, for the pleasure of fishing; but yesterday, luckily, Mrs Byng informed me in her letter that Mr King could not attend her, owing to the indisposition of his wife.

Well then, I was obliged this morning to wait upon Dr King (a note would not have been so civil). And after a long sitting with him and his family at a late, idle breakfast, opened my desire, to which he answered, 'Oh, that was impossible; he had no power; that permission came from the Duke; that he could not even take me with him!' I believe I stared a little at finding myself such a fool, for had I known all this, I could have written to the Duke e'er I left London. After this failure, I again tried what garden success I might have (though I felt faint-hearted), but here I was received by Mr Shipley (who holds a situation beyond the power of a minister to give) in an open-hearted manner, who made me eat fruit and walk about with him. When I was at Dr King's, I spake out, in my old way, 'What a fine kitchen garden he must have at Blenheim; and that I concluded a cart load of vegetables and fruit was brought to his door every morning.' But he showed me his own small kitchen garden under his window, saying 'that supplied him'. I could only

[1] Possibly, riding side saddle.

answer, 'Were I Duke of Marlborough, I should say, "Make that a pleasure ground, for Mr Shipley is your gardener!"'

To Mr Shipley I spake not about singing birds, but took courage about fruit and of Mrs Byng's liking of it, and that I hoped. So he answered, very civilly, 'Send a boy down from the inn'; he then walked with me to the newly-made pleasure ground near the cascade, where he left me, and left me with a master key too! So I found myself here, as I should be.

Much did I enjoy this delightful spot, which is all in right except the fountain and its figures, which savour too much of the Apollo Garden, St George's Fields!

> . . . It was a place
> Chos'n by the Sovran Planter, when he framed
> All things to man's delightful use; the roof
> Of thickest covert was inwoven. Shade
> Laurel and myrtle, and what higher grew
> Of firm and fragrant leaf.
>
> Milton, *Paradise Lost*

I kept my slow pace of pleasure (with a *hydrophobic eye* at the water) till I let myself out near the house, and was home by two o'clock, in my way encountering Dr King (an uncertain-absent, vulgar, —) who had enjoyed his fishing and expected me to dinner. But no, no, I had, at mine inn, my roasted rabbit and my cherry tart, and sat in my hat. 'But where's the wine?' Of the several sorts of port I tasted, they were all either rough or sour! Master Cross is profoundly ignorant!!! So my stomach gets hard. I took a long evening ride upon my mare towards the heronry, a noble assemblage, and only to be had in old parks upon very old trees.

But all such pleasures are only allowed to an absolute master; for I find that these, here, are nearly destroyed, as *potent of mischief*! The rooks are destroyed, as potent of mischief! The squirrels are destroyed, as *suckers of pheasants' eggs*!! And the singing birds are destroyed, as *destroyers of fruit*! So man, instead of encouraging delights and the companions of his walk, becomes from ignorance and idleness the ruin of his own pleasures! However, I get mine own way, upon my own mare, at mine own pace; and the deer seemed to understand me. I looked at the horses, I admired the cows, I disturbed some hares, and was as abandoned to rural sequestration as I could wish.

At much expense, the Duke of Marlborough has lowered the hill on the opposite side of the lake, upon which the old manor house stood, but in my opinion without any advantage to the place – as broken views I think preferable to a flat stare. Soon after eight o'clock I returned home; and then, by way of variety (and must we have variety, and even here too!) walked along the Oxford Road to Campsfield, and back.

> Tired of the joy, parterres and fountains yield
> He sometimes thinks he better likes a field.

Minced veal and tart for supper. That closed this day's business.

7 July   This finished my sixth week! Oh, that I had stayed in London till this day and that now my holidays were to begin, for this was a summer's day, with a high and blue sky. My early morning was rendered miserable by a letter from Mrs Byng, making doubts of her coming from Mr Frek's earache; but I will hope. My horses so ill-shod, and without steeling, at Clitheroe, were now obliged to undergo another shoeing; and to this did I and Garwood assiduously attend, to prevent the buttress. Cross offered to show me a new ride; and (the shoeing business safely over, I hope) he and I rode together whilst Garwood was to look to the bed arrangement, being appointed chamberlain as well as master of the horse. Our ride (warm, as I like, never too much sun for me) was to the new pheasant grounds, planted, defended and gated for the Duke's private sport. These grounds, of which I opened the gates (to C.'s great surprise, who came without a key!!) are of a wild, foresty nature, with wide drives; and at the top of a hill, above Campsfield, there is an appearance of castellated ground. This adds much to the grandeur of the Blenheim circuit, and is in a noble and judicious style.

This drive continues through Bladon Wood, the Duke's own farm, and so, crossing the road, enters the park below Bladon village; passing by the lower water and the cascade, we came into the meadows, which now exhibit the richest display of country felicity. For the hay is now cutting, and under one large tree the group of hay-makers was clustered at their homely and jolly meal. Let them enjoy what they can, for their days of happiness are but few and short! In this back river, I saw a clergyman trolling. Trolling is a sport I try sometimes; but a perch-hile for my money. Trolling is like fox-hunting, a thing to brag about and commonly unsuccessful. Ground fishing resembles hare-hunting – six good days' sport in a week. But then, indeed, there is a lack of boasting, and great trouble!!

Cross left me to attend the racket of his inn, which begins about two o'clock, to take a sweet, solitary ride in the park, 'beneath the shade of melancholy boughs' by the riverside, Rosamund's Well, and over the bridge home.

Settling beds: mine with clean sheets and little Frek's little tent bed. An old acquaintance, General J., was at this inn with some military friends and some ladies, and he pressed me to dine with them, but I excused myself to mine own eel, cold beef and tart. Garwood was then detained with directions to Oxford, to escort back Mrs Byng; and soon after I sent a boy to Mr Shipley, the Duke's head gardener; then loitered about till I could begin my walk of meeting, when my impatience had to encounter many disappointments – as, 'Here's a chaise, a man in it!' 'There's another coming?' 'That's a cart!' 'Well, here they come, a gentleman's coach!' So I fatigued both mind and body, and waddled about till dark. At my return, almost tired, I found a magnificent basket of fruit (and another, at my desire, of roses); these I kept for Frek to open and to enjoy, but at ten o'clock, all my hopes withered by the return of Garwood from Oxford, with a letter from Mrs Byng sent down by post coach, saying that poor Frek was not well enough to travel, but that she hoped on the morrow. So now I had an opportunity of being gallant to General J. and the ladies, by sending them up it, and roses, receiving, in return, many compliments of thanks and of invitations, and at last the General in person came down to sit with me.

Not supping till past ten o'clock made a late night.

8 July　　My first salutation this morning was a letter from Mr N. in London, speaking of poor Frek's incapacity to travel till Monday, so here must abide alone two more days. Shall I go to church? No; I shall commune in my chamber. The preaching here is bad, and I can easily believe it. So sat at home till twelve o'clock, when I rode for two hours gently in the right-hand verge of the park, with the home farm, to the Ditchley Gate and back. It is a cool and shady drive, and I saw several deer who had come in without privilege and without a key. My dinner was from Mr Cross's table, very good and truly rural, beans and bacon and some slices of roasted fawn, which was excellent! But I cannot find a glass of drinkable wine. Oh, that I were at Biggleswade, where the house is so well-managed. Here, all is noise and confusion: C. Bawling for the waiter (Hanks), H. Bawling for the chambermaid. At Biggleswade, Mrs Knight governs all in quietness; there are no children – and no tap; here they come for pints of beer! My dinner finished, a one-horse chaise appeared at the door, with Mr & Mrs D., who came out of Gloucestershire to make us a visit and were much disappointed not to find Mrs Byng. Now their dinner was to be prepared. For one who can dine at such foolish early hours as I do? Then we walked into the park and, under my direction, to the private cascade garden, which could not but be admired by them.

In our return there is a most beautiful view of the lake and of the opposite wood etc, etc, which my weak pencil has feebly attempted to describe.

The evening was very serene, and the park full of walking company. I had a subsequent ride alone, and was obliged to enter into conversation with the rector, whose discourse is like a water-mill.

We supped at half-past nine o'clock; our lady retired soon, but we males sat up till near twelve o'clock.

9 July   I love early rising, for my mind was always upon some new pursuit. Not that I was up today till past seven o'clock; but then this is a dawdling, ill-managed house. However, I had finished breakfast at 9 o'clock when Mr D. descended, saying, 'To Dr B., who lives a mile off, have I communicated your wishes of fishing. He is just arrived; and the fisherman, with his boats, awaits your command.' Now what think ye of the little, dirty, subservient Tickle-Text? Who never made, nor dared to make one trial to serve me, afraid, perhaps, of the Duke of Marlborough's servants, afraid of not being sufficiently supple to His Grace, or His Grace's dependants!! This may be, this too often is the road to preferment (but I have taken, and will pursue another path); so this family is prospering.

After an early breakfast, and Mr and Mrs. D.'s very late one, we embarked aboard a flat-bottomed boat in the lake, with Dr B., and going under the Great Arch, we had most excellent sport at perch-fishing, with minnows. (An Irish gentleman said that the properest place to fish in, in rain, was under an arch, as the fish would come there to be out of the wet.) Mr B. wasted his time in trolling. We caught many and very handsome perch; the biggest, taken by Mr D., weighed two pounds and a half, and several of a size little inferior! It was the grandest capture of perch I ever saw made. We, with Dr B., returned to dinner at four o'clock; when I was surprised at the honour of a visit from Colonel Bertie, parting for some hours from those agreeable females to whom he (with much judgment) devotes his time.

(Had Colonel Bertie ever signified a wish of touring with me, when his London engagements permitted him, I had postponed my early travel, nor had thus wandered about alone; or had he ever signified to me that he would have met me at my return, as at Shifnal, Wolverhampton or Birmingham, I had awaited him with recruited spirits for another ride. But instead of that, instead of friendship, he now comes down to Oxford, Gentleman Usher to two old —! So that I cannot help meeting him with a cold and jaundiced eye – and then in the moment of such recollection, he makes me a formal dinner visit!)

In the evening, after bad society and bad wine, I was to take my ride to meet Mrs Byng, Colonel Bertie rode with me on his return to his company, and were soon overtaken by Mr D. hurrying to Oxford to see a horse; accordingly they pushed forward, and I was soon met by Mrs Byng and Frek. Mrs Byng was jaded to death by the heat and dust of the journey, and he, poor fellow, wrapped up in night caps after his sufferings from the earache.

I returned with them to Woodstock, Garwood leading back my mare. It was now a proper hour for supper, which I hurried on, though Mr D. and Dr B. were then at tea. (Ladies are always for tea, at all time and at all hours!)

Supper soon came in, and at the end of it a Mrs A., a lady of Mrs D.'s acquaintance from London, who was going to their house, so had that been known, she and Mrs Byng might have come down together.

10 July   During the last night there fell a heavy rain; so now, dullness, and our 24 hours summer is at an end. No pursuit abroad, and nothing to be done within, for we have no card players! To my great surprise, the D.'s were preparing to depart! Mrs D. must go off (instantly!) to see her children!! Mr D. would, however, stay till evening if more fishing could be procured; so I resolved upon a personal embassy to Mr W., the Duke of Marlborough's agent, who received me (as most great men receive little men) very pompously, and at last, when I fancied I was departing without hope, honoured me with a permission to catch perch. So, Mr D. and I had then to find the fisherman, who had no minnows and with difficulty procured worms; and then encountered as cold and comfortless a setting in a boat (wind north-east) as could be supposed at any season of the year. But, to my surprise, we did catch about a dozen perch, some of near a pound weight.

During this time my son Frek, for whom I had engaged a small pony, was taking his first ride with Garwood. I was glad to leave the chill boat, and to come in to dinner, though here is no drinkable wine, so neither comfort nor consolation. The rain returning, we prosed through the evening.

11 July   Rain; rain; with the gloom and chill of December! Mr D. says that this weather is caused by a comet. I thought that the tail of a comet was laden with fire. Mr D. busied himself in alterations of his one horse chair, I upon my drawings, else there was nothing to do, and surely there never was so cruel a time! An end put to fishing, of getting Mrs Byng to ride, and seeing the gardens in perfection. What a summer is this? But one or two tolerable days to receive us, and then going back into November! I voted for a game of dummy whist, but was not seconded. For hope and consolation, I despatched Garwood to Oxford, for some port wine from the King's Arms and to bring an artificial minnow to try in case of better weather, and of no live minnows to be procured.

At one o'clock, he returned with the cargo; the minnow was excessively dear, and probably will never be of use; as for the port wine, we drank one bottle of it and thought it better, though bad, than the wine here. Now Mr D., no longer to be restrained, would get off, notwithstanding the wet, in his one horse chair, after having accomplished a gloomy visit. The rain continued so violently that I could only make little crawls about the town and to the stable. My worst touring weather was charming, in comparison to these two last days.

12 July   Another dark day, with the wind at north and very cold. So my joint orders are for a good fire. I heard yesterday from Colonel Bertie at Oxford, that he would honour us with his company today at dinner, but not mentioning an hour! So I ordered dinner at an hour later than my intentions, three

o'clock. And as the day was melancholy, and Mrs Byng showed
no inclination for moving, I delayed my ride till twelve o'clock,
when my son and I rode together, first to the kitchen garden,
when I viewed with pleasure his abandonment to the fruit; we
then went to the cascade garden, there enjoying ourselves in the
delights of that little paradise for half an hour (our horses held
at the gate by a boy); and so we returned home, by the detestable
column, before three o'clock. No Colonel arrived! His valet
informed us that his master would come, so our dinner was put
back, and at four o'clock the Colonel did arrive!! Nothing could
be said, but, 'you never mentioned the time of your coming!' I
received fruit in abundance from Mr Shipley, the Duke's
gardener. The Colonel's ladies arrived, too, at this inn; odd and
diverting that?? Why such sharp embarrassments and total
subjection!! The best part of his visit was his taking off my
hands that noble horse Bumper, so often mentioned in this
adventurous travel. To keep the peace, I was even obliged to
pay *my respects to the ladies*! A short ride of return with the Colonel
over Campsfield was hurried over by the rain, then a want of a
card party; neither Frek nor his Pappa knew how to employ
themselves, I have nothing to relate and am unstrung by the
weather. We languish from meal to meal – last stage of all is
bed. To which I was as willing to go as Mr Frek, but not so
willing to talk as he was after we were in bed.

13 July   The steeple of Woodstock church has been lately
rebuilt; and as the Duke of Marlborough contributed largely, and
for an ornament to the park, he might have attended to the plan
and not suffered a conceited Grecian building to be set up, instead
of an elegant Gothic one. A family of the Bruces, all of great age,
lay buried in the churchyard, as also the man killed here at the
rejoicings of the accession of King George I. But why is a rector
not to preserve such a tombstone with such an inscription:

> ANNE CELLAR
> All women that lives is born to die
> And none can boast secure felicity.

227

or suffer the churchyard to be overrun with weeds? But the idleness of churchmen is intolerable, and they will not endeavour to prevent some useful reform though the mischiefs of France stare them in the face.[1]

In Blenheim Park, I was pleased to discover without being told the old Roman road that boldly crosses the north part of the park. The two ugliest things about the Blenheim drive is, the horrid, staring pillar of vanity and proclamation which from its height renders the trees dwarfish and the park ridiculous, and the other is the ill-placed foolish, fountain in the cascade private garden, a paltry, mean piece of Art amidst the beauties of Nature. There is likewise in that garden an old stone, over the mineral stream, of most indelicate workmanship which Virtue examines with the coldest eyes, as I have often seen Italian-travelled ladies examine prints, sculptures, etc.

It rained through the night, even Noah's dove could not be sent forth. I crawled downstairs to coffee and hot rolls, and to my great surprise Mrs Byng soon followed! Perhaps this was in consequence of my saying, 'This is lay-in-bed weather. Lay in bed now, if you like it.' Woman is a pleasing contradiction? Shall I get any more angling? For this and to show to Mrs Byng the garden, I will outstretch my time; and though the weather be bad, it comes better now to me in company than had it happened when I was alone at Barnard Castle, or at Askrigg, or at Skipton? Poor Mrs Byng came down in the only hot, dusty day, to be shut up here in the rain. Poor Frek parades the inn yard with his bow and arrow, shooting at pigeons, sparrows and stable doors. It cleared up before dinner time, when I sought the fisherman, whom I found engaged with the doctor; but I secured him for the evening, which was cold and unproductive of sport. Frek came to me in his ride, and then his mother, when we had a long walk in the kitchen and pleasure gardens and returned late to supper.

[1] France was in the grip of the French Revolution.

14 July   This was a fine morning, but I now feel weather strangely. Something like summer. Our progress of this day was round the park (Mrs Byng, Frek and Miss Cross, a very pretty and well-behaved girl, our landlord's daughter, in a post-chaise, myself on horseback) and to the cascade garden; and then, by the further road, to Ditchley, formerly the residence of English nobility. (Of this place and its pictures, so well known, I have spoken before.) Why not a tax here upon absentees, if they presume to hint it in another country? Having viewed this place, as soon as another company would get away, I trotted back to hurry dinner and to bespeak the fisherman and his boat (for the last time), which was not productive of much success, for perch fishing requires a hot midday sun and smooth water.

Frek came to me in his ride. We then, together, took our garden walk; and at my return, had only to collect my bills at this dear house.

The first hot night I have passed. Bills arranged (not paid), I depart upon tick. Our drive was to the King's Arms, Holywell, Oxford, to put up there, in case we meet with no *extraordinaries*. But these not being in our way, we ordered dinner and invited Mr R. F. of Brazen-Nose College. Miss Cross came with Mrs Byng in a post-chaise. I proposed the going to the evening prayers at Christ Church, which was miserably performed! Our Church is terribly upon the decline, which as a gentleman and a Churchman I grieve for; some management, or teaching, we should have for our money.

Every minister of a sectary comforts himself with a deanery, whilst the slumbering Dean or the sporting curate equally disgrace our Church!

I then by dint of eloquence prevailed upon Mrs Byng to take the round of Christ Church Meadows. (Some people take pleasures as pills.) Upon the Isis bank, seeing a very pretty cabined boat, I bethought me of finishing this highly-finished tour by an aquatic expedition; and having demanded the prices, hastened to the inn to charm Mrs Byng with my scheme. This being approved of, and

Mr Frek invited to be of the party, Garwood was sent to make the agreement with the boatman for tomorrow.

We supped by ourselves, as Mr Frek was obliged to attend his college. Warm weather I love. I was formed by the West Indies. Whoever is warm may be languid, but the chilly are always peevish.

16 July   It was a warm night; and our bedroom lay over the kitchen, which made the air of it very close. Luckily Mrs Byng slept with her son, so I had a whole bed to sprawl about.

I lounged to the bookseller's, but whatever game comes there is instantly snapped up by the old dons. Mr Frek came with a strange request for more company! However, when he returned to breakfast (having seen my astonishment and dislike) he said that his friends were engaged. Our breakfast was bad: no cream, and the Brown Georges are a sad provincial nastiness.

After much delay on the boatman's part, and impatience on mine, we at last did embark, opposite to where Friar Bacon stood, and found ourselves in a comfortable cabin aboard this *coche d'eau*. One man punted and the other dragged, and thus in tedious novelty were we pulled along, but all in the way of pleasure! Our boat questions were soon exhausted.

The meadows at Oxford afford no beauty till the country rises near Iffley. The weather was hot, but the breezes from the water and the opposite wind sufficiently cooled and too much retarded us. Our boatman had done right, I thought, to have rowed instead of this punting and dragging, which wobbles us strangely along. Two idler fellows I never saw.

Passing Iffley Lock, we came in front of Mr Nowell's house, which took our fancy much as a summer residence. Thence we came in due time to Sandford Mill and Lock (at the operation of raising the water we get out), where is a neat public house frequented by the Oxonians; and our bread and cheese and cider was handed to us by a gay dressed-out lass, an additional incitement to parties of pleasure? Beer for the boatmen.

Lord Harcourt's seat at Nuneham looks gaily from the river,

which appears to run in a wrong upward channel. All round the haymaking business (the delight and beauty of the country) was going on merrily. But who would wish to live so near Oxford, subject to a novelty of insults? The view of Abingdon gave me pleasure, as I tired of our tiresome boat and I was glad to disembark, though our day had been hot and highly favourable. The entrance and canal reminded me of Holland. We passed by the old wall, and under the gateway of the old Abbey, wherein the county prisoners are now confined, in dreadful waiting for the judges who are expected tomorrow. 'A terrible show.' The list of these unfortunate men is cried about as the list of the running horses!

Our inn in the market place, of the old-fashioned cut, was now overrun by barristers and their attendants. Our dinner consisted of cold meat – very good; this inn would not have been unacceptable to turn in my travels. Taking leave of Mr Frek, I had to encounter all the insolence and extortion of the boatmen (though the freight had been paid at Oxford); for these gentry are never contented, and though I paid for two quarts of ale out of the four they pretended to have drunk, they went grumbling away.

I was now in a post-chaise with Mrs Byng and Frek, 'cribbed, cabined and confined'. From Abingdon we cross, over Culham bridge and a pleasant country, to the village of Clifton upon the banks of the Thames, one of the prettiest and Flemish-looking villages I ever saw. We soon trotted along to Dorchester and so to Benson, where I remounted my mare, ridden here by Garwood, and leaving Mrs Byng and Frek at tea, I took the straight road which leads to the long straggly village of Ewelme, whither I went to observe the remains of the Palace built by de la Pole, Duke of Suffolk. What remains of very old brickwork may have been offices of a stable, and are now inhabited by poor families.

Crossing the open country, I overtook the chaise about two miles from Benson; then mounting Frek before me, gave him – poor fellow – the last ride he may have for a long time. The short summer seemed now to be closing; and in a threatening rain hurried me on to Henley, to the Red Lion – nasty, crowded inn – about which, gloomy as the weather, I took some short walks until our supper time. Return very dull!!

17 July   Wake early, and arise to a dark morning; on horseback before 8 o'clock, leaving Mrs Byng to settle bills. Trot away. Hurley Bottom, and so on to Slough, the Red Lion – Jemmy D. wearing out, the waiter a driveller. After breakfast, and newspaper, I walked into the back garden where I sketched the workshop of Dr Herschell, who here frames his Microscopers to peep into the moon.

At Cromford Bridge I left the high road, where is this view, taken below the clump of fir trees passing by Southwell Green where I entered the Uxbridge Road. All this has been seen; nothing new to remark. Nor did I stop but to sketch Lord Holland's lodge by the roadside, leading to Mr Hall's farms at Kensington gravel pits; where, leaving my mare to enjoy the luxury of ease at grass, I was conveyed home by past three o'clock in a hackney coach which offered its services for a sixpence.